THE DUKE

100 CHAPTERS IN THE LIFE OF PRINCE PHILIP

IAN LLOYD

DEDICATION

To Debbie Clayden,
the truest of friends.

First published 2021

The History Press
97 St George's Place, Cheltenham,
Gloucestershire, GL50 3QB
www.thehistorypress.co.uk

British Library Cataloguing in Publication Data.
A catalogue record for this book is available from the British Library.

ISBN 978 0 7509 9608 2

Typesetting and origination by The History Press
Printed and bound in Great Britain by TJ Books Limited, Padstow, Cornwall.

MIX
Paper from
responsible sources
FSC® C013056

Trees for Life

CONTENTS

FOREWORD

The present reign has, to all intents and purposes, been a joint one. For sixty-five years, from the accession in 1952 to the Prince's retirement in 2017, many events in the royal year, from the State Opening of Parliament to the opening of a factory in Birmingham, were 'in the presence of HM the Queen and HRH the Duke of Edinburgh'.

Elizabeth II is the most travelled monarch in British history, having made some 266 overseas visits to 116 countries. It has been calculated that she has travelled 1,032,513 miles – the equivalent of lapping the globe forty-two times. Equally amazing is that for every one of those million-plus miles, the Duke of Edinburgh has been by her side (or, more often than not, three steps behind). In addition to all those joint tours, the Duke carried out 637 overseas tours on his own as well as 22,219 solo engagements between the Queen's accession in 1952 and his retirement in 2017.

The aim of this book is to present an overview of the Duke's life in 100 chapters. It is by no means a complete biography of Prince Philip but will try to highlight certain themes or topics that may be unfamiliar to many readers.

His has been a fascinating life, dominated by two family tragedies. The first was his mother's manic depression which led in 1930 to her incarceration in the first of two sanatoria and, crucially, a seven-year separation from her only son. That same year, his father left for the South of France with his mistress and, between December 1930 and August 1931, his four sisters married. Nine-year-old Philip was effectively orphaned and, since the family home in Paris was closed down, more or less homeless, forcing him to spend his school holidays with friends and relatives. His unstable teen years probably account for his prickly character and defensive comments. Contemporaries recall he never felt sorry for himself, though he once revealed to a courtier: 'I used to wonder who I was.'

The second family tragedy came just over four years after his wedding to Princess Elizabeth with the death of her father King George VI at the age of only 56. Had the King died at, say, 80 years of age, then Elizabeth II would have succeeded just short of her fiftieth birthday and Philip would have been 54, and would almost certainly have enjoyed another two decades of naval service.

There was another problem. According to her friends, American-born Meghan Markle felt 'totally unwelcome' in the Royal Family, but her story pales into insignificance against Philip's. At the time of his engagement, a newspaper poll found 40 per cent of readers objected to Elizabeth marrying someone 'foreign', despite the fact he had spent the whole of the Second World War serving in the Royal Navy. Senior members of the Royal Household disliked and distrusted him, whilst, continuing the 'foreign' theme, the King's friends dubbed him 'Charley Kraut'. Even today he is satirised by the press and public as 'Phil the Greek'.

He was even an outsider constitutionally. As a male consort his role was less defined than that of a female consort, as he explained to one of his biographers: 'If you have a King and Queen, there are certain things people automatically go to the Queen about. But if the Queen is also the *Queen* they go to her about everything.' In the end he tried to carve out his own role, supporting some 800 organisations. These included the Duke of Edinburgh's Award, founded in 1956 as a series of self-improving exercises for adolescents and young adults involving a wide range of activities. An ongoing success story, in the UK to date over 3 million awards have been achieved. The scheme has expanded to 144 nations over its six-decade history.

While the D of E Award is part of his legacy, so is his reputation as a ladies' man and his propensity to make gaffes. The former haunts him, much to his obvious annoyance, and reports of his alleged flings have often been based on the flimsiest of evidence. His quips and gaffes have always been a constant delight to the press. As 97 per cent of royal engagements are boringly routine, the few that fail to go to plan are relished by the media. During the state visit to the Czech Republic in 1996, the Queen and Duke followed separate itineraries for one day. Two coaches waited to take journalists and photographers on the two away days. I climbed aboard the one for the Duke and was surprised to find half of Fleet Street following me. The reason soon became apparent, as one royal tour veteran claimed: 'Well, he's bound to stick his foot in it.' In print his comments veer towards the downright offensive. One I was told hasn't ever made it in onto the list as it is so jaw-droppingly awful it's hard to believe. The majority are actually very funny, said with a twinkle in the royal eye and, more importantly, well received by those he's talking to.

In writing this book I have drawn on my past interviews with the Duke's cousins, Lady Pamela Hicks and the late Countess Mountbatten, as well as several interviews with the Queen's cousin, the late Hon. Margaret Rhodes, and a former assistant private secretary, Sir Edward Ford. I am also thankful to David Gorringe and the late Peter Bartlett for sharing their memories of filming the *Royal Family* documentary, and a former charity executive for recounting, off the record, his many anecdotes about the Duke at the Royal Variety Performance.

The book could not have been written without the invaluable help of the published sources written by biographers who have had access to the Duke and his circle. Philip Eade's *Young Prince*

Philip: His Turbulent Early Life is a superbly researched account of the first three decades of the Duke's life. Gyles Brandreth's *Philip and Elizabeth: Portrait of a Marriage* is a witty overview of the royal couple's life together and benefits from access to many 'new' sources including the Duke's alleged *amoureuses*. Basil Boothroyd was the first to interview the Prince about his life in detail for his *Prince Philip: An Informal Biography*.

Over the years, I have also seen the Duke in action during more than 500 public and private engagements and several state visits abroad.

I would like to record my thanks to Joe Little, managing editor of *Majesty* magazine, for reading the manuscript and offering advice, to portrait painter Richard Stone for recalling his sittings with the Duke and to graphologist Tracey Trussell for analysing the Duke's handwriting for me. Finally I am indebted to Simon Wright, commissioning editor of The History Press, for agreeing to publish the book and for coping with the author's tardiness during this oddest of years.

Ian Lloyd
Oxford
November 2020

1

BORN WITH TWO BIRTHDAYS

The Queen is not the only member of the royal family with two birthdays: Prince Philip has two for an entirely different reason. Elizabeth II enjoys a private celebration on 21 April to mark her actual arrival into the world and an official one in June marked by Trooping the Colour.

At the time of Philip's birth, Greece was still using the Julian calendar, under which the date was 28 May 1921. When the country adopted the Gregorian calendar two years later, the date was put forward by thirteen days to 10 June – the date it's been celebrated on ever since.

With his father, Prince Andrew, away on active service, it took four months to officially register his son's birth, which was done on 24 October 1921 – Julian date – and 'Entry No 449' tells us that Prince Philippos of Greece, sixth in line to the throne, 'was born on the day of the twenty-eighth of the month of May in the year 1921 on the day of the week of Friday at 10 o'clock in the morning'.[1]

2

'MY PLACE OF REST'

'Mon Repos' might sound like a bed and breakfast in Eastbourne, but it's also the name of a neoclassical villa on the island of Corfu and the birthplace of Prince Philippos of Greece and Denmark. Built in the late 1820s for Sir Frederick Adams, Lord High Commissioner of the Ionian Islands, it was given by Greece to Philip's grandfather as a summer residence. It was bequeathed to the Prince's father Prince Andrew and remained with the Greek royal family until its overthrow in 1967.

Philip's cousin, Queen Alexandra of Yugoslavia (the former Princess Alexandra of Greece), recalled 'the broad, sunny hall, the wide staircase curling up to the upper floor'. Outside was the all-pervading 'scent of orange and wisteria' and the garden was 'thick with eucalyptus, magnolia, cypress, olives and orange and lemon trees'.[1] According to Alexandra, Andrew 'loved every part of it' and 'it was a particular joy and pride to him that his son should be born there'.[2]

Princess Alice was 36 and in a high state of anxiety when her baby was due and for some reason the local doctor thought it was more expedient for the mother to give birth to her son on the dining room table rather than her bed and carried her downstairs himself.

Afterwards, the recuperating Princess wrote to a relation: 'He is a splendid, healthy, child thank God. I am very well too. It was an uncomplicated delivery and I am enjoying the fresh air on the terrace'.[3]

Like many of Queen Victoria's descendants, Princess Alice was assisted by no-nonsense, salt-of-the-earth, English women. Nanny Miss Roose, 'Roosie', had already looked after Philip's cousin Princess Marina of Greece and her sisters. Now once again she stocked up on English baby foods and ordered infant woollies from London.

Housekeeper Agnes Blower avoided 'those messy foreign dishes which the Greek cook concocted' and opted for soundly British 'rice and tapioca puddings and good wholesome Scots porridge' for the baby.[4] Miss Blower was clearly no fan of the locals and recalled being assisted by 'a few untrained peasant girls', 'and two unwashed footmen who were rough fellows'.

Meanwhile Philip was oblivious to the unclean staff and contented himself playing with nanny's pin cushion, 'for hours, sat quietly in his cot, pulling the pins and needles out and pushing them in again'.[5] Stabbing a pin cushion for hours sounds a bit alarming for a 6-month-old baby but, looking back, he would no doubt have said his usual mantra: 'it did me no harm'.

3

KEEPING IT IN THE FAMILY: HOW PRINCE PHILIP AND THE QUEEN ARE RELATED

The Duke is related to the Queen through the ancestry of both his mother and father.

THE MATERNAL LINE

His mother, Princess Alice of Battenberg, was the granddaughter of Queen Victoria's second daughter, Princess Alice, who married the future Grand Duke Louis of Hesse.

The Queen is descended from Victoria's eldest son, Edward VII.

In other words, both Philip and Elizabeth are great-great-grandchildren of Victoria and are therefore third cousins. Queen Victoria is known as the 'Grandmother of Europe' and her living descendants also include Harald V of Norway, Margrethe II of Denmark, Carl XVI Gustaf of Sweden and Felipe VI of Spain.

THE PATERNAL LINE

Philip's father, Prince Andrew of Greece and Denmark, was the son of King George I of Greece. George was the younger brother of Britain's Queen Alexandra, consort of Edward VII.

So both Philip and Elizabeth are descendants of George and Alexandra's father, King Christian IX of Denmark. Since Philip is Christian's great-grandson and Elizabeth is his great-great-granddaughter, in this line they are second cousins once removed.

Due to the fact that his six children made upwardly mobile marriages in the other courts of Europe, King Christian was dubbed the 'Father-in-Law of Europe'. Like Victoria, he is an ancestor of Margrethe II, Harald V and Felipe VI, though unlike her he is also ancestor of Philippe of Belgium and Grand Duke Henri of Luxembourg.

4

A SLICE OF BATTENBERG

'My grandmother was an extraordinary character,' recalled Prince Philip in a 1968 interview, some eighteen years after the death of the Dowager Marchioness of Milford Haven. 'Tremendously well informed and with an ability to argue and discuss intelligently any subject you care to mention. She was the nearest thing to a perambulating encyclopaedia that anyone could possibly perceive.'[1]

His admiration is unsurprising: the two had much in common. 'Radical in her ideas, insatiably curious, argumentative to the point of perversity', says the official biographer of her son, Earl Mountbatten.[2] It's a description with a familiar ring – neatly summing up her grandson too.

Louis Mountbatten himself labelled his mother 'outspoken and open-minded',[3] something his exact contemporary Queen Elizabeth the Queen Mother echoed: 'She was rather like a man … She was quite dictatorial. I remember she would say: "Now, I am going to tell you this."'[4]

Born Princess Victoria of Hesse in 1863 at Windsor Castle, she was the first of Queen Victoria's grandchildren to be born in Britain, the first to be named after her and the first of many to have been born in her presence. Princess Victoria's mother was Queen Victoria's second daughter Princess Alice, who in 1862 married the future Grand Duke Louis IV of Hesse. Their five daughters included ill-fated Alexandra, Empress of Russia, who was murdered by the Bolsheviks in 1918 alongside her husband Tsar Nicholas II and their five children. The Empress Alexandra and another sister, Princess Irene – who married Kaiser Wilhelm II's brother Henry – were carriers of the haemophilia gene. Their brother Frederick was a haemophiliac and died at the age of 2 following a fall from his mother's bedroom window. Fortunate for the British royal family, Princess Victoria was not a carrier.[5]

Victoria married Prince Louis of Battenberg in 1884 at a lavish celebration at the Hessian court in Darmstadt in a ceremony attended by Queen Victoria. Legend has it that the famous Battenberg cake was created for the wedding banquet. Victoria's granddaughter Lady Pamela Hicks likes to think it was: 'It is very likely, though what's the harm if it wasn't! We were told about it, growing up, and that the four squares represented the four Battenberg brothers.'[6]

After the death of Princess Alice from diphtheria in 1878, when Victoria was 15, her grandmother acted in *loco parentis* and was a frequent correspondent with her Hessian granddaughter. She was concerned that the newly married Princess showed 'a certain coolness and detachment' (something her grandson would be accused of, particularly in his relations with his eldest son) and thought she failed to convey sufficient love and affection towards her husband.[7]

Certainly Princess Victoria's grandchildren found her a rather imposing figure and they were expected to treat her with deference, as Lady Pamela recalls: 'On meeting her we had to kiss her hand, then kiss her cheek before curtseying to her.'[8] Prince Philip kissed her and bowed with similar deference.

Princess Victoria's apartment at Kensington Palace was one of several bases the teenage Philip used during school holidays and then later when on shore leave from the navy. A Mountbatten family butler, Charles Smith, recalled, 'The patience of Grandmama was sometimes a little exhausted by his restless enquiring nature. She would always keep a good eye on him, tidying up behind him and ensuring his clothes were in good order, but inevitably she needed breathing space to collect her thoughts.' That's where Charles the butler came in useful, and he was deputised to take young Philip to see a series of swashbuckling films, from *Treasure Island* to Charles Laughton in *Mutiny on the Bounty*.[9]

The boy Prince's film choices show a maritime theme and it's no surprise that, with war looming, a career in the British Royal Navy – following the path of his grandfather and uncles George and Louis – was inevitable. Princess Victoria surprisingly thought he might have stayed in Greece, which he visited in the late 1930s with his mother, and was 'where he belongs … War is too serious a matter for boys of foreign countries to have to undergo the risks,' she wrote to her younger son Louis, adding, 'and they can only be an encumbrance & of no real use to our country'. Nevertheless, as both Lord Louis and the King of Greece felt Philip would be better serving in the Royal Navy, she acquiesced.[10]

The Princess lived to see her grandson serve with distinction in the Second World War. She attended his wedding to the granddaughter of her cousin George V and she was godmother to her great-grandson Prince Charles. Philip was serving at sea when his grandmother died peacefully at Kensington Palace on 24 September 1950, though a few weeks earlier he had been able to tell her of the birth of his daughter Princess Anne.

5

PHIL THE GREEK

When he first arrived on the scene as a suitor for Princess Elizabeth, sniffy courtiers dismissed him as 'a penniless Greek prince'. By royal standards he was certainly impecunious but genetically he was faultless. In fact, his pedigree was far more royal than his future wife's.

Through the Queen Mother's 'commoner' family tree, Elizabeth II's great-grandparents include run-of-the-mill land-owning stock – Caroline Burnaby and Frances Smith. Among her eighteenth-century ancestors are John Edwynn, Sheriff of Leicester, George Smith MP and Thomas Bird, a silk manufacturer.

On the other hand Prince Philip's great-grandparents are all pretty august including one king, two grand dukes and one of

Queen Victoria's daughters. Only his great-grandmother Julia Hauke, a lady-in-waiting at the Hessian court whose marriage to Prince Alexander of Hesse was declared morganatic due to her 'low' status, was not of blue blood.

The Duke's family tree shows a fascinating link with Tsarist Russia. His paternal grandmother Grand Duchess Olga Constantinova of Russia was the granddaughter of Tsar Nicholas I. On his mother's side Philip was the great-nephew of Tsarina Alexandra Feodorovna (born Princess Alix of Hesse) and her sister the Grand Duchess Elizabeth Feodorovna, who were both massacred with other members of the imperial family following the overthrow of the Romanov monarchy during the Russian Revolution.

In 1994 Philip visited his great-aunt Elizabeth's convent in Moscow during the Queen's state visit to Russia. Four years later, he and the Queen attended a commemorative service at Westminster Abbey for the restored West Front which included ten new statues of saints – among them one of Elizabeth, canonised in 1992 by the Moscow Patriarchate.

The following year a blood sample from the Duke of Edinburgh allowed scientists to compare the mitochondrial DNA of bones thought to be those of the murdered imperial family with matrilineal living relatives. They were able to prove beyond doubt that the bones included those of the Tsarina Alexandra and her daughters, and confirmed their fate at the hands of a Bolshevik firing squad in the cellar of the house in Yekaterinburg.[1]

Although the Prince has been fondly nicknamed 'Phil the Greek' by cheekier elements of the press for over seventy years, he hasn't a single drop of Greek blood in his veins. The modern-day Greek royal family was imported from the Danish royal house when Philip's 17-year-old grandfather Prince William of Denmark was invited to be King of the Hellenes, opting for the regnal name of George I. Thanks to this mid-nineteenth-century

Philip at his great-aunt Grand Duchess Elizabeth's former convent in Moscow, which at the time was being used as an icon and painting restoration studio, October 1994. (© Ian Lloyd)

job swap, Philip's DNA is Viking rather Mediterranean and he is part of the very un-Greek-sounding dynasty of Schleswig-Holstein-Sonderburg-Glücksburg. Certainly he has always thought of himself as Danish.[2]

Not only does he lack a Greek bloodline, but the Prince can barely speak the language, although he told one interviewer that he 'could understand a certain amount'. In childhood he and his family spoke English, French and German.[3]

6
PARIS AND A BOHEMIAN AUNT

From the spring of 1923 until Princess Alice's mental collapse in 1930, Princess Alice and Prince Andrew and their children divided their time between Paris and London. They were given a lodge on the estate of Philip's aunt, Princess George of Greece, at St-Cloud, some 6 miles from the centre of the French capital.

Princess George was a fascinating character, famed for her all-consuming interest in psychoanalysis, her friendship with Sigmund Freud and her unconventional lifestyle. Born Marie Bonaparte in 1882, she was the great-granddaughter of Napoleon I's rebellious younger brother Lucien. She was fabulously rich thanks to her maternal grandfather François Blanc, who made his fortune on real estate development in Monaco, buying 97 per cent of the casinos in Monte Carlo.[1]

Her wealth made it possible for her to bankroll Philip's family. This included sending the young Prince and his sisters to private schools in Paris in the belief that this would have been their right had they not been exiled. Paradoxically she sent her own children, Prince Peter and Princess Eugénie, to the local state-run *lycée*, feeling it was important they should mix with children of all backgrounds.

In 1907 Marie married Philip's paternal uncle Prince George of Greece. George has a footnote in history for saving the future Tsar Nicholas II of Russia from assassination during a visit to Otsu, Japan, in 1891. The Tsarevich was attacked by a sword-wielding policeman who turned out to be a former samurai with a grudge against Westerners. George managed to knock him to the ground using his cane. George was also passionately in love with his own uncle, Prince Waldemar of Denmark, the youngest brother of Britain's Queen Alexandra. The Queen of Greece had brought the young George to Copenhagen to serve with the Danish Navy, lodging him with Waldemar, who was ten years his nephew's senior. 'From that day, from that moment on, I loved him and I have never had any other friend but him,' wrote George.[2] So passionate was their relationship that whenever the younger Prince had to depart his uncle's estate at Bernstorff he would weep and Waldemar fall sick.

Unsurprisingly, George and Marie's own relationship was passionless. The groom never allowed his new wife to kiss him on the lips and after the honeymoon she wrote: 'You took me that night in a short brutal gesture, as if forcing yourself. You said "I hate it as much as you do. But we must do it if we want children."'[3] Marie would seek passion elsewhere, even to the extent of romancing Uncle Waldemar while her cuckolded husband sat and watched or lay next to them. Tiring of the older man, she then enjoyed a liaison with his eldest son Prince Aage. After accruing a list of willing sexual partners, Marie documented them in her unpublished 1918 memoirs *The Men I Have Loved*.

Marie enjoyed an equally fulfilling life out of bed. She was a very close friend of Sigmund Freud, who mentored her interest in psychoanalysis and who once memorably asked her, 'What does a women want?', presumably feeling if anyone would know, it would be the Princess. After all, she had carried out her own study on frigidity under the pseudonym A.E. Narjani. Her theory was that the closer the clitoris was to the vagina the more chance a woman had of achieving an orgasm. To back up this notion she personally measured that crucial distance in 243 women. Satisfied she had discovered the truth, she had her own clitoris surgically shifted a few inches in the right direction. Unfortunately both this and a subsequent operation failed in their ultimate goal.

So focused was she on the benefits of psychoanalysis that when she was once 'flashed at' on the Rue de Boulogne she handed the baffled perpetrator her card and the offer of a free session on her analyst's couch – a gesture that sent him scuttling away.[4]

Marie also had an interest in the criminal mind, describing Jack the Ripper as 'a supermurderer and a superanarchist'.[5] In 1934 she published *The Life and Works of Edgar Allan Poe: A Psycho-Analytic Interpretation*, with a foreword by Sigmund Freud.

The Princess's writings also give a vivid picture of some of Philip's relations. She describes his mother as 'a beautiful blond, Englishwoman with ample flesh, smiles a lot and doesn't say much as she's deaf'. The tall gangly Prince Andrew, she thought, 'looks like a thoroughbred horse'.[6] She has also left us a fascinating vignette of Queen Alexandra, whom she found 'sixty-three years old [in 1907], surprisingly young, enamelled skin. Disturbing when youthfulness covers an old skin. She seems kind and friendly, but also insignificance personified'.[7]

Marie and George maintained strong links with the British royal family, particularly after Prince Philip joined what George VI referred to as 'the firm'. They represented King George I of Greece at the 1911 Coronation of George V and Queen Mary and half a century later stood in for King Paul at the 1953 Coronation of the present Queen. They were also present in Westminster Abbey to witness the marriage of their niece Princess Marina of Greece to Prince George, Duke of Kent, in 1934 and again thirteen years later for Philip's marriage to Princess Elizabeth.

Philip stayed in touch with Marie for the rest of her life and she was present with George when the Greek royal family were reunited at Tatoi Palace for a private visit by Elizabeth and Philip in December 1950, enabling the Princess to meet her husband's extended family. The Edinburghs enjoyed several private dinners with George and Marie. Less to the latter's liking were the official palace dinners hosted for the British Princess by King Paul and Queen Frederica. Princess George wrote to a friend: 'Grand dinner at court for Elizabeth and Philip, decorations, tiaras, horror!'[8] Marie, the most unconventional of princesses, remained a maverick to the end.

7

BABY STEPS IN BRITAIN

By the time he was 18 months old, Prince Philip had made two visits to the country he would one day make his home.

In September 1921 Philip's only surviving grandfather, Princess Alice's father Louis, Marquess of Milford Haven, died suddenly from heart failure in London. Alice and her baby son arrived too late for the funeral service at Westminster Abbey or the interment at Whippingham Church on the Isle of Wight.

Like Philip, Prince Louis was a foreign national who had a distinguished career in the British Navy. Queen Victoria kept a keen eye on his progress in her armed forces and was unafraid of voicing her 'belief that the Admiralty are afraid of promoting Officers who are Princes on account of the radical attacks of low papers and scurrilous ones'.[1] He spent forty years in the British Navy, rising to the rank of First Sea Lord, but had to resign from the post due to intense anti-German feeling during the First World War. He was also forced to change his name from the Germanic-sounding Battenberg to its anglicised version Mountbatten.

In a touching gesture, Philip carried his grandfather's ceremonial sword with him at his 1947 wedding to Princess Elizabeth and used it to cut their wedding cake.

The second visit was the following year. After exile from his homeland as a result of the Greco-Turkish War (1919–22), Prince Andrew and his family visited London en route to their eventual home in Paris. They were based at Spencer House, St James's – the ancestral home of Philip's future daughter-in-law Diana, Princess of Wales – leased to Princess Christopher of Greece. The Princess was the fabulously rich American heiress Nancy Leeds, who had married Andrew's brother and was known as Princess Anastasia of Greece and Denmark, during her three-year marriage before she succumbed to cancer in 1923. Nancy/Anastasia kept Spencer House permanently staffed and ready for visits such as Andrew and Alice's.

While in London the royal couple and their son visited Philip's great-aunt Queen Alexandra, the widow of Edward VII. Born in 1844 in Denmark, Alexandra had married a future British monarch and spent the majority of her life in Britain – as Philip was to do. Joining the group was Andrew's widowed mother Queen Olga of Greece, who was married to Alexandra's younger brother King George I of Greece. This visit took place at Marlborough House, the Dowager Queen's London residence, on 18 December 1922.[2]

8

FAMILY TRAGEDY NO. 1: PHILIP'S MOTHER IS FORCIBLY REMOVED

On 2 May 1930, in Darmstadt, Germany, Prince Philip was taken out for the day by his grandmother Princess Victoria. He enjoyed a carefree picnic with plenty of opportunity for the rough and tumble Prince to run off his boisterous energy.

He was a month short of his ninth birthday and would have had no idea the day out was in fact a diversionary tactic. A few miles away at Neue Palais, a group of men in white coats arrived in a car and forcibly detained his mother, giving her a powerful sedative concealed in an orange. When she awoke she was hundreds of miles away at the Bellevue Sanatorium at Kreuzlingen in Switzerland.

In 1928 Princess Alice had converted to the Greek Orthodox faith and had become increasingly religious. She began to suffer religious delusions, thinking she was in a sexual relationship with Jesus Christ and that she even had a signed photo from him. Alice, in the words of her mother, was 'in quite an abnormal state', wandering around the house praying and believing she was about to be given a message from Christ to share with the world.[1]

The family turned to the still largely experimental treatment of psychology and in February 1930 they sent Philip's mother to a psychiatric clinic, Sanatorium Schloss Tegel run by Dr Ernst Simmel near Berlin. Here Alice was diagnosed as a 'paranoid schizophrenic', to use the insensitive pre-war parlance.

A lady-in-waiting revealed to Simmel that Alice had had a passionate, unrequited, crush on an unnamed Englishman for several years. The psychiatrist believed the repression of Alice's highly emotional feelings accounted for her state of mind.

At this point the clinic was visited by Sigmund Freud, the founding father of psychoanalysis. In March he examined Alice's case notes and recommended the alarming treatment of X-rays to the ovaries to bring on the menopause. This, he maintained, would cure her excessive libido and improve her mental illness. There is no evidence Alice had any choice but to submit to the procedure or that it worked. Shortly after, she discharged herself from Schloss Tegel and returned to St-Cloud and to Philip.

The Princess's health must have rapidly declined at home since it was only a matter of weeks later that she was detained in the Bellevue Sanatorium.

Her two nieces were particularly sympathetic to Alice's plight. 'I think my aunt would have suffered very much,' was the verdict of Countess Mountbatten, speaking in 2012. Her sister, Lady Pamela Hicks, agreed: 'It was difficult to talk to other people about it because they were embarrassed or ashamed … In those days it was something to be kept quiet about.'[2]

Alice's suffering is evident in her case notes, which show that on 27 July she climbed through a window at the sanatorium and ran away. She managed to get onboard a train bound for Germany but was apprehended and returned.

At the end of September it was decided that Alice was well enough to leave. At this point she found out she had been

Prince Philip appears delighted to be reunited with his mother at the marriage of her granddaughter Princess Margarita of Baden to Prince Tomislav of Yugoslavia, at Salem Castle, Germany, in June 1957. (Keystone-France / Getty)

detained on the orders of Princess Victoria. She never entirely forgave her mother. Since Prince Andrew had already left for the South of France with a mistress, and the household in St-Cloud had been disbanded, Alice made the decision to adopt a nomadic existence, staying in modest hotels or boarding houses in different parts of Germany. It would be another five years before she was reunited with Philip.

Oddly, it was another family tragedy, the death of her daughter Cécile in an air crash in 1937 with her husband and three of her children, that once more propelled Alice back into Philip's life. The shock somehow made her feel needed by her family. She would remain close to her only son and died in apartments the Queen provided for her in Buckingham Palace in December 1969.

9

FIRST MEETING

They don't remember it, but the first time Elizabeth and Philip saw each other was at the wedding of the Princess's uncle George, Duke of Kent, to Philip's first cousin Princess Marina of Greece, on 29 November 1934.

Eight-year-old Elizabeth was one of the two bridesmaids, charged with looking after Marina's frothy white veil. Philip was sitting in the second row of assembled royal guests just below the five steps up to the high altar. Photos show the tiny bridesmaid intent on her job and, just to her left, the back of Philip in his Eton suit.

'One of the most interesting guests', noted one journalist, 'was a fourteen year old [sic – he was 13] flaxen-haired schoolboy Prince who had made the long journey of over five hundred miles from Elgin alone.'[1] Poignantly, when he revealed to his school mates that he didn't have collar studs or cufflinks, they had a whip-round to get him some.[2] He might have been the only prince at Gordonstoun but he remained an impoverished one.

While Europe's royal families had arrived by train and sea in a variety of groups, Philip as usual had to cope by himself.

He left school at Gordonstoun two days before the wedding, travelling in a sleeping berth reserved for him under the name of Mr Phillips on the afternoon mail train. He returned four days later.

10

QUIPS, GAFFES AND BANTER: THE DUKE'S MEMORABLE CLANGERS 1–10

UPSETTING THE WORLD

01 **China:** To British students during the 1986 state visit, '*If you stay here much longer, you'll all be slitty-eyed.*'

02 **Paraguay:** To Alfredo Stroessner, the Paraguayan dictator, '*It's a pleasant change to be in a country that isn't ruled by its people.*'

03 **Germany:** In 1997, he welcomed German Chancellor Helmut Kohl at a trade fair as 'Reichskanzler'; the last German leader who used this title was Adolf Hitler.

04 **Hungary:** To a Briton in Budapest, in 1993, '*You can't have been here that long – you haven't got a pot belly.*'

05 **Cayman Islands:** To a wealthy islander in 1994, '*Aren't most of you descended from pirates?*'

06 **Thailand:** In Thailand, in 1991, after accepting a conservation award, '*Your country is one of the most notorious centres of trading in endangered species in the world.*'

07 **Another Oriental slur:** Addressing the World Wildlife Fund on the topic of endangered species in 1986, '*If it has got four legs and is not a chair, if it has got two wings and it flies but is not an aeroplane, and if it swims and is not a submarine, the Cantonese will eat it.*'

08 **Germany:** Asked what he thought of the new £18 million British Embassy in Berlin in 2000, '*It's a vast waste of space.*'

09 **Ethiopia:** On being shown some local art during the 1965 state visit by the Queen, '*It looks like the kind of thing my daughter would bring back from school art lessons.*'

10 **USA:** Visiting President and Mrs Reagan in California in 1983, Philip was bothered by over-zealous secret service-men. '*Are you expecting any trouble?*' he asked one, and, after being told they weren't, he snapped, '*Then back off!*'

The South Seas? Actually, it's Morecambe in 1999, and Philip makes a characteristic quip to exotically dressed band members on the seafront. (© Ian Lloyd)

11

NO FIXED ABODE

From 1930 when he was aged 9, to the summer of 1949 when he was 28, Prince Philip had no permanent family home, with the exception of a weekend retreat given to Elizabeth and her new husband in early 1948. Quite what this lack of a fixed base did to Philip's personality as he grew up is anyone's guess. 'The effect of not having a home is imponderable,' his lifelong friend Lady Myra Butter once reflected. 'You didn't go into those things then, but now people like Philip would be counselled all the time.'[1] The Prince himself decided at an early age to drop an iron curtain around the sensitive topic, merely stating: 'I just had to get on with it. You do. One does.'[2]

For the next decade and a half, when he wasn't either at school or in the navy, Philip was shunted from pillar to post, staying with a variety of relatives and friends in Britain and Germany.

The British contingent was led by his formidable grandmother Princess Victoria, Dowager Marchioness of Milford Haven. She tended to be the one who organised where Philip would spend his holidays and he always kept a couple of trunks of clothes at her Kensington Palace apartment, ready to take with him. He would often touch base with her in London before heading for another location. A typical grandmotherly instruction from 1935 began: 'You might spend the few days after leaving Gordonstoun & starting for abroad with me at Kens. Pal.,' asking him to let her know when he would be arriving.[3]

Shorter school holidays were often spent at Lynden Manor, home of Philip's uncle George, Marquess of Milford Haven, and his wife Nadeja ('Nada') at Holyport, near Windsor. Uncle

George was Philip's guardian in Britain, though not a particularly hands-on one since, during the Prince's five years at Gordonstoun, he never visited his charge there. Following the Marquess's death from cancer in April 1938, his younger brother Lord Louis Mountbatten (known to his friends and family as 'Dickie') stepped in *loco parentis* and Philip stayed with him and his wife Edwina at their Brook Street apartment in London or Adsdean, their country estate near Chichester. During the war, Philip often crashed at the Mountbatten's small house at 16 Chester Street.

Other UK-based holiday destinations included Coppins, the country home of his cousin Princess Marina and her husband the Duke of Kent at Iver, Buckinghamshire. There was also the estate of Nada Milford Haven's sister Zia and her husband Sir Harold Wernher at Market Harborough. The couple again took on a near-parental role for Philip, and he remained a lifelong friend of their two daughters Gina and Myra. Gina Wernher, later Lady Kennard, remembered, 'it was never ever "poor me!"' from Philip, though he did once say: 'Where is home? Except for all of you, I don't have a home to come back to.'[4]

Philip also holidayed in Germany with his four sisters, their German husbands and a growing brood of children. Aged 12, he spent several months at school there during the winter of 1933–34. He appears to have taken this peripatetic lifestyle for granted at the time, but over the years occasionally dropped his protective carapace to show how his nomadic youth had affected him. 'Looking back at my childhood,' he revealed to a close female friend, 'it really is amazing that I was left to cross a continent – taxis, trains, boats – to get to my sisters' homes in Germany. There was no one to pick me up.' The friend thought he sounded like an orphan.[5]

His cousin, Princess Alexandra of Greece, holidayed with Philip, then aged 17, in Venice in 1938 and remembered how grateful he was to be included in the family party. 'Philip gave the impression at the time', she wrote in 1960, 'of a huge, hungry dog; perhaps a friendly collie who had never had a basket of his own and responded to every overture with eager tail-wagging.' Like Gina Kennard, she noted there was never any self-pity: 'Though never sorry for himself, to be fed and looked after meant such a lot to him.'[6]

Two entries in separate visitors' books, both in 1946, show that sixteen years after the family home broke up, Philip hadn't come to terms with his rootless existence, even if he might have meant the comments in his usual jokey fashion. 'Whither the storm carried me, I go – a willing guest,' he wrote at one home in June, and, staying with his cousin, Patricia Knatchbull, elder daughter of Lord Mountbatten, a few days before Christmas, he put 'no fixed abode!'[7]

Decades later, in another uncharacteristically revealing comment, Philip told a courtier, 'I used to wonder who I was.' Around this time the American writer Rabbi Arthur Herzog, who had known Philip well, reflected on the damage the Prince's rootless existence as a youth had had on his character. 'He does not know who he is,' he said at the time of the Duke's eightieth birthday. 'He has lost his real identity. He once told me he thinks of himself as a cosmopolitan European.'[8]

Marriage to Princess Elizabeth, and their four children together, not only gave Philip a family but a sense of belonging. 'I think he'd always thought how marvellous it would be to have a home and family,' said Gina Kennard, adding, 'and he knew there would be a home of real security with the Queen.'[9]

His cousin David Milford Haven summed it up in that winter of 1947: 'at long, long last … he's got a settled home.'[10]

12

NOT A HARD ACT TO FOLLOW: PHILIP AND THE STAGE

While the Queen, Margaret, Charles and Edward all trod the boards on several occasions in amateur productions, Philip only managed three very forgettable performances.

On 17 December 1935 the front page of the *Dundee Evening Telegraph* tells us that Gordonstoun School is to put on a performance of the Oberufer Nativity Play the following day and 'Prince Philip of Greece will have one of the leading roles'. It was a far cry from the royal nativity at Windsor in 1940 when Princess Elizabeth played one of the three kings and her sister Margaret made their father cry his eyes out by singing 'Gentle Jesus'. Instead, this was a traditional German version that used three plays to focus on the expulsion of Adam and Eve from the Garden of Eden, the proclamation of the birth of Jesus to the shepherds and the visit of the magi to see the Christ child. Thanks to the Gordonstoun ethos of supporting the local community, the nativity was put on in nearby Hopeman to raise money for the school's newly opened coastguard service. It's unclear which of 'the leading roles' Philip was assigned in the all-boy school of less than fifty pupils, but it's a safe bet it wasn't Mary.[1]

The previous summer Gordonstoun had put on its first production, an aptly chosen rendition of Shakespeare's 'Scottish play'. Fourteen-year-old Philip was chosen for the minor role of Donalbain, younger son of the about-to-be-murdered King Duncan, and would no doubt have been aware that the site of

Fourteen-year-old Philip prepares to make his acting debut as Donalbain in the Gordonstoun School production of *Macbeth*, July 1935. (Fox Photos / Stringer / Getty)

the 'blasted heath' where Macbeth meets the three witches was 20 miles west of the school, on a low hill near Brodie Castle.

A crowd of 300 was said to have enjoyed the outdoor production characterised by 'vigour and youthful enthusiasm' and 'particular interest attached' itself to Philip's performance, which was limited to three silent appearances in Act One and ten lines in Act Two.[2] The following July he had the tiniest of stage appearances as an unspeaking sentry in *Hamlet*.

Exactly thirty years later Philip returned to watch another version of *Macbeth*, starring Prince Charles, who was widely praised in the eponymous role. It's a shame the Duke wasn't as good at acting the part of a proud father, since at the point

when Macbeth/Charles was thrashing about in emotional tur-
moil while lying on a fur rug, all he was aware of was the sound
of his father's laughter. 'I went up to him afterwards and said:
"Why did you laugh?" and he said "It sounds like *The Goons*."'[3]

Official theatre visits have been a staple of the royal engagement list throughout the Queen's reign. For instance, in March
1984 the Queen and Duke attended a charity gala performance
of Andrew Lloyd Webber's *Starlight Express*. Five years later they
attended *Aspects of Love*, where as well as the musical they could
observe Prince Edward, one of the production assistants working
for Lloyd Webber's Really Useful Theatre Company. Spotting her
youngest son standing behind a posse of photographers in the
foyer, the Queen said, 'Hello!' and feigned a look of surprise.

One of the oddest theatrical outings of the reign was for the
official opening of the Globe Theatre in Southwark in June 1997,
modelled on the Tudor original. The Queen and Duke made the
journey in suitably Elizabethan fashion, embarking on a barge
at Lambeth and arriving at Emerson Street Stairs accompanied
by the Queen's Bargemaster and Watermen. The couple were
amused during the performance of 'Triumphes and Mirth'
when Tudor costermongers among the groundlings pelted the
stage with currants.

Off-duty, during their long marriage the Queen and Duke
have been occasional theatre-goers, preferring to remain as
inconspicuous as they can be, though inevitably word spreads
through the cast, audience and passers-by. As the curtain falls it
might as well be yet another royal gala with applause from the
stalls and, latterly, a blitz of smartphone flashes.

Until the mid 1980s they paid an annual visit to the local
Theatre Royal in Windsor with their house party during Royal
Ascot week.

In London they tended to arrive by taxi – their own, a liquid petroleum gas-powered Metrocab bought by Philip in 1999 in which to whizz round the capital. They used it in 2006 when they went to see *Billy Elliot the Musical* at the Victoria Palace Theatre for an eightieth birthday treat for the Queen. Six years later, in Diamond Jubilee year, they went in it to see *One Man, Two Guvnors,* at the Theatre Royal, Haymarket, with grandson Peter Phillips and his wife Autumn.

An undeniable treat for the equine-loving pair was their night out at *War Horse*, when an onlooker noted they were 'incredibly apologetic for asking people to let them pass' as they took their seats in the stalls.

13

FAMILY TRAGEDY NO. 2: THE DEATH OF A BELOVED SISTER

Early evening on Tuesday 16 November 1937, and as darkness enveloped the grey seventeenth-century edifice of Gordonstoun School, headmaster Kurt Hahn summoned Prince Philip of Greece to his study to tell him the traumatic news that his sister Cécile, his brother-in-law Georg Donatus, known as 'Don', and their two sons had been killed in an air crash.

Born in 1911, Cécile was ten years older than Philip and according to their grandmother stood out from her sisters as 'the prettiest of the lot'. Philip had attended her wedding in February 1931 to Georg Donatus, son of Ernest Louis, Grand Duke of Hesse, one of Queen Victoria's many grandsons. In

May 1937 Philip and Cécile were reunited in London during the Coronation festivities of George VI in London. That same spring Cécile and Don took Philip to visit Princess Alice over lunch in Bonn – the first time mother and son had met since 1932.

The Hessian royal family were flying to England for the wedding of Don's brother Prince Louis (known by the diminutive 'Lu') to the Hon. Margaret ('Peg') Geddes, daughter of Sir Auckland Geddes, a former ambassador to the United States. Cécile, Don, their two young sons, Ludwig and Alexander, and Don's widowed mother Grand Duchess Elenore boarded the three-engined Junkers monoplane at Frankfurt shortly before 2 p.m.

Philip's sister was reputedly so terrified of flying that she always wore black when she flew, although it must have been reassuring that the experienced pilot, Tony Lambotte, was the personal pilot of King Leopold III of the Belgians.[1] She was also eight months pregnant with her fourth child.

The aircraft was due to stop en route to pick up two more passengers near Brussels. However, thick fog sweeping in from the North Sea forced them to divert to Steene aerodrome on the coast near Ostend. With visibility down to a few yards, ground staff set off three flares to help Lambotte, but only one went off. Flying blind, the pilot hit the top of a 150ft-high brickworks' chimney at about 100mph, severing a wing and an engine. The rest of the plane crashed some 50 yards further on, bursting into flames and killing everyone on board.

Rescuers, removing the bodies, found the remains of a stillborn child in the wreckage, suggesting Cécile had gone into labour on the short flight, which must have influenced the pilot's decision to land rather than attempt to fly straight on over the Channel.

In later life, Prince Philip recalled hearing the news in 'profound shock'. Hahn noted that, on being told what had happened, the 16-year-old boy 'did not break down', adding, 'his sorrow was that of a man'.[2]

It was the first of a series of tragedies that befell the teenage Prince in the late 1930s. The following April his uncle and guardian George, Marquess of Milford Haven, died from bone marrow cancer aged 45. Then in June 1939 Philip's niece, Johanna, the only surviving child of Cécile and Don, who had not been with her parents in the air crash, died from meningitis aged 2½. The orphaned child had been adopted by Lu and Peg, who poignantly would never have children of their own.

It's hard to say the effect the deaths would have on Philip. Like many of his contemporaries he just robustly got on with his life, adopting the 'stiff-upper-lip' approach which his grandson Prince William condemned in 2017, saying, although there was a time and place for it, it should not be at the expense of people's health.

In 2004 Philip's childhood friend Gina Kennard recalled that Cécile's death 'affected him deeply'. She remembered him pulling out of his jacket pocket a small piece of the damaged aircraft. 'He was very quiet. He didn't talk about it much, but he showed me a little bit of the wood from the aeroplane. It was just a small piece, but it meant a lot to him.'³ Gina was herself part of that stiff-upper-lip generation and she said she always regretted not giving him a hug.

14

THE NAZI LINK

Surviving photographs show a sorrowful Prince Philip following the coffins of his sister Cécile, his brother-in-law Georg Donatus and his two small nephews through the streets of

Darmstadt following the tragic air crash that killed them all in November 1937. The 16-year-old's white-blond hair contrasts with his plain black mourning clothes and his understated look contrasts with the military uniforms of the others in the procession. Alongside him march four men in German uniform. They are Philip's three remaining brothers-in-law and another relative. One is dressed in an SS uniform, another as a stormtrooper.

As he walked through the cobbled streets of the German city, the Prince would have been aware of the all-pervading symbols of the Nazi regime around him. Troops from the Nationalist Socialist Party lined the route, huge swastikas were flown from building after building, and jutting out from the dense crowd was a sea of arms held aloft in the 'Heil Hitler' salute.

Adolf Hitler and his minister of propaganda, Joseph Goebbels, sent messages of sympathy to the family and, another leading Nazi, Hermann Göring, marched in the procession a few rows behind Philip. The Prince no doubt knew that six months earlier, on 1 May 1937, Cécile and her husband had joined the Nazi Party, and that they were not the only members of his close family to be involved.

Witnessing the growing strength of the German fascist regime, he must have felt relieved he himself had left the country before the full impact of Nazism took hold.

Having left Cheam School in England in late 1933, Philip was enrolled at the Schule Schloss Salem, founded by Kurt Hahn on the estate of Prince Max of Baden, the last imperial chancellor of Germany. Hahn had been the Prince's private secretary and was headmaster of the school until, as a fierce critic of Hitler and a Jew, he was forced to leave the school and managed to escape to Scotland, where he eventually founded Gordonstoun School.

Philip's sister Theodore had married Max's son Berthold, Margrave of Baden, and they offered the 12-year-old Prince a place at Salem, as he later explained: 'The suggestion came from my sister and brother-in-law who owned the school: it had the great advantage of saving school fees.'[1]

After Hahn's departure, Berthold became the headmaster. He was put under pressure by the Ministry of Education to introduce a rigid pro-Nazi regime in his classes or to face closure. 'There was much heel-clicking and shouts of "Heil Hitler" were compulsory for German nationals,' recalled Philip.[2] During his two terms at Salem he was also aware of 'inhibitions about the Jews' and 'jealousy of their success', though he was keen to emphasise he 'was never conscious of anybody in the family actually expressing ant-Semitic views'.[3]

Alone of all the schoolboys he was allowed to stay in Berthold and Theodore's castle and was therefore in the position of an outsider looking in. He thought it hilarious when the boys performed the Nazi salute since, back at Cheam, his classmates had used the same raised arm gesture when they wanted to be excused for the lavatory. On a more serious note, he knew 'the Nazis were moving in', much to the consternation of the Margrave and his wife. 'As none of that family was at all enthusiastic about them', recalled Philip, 'it was thought best that I should move out!!' He added, 'It was certainly a great relief to me.'[4]

Philip's sisters had all married into German nobility and three of the families had links with the Nazi Party, which was part of the reason Philip's love match with the heiress presumptive of the British throne presented problems to some, including the Princess's own mother.

His eldest sister Margarita married Gottfried, eighth Prince of Hohenlohe-Langenburg, a great-grandson of Queen

Victoria. He joined the Nazi Party in March 1937, the same month as Cécile and Georg Donatus joined, and offered to liaise with the British royal family. He went on to serve in the German Army.

The closest link between the family and the new regime was via Philip's youngest sister Sophie, known to her siblings as 'Tiny', who, aged only 16, married Prince Christoph of Hesse, another of Victoria's great-grandsons. The couple became friends with Göring before the Nazis seized power and he persuaded them to meet Hitler. In an unpublished memoir, Sophie later recorded: 'As Göring was insistent that we should meet Hitler personally we decided to ask him to lunch at our flat … I have to say that though Chri [her husband] and I changed our political view fundamentally a few years later we were impressed by this charming and seemingly modest man.'[5] In April 1935 Sophie was also photographed sitting opposite Hitler at the reception following Göring's wedding.

Prince Christopher became an SS colonel and head of one of the Nazi intelligence agencies. He was killed in 1943 flying back from Italy. Prince Philip of course served in the British Navy and at one point was almost directly fighting his brother-in-law. 'We have reason to believe', wrote Sophie later, 'that at one time during the Allied invasion of Sicily my brother and my uncle [Lord Mountbatten] were fighting on the same section of the island where my husband was serving.'[6]

Christopher's older brother Prince Philipp of Hesse (who walked next to Philip at the 1937 funeral) became a stormtrooper in 1932, an Oberpräsident (governor) of the province of Hesse-Nassau and a Luftwaffe reserve officer. He was Hitler's personal emissary to the Italian leader Benito Mussolini and, next to Albert Speer, was one of Hitler's closest personal friends at the beginning of the war.[7] In 1943, like many German aristocrats used by the Nazis for their social and political links, Philipp dramatically fell from favour and was sent to a concentration camp.

Christopher and Philipp of Hesse weren't the only Nazis in the Hessen family. Their mother, born Princess Margaret of Prussia, one of Queen Victoria's many granddaughters, became a member of the party in May 1938 and invited Adolf Hitler to tea.[8] She even flew the swastika from her home, Schloss Kronberg.

Christopher, Philipp and Sophie all radically lost faith in the Nazi Party as the war progressed. In May 1945 Sophie wrote to her grandmother, Princess Victoria: 'Since two years my eyes have been opened and you can imagine what feelings one has now about those criminals.'[9]

Philip was reunited with Margarita, Theodore and Sophie at the latter's second wedding, on 23 April 1946, to Prince George of Hanover. It was the first time the siblings had been together for seven years and they wept and hugged each other.[10] In 1954 Elizabeth II became godmother to Sophie and George's daughter, Princess Fredericke.

Sophie was the first of the sisters to visit Philip and Princess Elizabeth, staying with them privately at Windlesham Moor with two of her daughters in the spring of 1948. The other two sisters visited in the same summer. At the Queen's Coronation in 1953 the three sisters sat with their mother Princess Alice in the Royal Box on the row immediately behind the Queen Mother and Princess Margaret. It was a very public show of family unity after the sisters were snubbed by not being invited to Philip and Elizabeth's wedding six years earlier.

15

GIRLS, GIRLS, GIRLS

The Prince has always had an eye for the ladies. Quite who they are has always remained a tantalising secret that only Philip himself knows.

Two sources very close to the Duke testified to his youthful appetite for the opposite sex. His cousin, Queen Alexandra of Yugoslavia, wrote a surprisingly frank account of Philip's life in 1960 and recalled: 'Blondes, brunettes, and redhead charmers, Philip gallantly and I think quite impartially squired them all.'[1] Later, on shore leave in Australia, 'Philip', she writes, 'with a golden beard, hit feminine hearts, first in Melbourne and then in Sydney with terrific impact.'[2]

Alongside him during leave in North Africa was the Prince's close friend from his naval days (and later his equerry), Michael Parker, who added to the picture with typical Aussie directness: 'We'd drink together and then we'd go and have a bloody good meal. People are always asking, "Did you go to the local estaminets and screw everything in sight?" And the answer is, "No! It never came into the picture. There was so much else to do."'

Unfortunately, after deflecting comments about his shipmate's love life, Parker slightly stuck his foot in it by adding the throwaway line: 'There were armfuls of girls.'[3] It was a remark that would come to haunt him as he told another biographer of Philip, Gyles Brandreth: 'Jesus, I wish I had not used that phrase,' he exploded, before oddly embellishing it with, 'Yeah there were "armfuls of girls", showers of them but nothing – nothing serious. What I meant was this: we were young, we had fun, we had a few drinks, we might have gone dancing but that was it.'[4] In case anyone missed the point, he added, 'There were girls galore, but there was no one special. Believe me. I guarantee it.'[5]

Queen Alexandra witnessed Philip squiring one of the many girls for herself. In the summer of 1938, the Prince, then aged 17, stayed with his cousin and her mother, Princess Aspasia of Greece and Denmark, for a holiday in Venice. After each party Philip gallantly insisted on escorting his latest squeeze back to dry land by boat. 'No need to keep the driver, Auntie Aspasia,' he would say, 'I'll take over. The boatman's had a long day.'

Each night his aunt futilely stipulated a twenty-minute curfew. Alexandra knew her cousin had met someone special when he asked for a time extension to the deal. Aspasia agreed so long as he promised to keep circuiting the island so she could hear the engine running. Boys will be boys, and after three or four circuits the engine cut out for five minutes, 'which we filled with surmise', recalled his cousin.[6]

The Duke's biographer, Philip Eade, has identified the unnamed girl as Cobina Wright, also aged 17 that summer, whose socially ambitious mother, also named Cobina, had hosted parties for Philip. In her only interview about Philip, Cobina Jnr recalls they met at Harry's Bar where her mother 'shoved her into his arms'. After three weeks of parties and romantic gondola rides, Philip followed Cobina back to London and later wrote passionate letters to her. In that same interview she revealed she kept photos 'of the three loves of my life' – including one of Philip – and that at that time, 1973, they still wrote regularly to each other. A royal source told Philip Eade that the Prince 'had fallen very heavily for Cobina'.[7]

Keeping it in both families, by a quirk of fate Cobina's daughter, Cobina Caroline (nicknamed CC III), later dated Prince Andrew before his 1986 marriage to Sarah Ferguson.[8]

16

FIRST LOVE

Just months after his teenage crush on Cobina Wright ended, the Prince began a second romance. This time it was with a stunning Canadian-born socialite called Osla Benning. Osla was born in 1921 and so the couple were both 18 when they met. According to someone who knew her, Osla had 'dark hair, alabaster white skin, an exquisite figure and a gentle loving nature'.[1]

They were introduced by Osla's close friend and flatmate Sarah Norton (later Baring). Sarah was a fascinating character in her own right who worked for *Vogue* during the war before becoming a linguist at Bletchley Park, the centre for Allied code-breaking, thanks to her fluency in German. Much later, she was mentioned in Prime Minister's Questions in the House of Commons when Prime Minister David Cameron revealed that a relation of his wife Samantha had worked at Bletchley. (Sarah was the mother of Samantha Cameron's stepfather William, 4th Viscount Astor.) Impeccably connected, Sarah was a god-daughter of Philip's uncle Louis Mountbatten. Once, during a visit to Bletchley by Mountbatten and other military top brass, she surprised her fellow code-breakers by exclaiming to him, 'Uncle Dickie, What are you doing here?'[2]

It was Mountbatten who asked Sarah to find someone for Philip, as she recalled to biographer Philip Eade: 'Uncle Dickie said to me, "I don't think Philip's got a girlfriend at the moment, I wish you could find a nice girl for him because he doesn't know anyone," so I said, "I know, I'll get them together," and he said, "Excellent!"'[3]

This seems to fly in the face of the conventional theory that Mountbatten was masterminding the future union of his nephew to Princess Elizabeth from as early as July 1939, when the distant cousins met at Dartmouth Naval College and the 13-year-old future queen couldn't take her eyes off the young, blond, athletic Philip. Perhaps Mountbatten wanted the Prince to fully experience the world of the opposite sex before finding the right partner. After all, it was this strategy that surfaced again almost forty years later when he counselled his great-nephew Prince Charles on the subject of relationships and marriage. Mountbatten wrote to the Prince of Wales: 'In a case like yours a man should sow his wild oats and have as many affairs as he can before settling down. But for a wife he should choose a suitable, attractive, sweet-charactered girl before she has met anyone else she might fall for.'[4] Mountbatten was murdered two years before Charles married Lady Diana Spencer and so never lived to see how spectacularly wrong his theory became in practice.

The wartime romance of Philip and Osla was an altogether more successful venture. Sarah Norton set up a blind date at a Soho nightclub, telling Philip to come along 'because I'd got a rather pretty girl I'd like to introduce him to, and anyway they became great friends, they had a lovely time together.'[5]

Osla and Philip both came from broken homes. Osla's parents had split up and her mother had gone on to marry several times. It was a situation the Prince understood very well from his own peripatetic childhood, just as two generations later Prince Harry – whose parents had separated when he was 8 – instantly bonded with actress Meghan Markle whose parents divorced when she was 6 years old.

In London Philip and Osla danced the night away in high-society venues from the 400 Club to the Café de Paris. The two also met up at the cottage shared by Osla and Sarah near

Slough while the girls both carried out war work at the Hawker Siddeley aircraft factory. The cottage was owned and also lived in by Sarah's father, the filmmaker Richard Norton, 6th Lord Grantley, who recalled the youthful Philip as 'the best of company' and admired 'his forceful intellect'.[6]

Philip and Osla's romance blossomed despite the inevitable disruption of wartime duties for both of them. Philip bought her a bejewelled naval cipher as a brooch and the two wrote regularly when he was overseas. Sarah Baring later recalled Osla showing her his 'very sweet, nice letters about how much he was looking forward to seeing her'. When he got back on shore leave it was Osla he always rang first.[7]

It may seem strange to the twenty-first-century reader but it is unlikely the relationship was a physical one if Osla was typical of her circle. In fact she once caused a stir in a nightclub by loudly chastising her then boyfriend for inconsiderately leaving his torch in his trouser pocket, which made it uncomfortable for her to dance with. Much to her embarrassment an older woman hissed, 'Grow up! That's an erection.'[8]

In old age, Sarah Baring reflected:

> Nobody told us anything about the facts of life. We were all ignorant, and if we had known we'd have thought it disgusting. Certainly, I and all my close friends would have considered ourselves defiled if we hadn't come to marriage as virgins. Even after you had become engaged, it made no difference. Virginity lasted right up until the wedding night … At deb dances there were a few girls of whom we'd say 'They do it, you know!'[9]

Word soon got round if a boy was too amorous and the acronym NSIT – Not Safe in Taxis – was not one a decent young man, especially a prince, wanted to be labelled with.

The relationship seems to have gradually fizzled out. Philip attended parties at the new flat Osla shared with another friend, Sylvia Heywood, and crashed out on the sofa there. He also bought Osla a large book of illustrations called *Scraps and Sketches* by the caricaturist George Cruickshank for Christmas 1943 – the one the Prince spent at Windsor and which seems to have been when he first grew enamoured with the increasingly attractive Princess Elizabeth. By the start of 1944 the relationship had broken down and later that spring Osla was briefly engaged to a young diplomat.[10]

Touchingly, as with Cobina Wright, Philip stayed in touch with Osla for the rest of her life and was godfather to her son Mark. When she died in October 1974 at the age of only 53, found among her possessions was a photo of a young and incredibly handsome Philip with his blond hair not slicked down as usual but curly and tousled.[11]

17

A PRACTICAL JOKER

Many people are practical jokers as children and then grow out of it. Prince Philip remained a lifelong fan of the art. Having said that, it was a one-sided practice and few, if any, have dared to prank him.

As a small boy in Paris, he and Ianni Foufounis, his Greek-born friend, would take the family's Persian rugs out to the garden to sunbathe on. One day they disappeared and, after an hour's search, were found walking from house to house emulating the Arab salesmen they had seen touting their wares on the beach.[1] Lifelong friend Gina Wernher – later Lady Kennard – first met Philip in the late 1920s and remembered him as 'a very, obstreperous, rough little boy' who once pushed her down the stairs.[2]

More childhood naughtiness was recorded by his cousin Alexandra of Greece. She and Philip were once holidaying on the estate of the Landgrave of Hesse when they decided to unbolt the pig-stalls to see what would happen. The occupants took no notice and remained in situ, happily grunting away. Philip therefore decided to liven things up by poking them with a stick. The result was 'pandemonium … squealing, screaming, freed from their sties, the pigs stampeded and scampered … towards the tea-lawn'. Here they ran riot, knocking over chairs, sending screaming aunts and uncles running in all directions and upsetting all the trays and tea things.[3]

Aged 16, Philip was best man at the wedding of his cousin Prince Paul of Greece to Frederica of Hanover. Mingling at the reception later, he passed his aunt Helen, mother of Princess Marina of Greece, and thought 'her bare back presented an irresistible target. Philip glided up swiftly and silently and devilishly pressed his cold champagne glass on her skin. Aunt Helen whirled round but Philip was gone.'[4]

At Gordonstoun School he was known for his boisterous sense of fun. Headmaster Kurt Hahn, in a very unheadmasterly moment, bet the head boy and the two helpers (of whom Philip was then one) that they couldn't break in to Duffus House, where some of the pupils boarded, and kidnap a junior boy. This proved too much for them but they did manage to steal some of the boys' clothes and when the school assembled for breakfast in the dining room the next day they found it festooned with shorts and underpants.[5]

Marriage to the heir to the throne did nothing to dampen his mischievous streak. When he and Princess Elizabeth were on their first visit to Canada, he used his playfulness to lighten the mood, which at times was very flat given their concern for the health of the King and also occasional criticism in the local press about Elizabeth's apparent unwillingness to smile. As they crossed the dominion on the royal train, Philip boobytrapped a tin of nuts for his wife to open and on another occasion chased her through the train corridors wearing a set of joke Dracula fangs.[6]

In later years it was members of his household that became victims of his sense of humour. During the state visit of Queen Beatrix of the Netherlands, Philip was escorting the visitor along a receiving line at Buckingham Palace. As they approached his private secretary, who was tucked away at the end of the line behind some palm fronds, the Duke said, 'I've no idea who this is. Must be some gatecrasher.'[7]

When private secretary Brian McGrath had only just started his job in 1982, he accompanied Philip to a series of meetings in Geneva. A working dinner was held and McGrath realised that only he was not wearing a name badge. Being a bit of a wine buff, 'I wandered along to inspect the line of promising-looking bottles that had been put out for the meal. Suddenly, to my astonishment, two large Americans moved up on either side of me and said that they didn't think I was meant to be there.'

McGrath explained who he was and who he was with but the unimpressed security guys said they'd checked with the Prince and he'd said to them: 'It's a funny thing you should ask, because I was wondering myself. We came in together but I've never seen the man before.' At this point the baffled private secretary was bodily lifted out of the room 'and, as I went, I caught sight of Prince Philip bursting himself with laughter'.

McGrath wasn't the first or last member of staff to realise 'that life with Prince Philip was going to be great fun, if a little unpredictable'.[8]

18

BREAKING AND ENTERING

Prince Philip and the Queen have probably never owned a set of door keys in their life. In his younger days this caused a few problems for Philip since he was second only to party-loving Princess Margaret in his fondness for a night on the town. The result was that over the years he has been locked out of Buckingham Palace, Kensington Palace and Clarence House.

In the run-up to his wedding, Philip and his cousin David Milford Haven slept in adjoining rooms in the Kensington Palace apartment of their grandmother, the Dowager Marchioness of Milford Haven. After partying in the West End clubs the cousins became adept at climbing over the rooftops and in through their bedroom windows to avoid the giveaway creaking floorboards outside the Dowager's bedroom. It wasn't the first time Philip had opted for an over-the-eaves approach. As a youngster he once climbed on the apartment roof and cheekily dared the policeman who ordered him down to come up and get him first.[1]

Philip wasn't the only one of his generation to break into Kensington Palace. When Princess Margaret was ferried back from the state banquet for the Italian president in 1990, clearly 'tired and emotional', slumped in her limousine, her security team found she was locked out of her apartment and none of them had a key. They decided to wake her chauffeur David Griffin at his flat in case he had one. Just as they set off, HRH called out from the back of the car: 'Don't bother with him. He'll be drunk!'[2]

Before Clarence House was ready for them to occupy in the summer of 1949, Elizabeth and Philip lived with the King and Queen at Buckingham Palace. Growing stir-crazy, from time to time the Duke and his old navy friend Mike Parker would escape for 'an evening stroll'. More than once they were locked out and Parker had to give Philip a leg-up over the palace wall. On another occasion the two men took a dip in the Buckingham Palace swimming pool after a late dinner. The member of staff detailed to look after the pool locked it up, little imagining anyone would be using it at that hour. It took much hollering before another member of staff was alerted to rescue them.[3]

It was a case of old habits dying hard when the Prince and Parker went in search of nightlife after the Edinburghs had moved to Clarence House. Finding himself locked out of his own home, Philip resorted yet again to a leg-up over the gates. Told about the escapade the following morning, Princess Elizabeth commented drily: 'Serves them right!'[4]

19

IT'S NOT FOR ME, IT'S FOR A FRIEND

One of the perks of being a royal prince is that autographs are, by tradition, not given out other than on official signed photographs or Christmas cards.

Philip avoided them even before joining the firm. As a prince of Greece, he was a minor celebrity in Scotland when he attended Gordonstoun School, and his activities, from playing in the hockey team to carrying out patrol duties for the Elgin coastguard, appeared in the local press. One day when he was approached by a tourist eagerly waving an autograph book he signed it 'Baldwin of Bewdley', the title given to former prime minister Stanley Baldwin when he was ennobled after leaving office in 1937.

According to one approved biographer, Philip's reluctance to sign 'comes from an abhorrence of being regarded as a "celebrity", most hollow of twentieth-century accolades'.[1]

Once at a dinner at St George's House, Windsor, the assembled guests signed their menu cards and passed them round the table. They eventually accrued next to Philip's coffee cup and when he was prompted to sign them he retorted: 'I am not a pop star!' Another time, while visiting an RAF base in Germany, the commanding officer ambushed him into signing the day's programme as he was about to board his aircraft. 'This is not usual,' said Philip in full Lady Bracknell mode before grudgingly signing and storming off.[2]

When his signatures do make it onto paper, what do they tell us about the man who wrote them? Leading graphologist Tracey Trussell says, 'The tall, regal, confidently large sized, and vertically composed arrangement of letters, usually firmly underlined, packs a prestigious image and transmits exactly what you would expect from royalty.' The first letter 'P' dominates the signature. 'The large size conveys pride and commands respect,' claims Tracey, 'and the stylish "bloated" loop, located in the upper zonal region, tells us he is undoubtedly achievement orientated and cerebrally charged, with a mind that is always one step ahead.' The final 'P' of his name also stands out with its broad loop, 'which is an indication of someone who can be outspoken and blurt things out without thinking. Stubbornness can be seen in the hooks at both the beginning and end of his name. The slight left slant of the writing is a nod to irreverence.' It would seem that 'you are what you write' clearly applies in the Duke's case.[3]

His cousin Lady Pamela Hicks points out that his signature reflects the land of his birth. 'I think it's rather marvellous he signs himself with the Greek "P" even if he doesn't have a drop of Greek blood in his veins.'[4] Lady Pamela is referring to the Greek letter 'phi' which later became 'ph' as in 'photo', 'anglophile' and of course 'Philip', written as a circle with a vertical line through it – Φ – which is how Philip usually signs himself on his paintings.[5]

As a fan of the now defunct magazine *Punch,* Philip attended one of its legendary weekly lunches. It was a tradition for the editor to ask the most distinguished guests to carve their names on the Victorian wooden dining table. Alongside the scratched signatures of Mark Twain and Charles Dickens, the Duke etched his letter 'phi'.[6]

Despite the rejection of his family by the Greek government and the assassination of his grandfather King George I on Greek soil in 1913, as a youngster Philip very much honoured the country in his signature. At school in Cheam he sent the headmaster, Harold Taylor, Christmas cards from 'Philippos' with the Greek version written underneath.[7]

Although he has been approached for autographs several times, there is no record of his ever being asked for a 'selfie', so historians can only imagine his response on that one.

20

QUIPS, GAFFES AND BANTER: THE DUKE'S MEMORABLE CLANGERS 11–20

UPSETTING THE COMMONWEALTH

11 **Canada:** In 1969, he forgot the name of the annex he was dedicating at Vancouver City Hall mid-ceremony, *'It gives me great pleasure to declare this thing open, whatever it is.'*

12 **Australia:** In 2002, talking to a successful indigenous Australian entrepreneur, *'Do you still throw spears at each other?'*

13 **Canada:** Responding to the gift of a white cowboy hat during a 1969 visit to Calgary, *'Not another one. You must give out dozens of these things.'* He told reporters that he could use it as a flower pot or to carry water.

14 **Papua New Guinea:** To a student in 1998 who had been trekking there, implying that the tribes there were still cannibals, *'You managed not to get eaten, then?'*

15 **Canada:** Philip was flying himself to Canada and stopped for refuelling at a Canadian forces base at Gander in Newfoundland. An official later recalled: *'The commanding officer says: "Hello. How was your flight, sir?" And the Duke says: "Have you ever flown before?" And the commanding officer says: "Yes." The Duke says: "Well, it was a lot like that." And he strides off to get a cup of tea.'*

16 **Bangladesh:** Bonding with the members at a Bangladeshi youth club, '*So who's on drugs here? … HE looks as if he's on drugs.*'

17 **Canada:** During a 1976 visit he snapped, '*We don't come here for our health. We can think of other ways of enjoying ourselves.*'

18 **Solomon Islands:** On being told, in 1982, that the islands' population growth was 5 per cent a year, '*You must be out of your minds.*'

19 **Canada:** Talking about French Canadians during a visit to Toronto in 1985, '*I can't understand a word they say; they slur all their words.*'

20 **Anguilla:** During a visit in 1965 he was told about a project to protect turtle doves. His response, '*Cats kill far more birds than men. Why don't you have a slogan: "Kill a cat and save a bird?"*'

21

TWO DEGREES OF SEPARATION: PHILIP AND THE DUKE OF WELLINGTON

It was the morning of 1 May 1850 and Queen Victoria was in labour with her seventh child. As protocol had dictated for over 150 years, members of the Privy Council gathered in an adjoining room to verify that the birth had occurred. (This was because when Mary of Modena produced a son for the deeply unpopular Roman Catholic James II, rumour had it that another boy had been smuggled into the delivery room inside a warming pan.) At seventeen minutes past eight, the Queen gave birth to a son, 'a very fine boy', as one of the ministers, Arthur Wellesley, Duke of Wellington, pronounced him.[1] It happened to be the Iron Duke's eighty-first birthday and the fresh prince was duly named Arthur after the hero of Waterloo, who became his godfather.

Fast-forward nearly a century to 16 January 1942 and the same royal personage, Prince Arthur, Duke of Connaught and Strathearn, departed this life aged 91 years. Among those gathered to mourn him a week later at the funeral in St George's Chapel, Windsor, was 21-year-old Prince Philip of Greece.

Wellington had been present at Prince Arthur's baptism at Buckingham Palace on 22 June 1851 and their relationship was immortalised in an oil painting by Franz Winterhalter – *The First of May, 1851* – which shows the aged victor of the Battle of Waterloo presenting his baby godson with a gold casket to mark his first birthday. A year later, on 18 June 1852, the anniversary of Waterloo, Wellington gave baby Arthur a guided tour of his London home, Apsley House.

Prince Arthur followed his godfather into the army, serving for forty years in various parts of the British Empire, and even wrote to his great-nephew, George VI, to offer his services at the start of the Second World War, when he was 89.

It was as a mark of respect that George ordered two weeks' court mourning following Connaught's death. Four kings – of Greece, Norway, Yugoslavia and Great Britain – attended the funeral at Windsor. They were followed in the procession by three Greek princes – Philip, Peter and Crown Prince Paul – as well as seven field marshals.[2]

As the coffin was lowered into its temporary home in the royal vault (before a later burial in the royal burial grounds at

Frogmore), George VI, in the khaki uniform of a field marshal, bowed. He was followed by Queen Elizabeth, heavily veiled and dressed in black, who gave a deep curtsey.

Then the other kings and princes, including Philip, bowed in obeisance at the passing of Prince Arthur, the last of Queen Victoria's sons.

22

FOR QUEEN AND COUNTRY: THE DUKE'S MEDALS

The Queen and Prince Philip have for many years been the world's last head of state and consort to have served in the Second World War.

Princess Elizabeth received the Defence Medal and the War Medal 1939–45. She last wore them in public at the 1986 Trooping the Colour ceremony.

Prince Philip's war service was rewarded with:

1939–45 Star: Campaign medal awarded to British and Commonwealth forces
Atlantic Star: Awarded in 1945 for service during the Battle of the Atlantic
Africa Star: Awarded in 1945 for service in North Africa between 1940 and 1943
Burma Star (with Pacific Rosette): Awarded for service in both the Pacific theatre of operations and the Burma Campaign between 1941 and 1945

Italy Star: Awarded for service in the Italian Campaign 1943–45
War Medal 1939–45, with Mention in Dispatches: awarded to
those who served in the armed forces or Merchant Navy for at
least twenty-eight days between 1939 and 1945. The oak leaf on
the ribbon denotes the Mention in Dispatches
Cross of Valour: Awarded for his contribution in fighting the
Italians when they invaded his homeland of Greece in 1941
Croix de Guerre (France) with Palm, 1948: A French military
decoration awarded to those in the Allied forces who fought the
Axis powers.

The Queen and Duke are both entitled to wear the King
George VI Coronation Medal, given to them when Elizabeth
was 11 and Philip a month away from his sixteenth birthday.

Medals worn by the Queen. Left to right: the Imperial Order of the
Crown of India, the Defence Medal, the War Medal 1939–45, the
Jubilee Medal of King George VI, the Coronation Medal of King
George VI, the Canadian Forces Decoration (silver). (© Ian Lloyd)

The rest of Philip's medals are commemorative ones for the Queen's Coronation and her Silver, Golden and Diamond Jubilees. He has also received honorary medals from New Zealand, Canada and Malta for his service to those countries as Duke of Edinburgh.

Having had more full-dress military events than the rest of us have had hot dinners, the Duke has become an expert on medals, ribbons and badges. When a parade of Chelsea Pensioners appeared on stage at the opening of the 2001 Royal Variety Performance, 80-year-old Philip squinted down at them from the royal box. 'God,' he muttered, 'none of them served in the war. It comes to something when I'm older than the Chelsea Pensioners!'[1]

Philip wearing his medals at a VJ Day commemoration at the Imperial War Museum in August 2005. (© Ian Lloyd)

23

NAVAL HERO

At 2100 hours on Sunday 28 March 1941 radar from the Allied naval fleet located the Italian Navy off Cape Matapan, the southernmost point of mainland Greece. What happened next led to Italy's greatest defeat at sea in the Second World War as well as Prince Philip of Greece's finest hour.

Philip had joined HMS *Valiant* on 2 January 1941. The battleship, launched in 1914, had seen action in 1915 at the Battle of Jutland during the previous war and had recently undergone a comprehensive three-year modernisation which included the latest radar and anti-aircraft guns.

Valiant was part of the Mediterranean fleet under the command of Admiral Andrew Cunningham, himself a Jutland veteran, and was engaged in convoying British troops from Alexandria to Crete and Piraeus to bolster the British Expeditionary Force in Greece. Hitler wanted the convoys stopped and the Italian Navy was given the task.

Back in Britain, Mavis Batey, code-breaker at Bletchley Park (and later a notable garden historian), deciphered messages from the Italian naval Enigma ordering an attack. This intelligence was passed on to Cunningham and, on 27 March, Philip noted in his ship's log: 'There were to have been three nights of all night leave in Alexandria but by Thursday forenoon there was a buzz going around the ship that some Italian cruisers had gone to sea.'[1] Cunningham headed towards Crete with four cruisers and four destroyers from the British and Australian navies. Five more destroyers joined them on the morning of the 28th.

British reconnaissance planes located the Italian fleet (which was hampered by its own lack of air power and radar) and two exchanges in the morning and afternoon of that same day severely damaged the Italian flagship *Vittorio Veneto* as well as the heavy cruiser *Pola*. The enemy neither expected nor was equipped for a night-time attack. They were located in the dark by radar before *Valiant* and the other battleship *Barham* opened fire at point-blank range from 3,500ft. Within five minutes Cunningham's men had sunk the two heavy cruisers *Zara* and *Fiume*, two destroyers and the already wounded *Pola*. The Italians lost 2,303 men, mostly from the cruisers. Another 1,015 were rescued by the Allied fleet. In contrast, the British lost a single torpedo bomber carrying three men.

During the night-time conflict Philip manned the searchlights, crucial in identifying the enemy targets. The Duke's biographer Basil Boothroyd was given access to Philip's wartime log, which gives a detailed account of his role. 'My orders were that if any ship illuminated a target I was to switch on and illuminate it for the rest of the fleet,' he recorded, adding, 'so when this ship was lit up by a rather dim light from what I thought was a flagship I switched on our midship light which picked out the enemy cruiser and lit her up as if it were broad daylight.'

She was only seen complete in the light for a few seconds as the flagship had already opened fire, and as her first broadside landed and hit she was blotted out from just abaft the bridge to right stern. We fired our first broadside about 7 seconds after the flagship with very much the same effect.

He was then ordered to train his lights to the left to pick out another cruiser:

The effect was rather like flashing a strong torch on a small model about 5 yards away … She was illuminated in an undamaged condition for the period of about 5 seconds when our second broadside left the ship, and almost at once she was completely blotted out from stern to stern.

At one point during the bombardment 'the glasses were rammed into my eyes' with the 'flash almost blinding me'. After estimating that 70 per cent of the shells must have hit, Philip concludes: 'When the enemy had completely vanished in clouds of smoke and steam we ceased firing and switched the light off.'[2]

At the age of 90 Philip reflected on the dramatic battle in a foreword to the 2012 book by J.E. Harrold. After pointing out that 'all these events took place 70 years ago, and, as most elderly people have discovered, memories tend to fade', he recalled:

I seem to remember that I reported I had a target in sight. I was ordered to 'open shutter'. The beam lit up a stationary cruiser, but we were so close by then that the beam only lit up half the ship. At this point all hell broke loose, as all our eight 15-inch guns, plus those of the flagship and Barham's started firing at the stationary cruiser, which disappeared in an explosion and a cloud of smoke. I was then ordered to 'train left' and lit up another Italian cruiser, which was given the same treatment.

The next morning the battle fleet returned to the scene of the battle, while attempts were made to pick up survivors. This was rudely interrupted by an attack by German bombers.

His conclusion, that 'The return to Alexandria was uneventful, and the peace and quiet was much appreciated', is a typically wry ducal reflection.[3]

Basil Boothroyd felt Philip's account, 'so calm, so controlled', was 'possibly a little underplaying'[4] and that he probably deserved more than being 'Mentioned in Dispatches' by Cunningham.

Philip's commander reported that 'the successful and continuous illumination of the enemy greatly contributed to the devastating results achieved in the gun action' and that 'thanks to his alertness and appreciation of the situation we were able to sink in five minutes two eight-inch-gun Italian cruisers'.[5] Not for the first time, and certainly not for the last, Philip's royal title may have stopped the navy top brass from looking at his actions objectively. 'When it comes to decorating princes, those responsible may be sensitive to suspicion of favouritism.'[6]

Further recognition for Philip's bravery came from the land of his birth. His cousin King George II of Greece awarded him his country's highest military decoration, the Cross of Valour. When another cousin, Princess Alexandra of Greece, congratulated him on the honour 'he simply shrugged', though he later admitted what he'd witnessed 'was as near murder as anything could be in wartime. The cruisers just burst into tremendous sheets of flame.'[7]

There was even a token gesture to Philip's battle heroics on his wedding day. The four-tier McVitie and Price wedding cake included a depiction of the Battle of Matapan and of *Valiant* among the many sugar decorations.[8]

24

1945: THE FINAL SURRENDER

The Queen memorably celebrated VE Day by joining thousands of revellers dancing through the streets of London when the war against Germany finally ended in May 1945. Later that same year, in the Far East, Prince Philip witnessed the official surrender of the Japanese Empire in Tokyo Bay and took part in VJ celebrations in Hong Kong.

When the Second World War began in September 1939, Philip was a cadet at the Royal Naval College, Dartmouth. By the time it ended he was second-in-command of the new destroyer HMS *Whelp*. He was appointed its First Lieutenant in February 1944 but it wasn't until the following August that the ship sailed from Glasgow to the Far East. Here, *Whelp* became part of the British Pacific Fleet under Admiral Fraser and under the ultimate command of his uncle Lord Mountbatten, the Supreme Allied Commander, South-East Asia.

In January 1945 Philip helped rescue the two-man crew of an Allied bomber shot down by the Japanese over Indonesia, after they had spent twenty minutes struggling to survive in the sea. The Prince ordered hot food and dry clothes for the pair, who were identified as pilot Roy 'Gus' Halliday and air gunner Norman 'Dickie' Richardson. The latter was reunited with the Duke in a 2006 radio programme.[1]

Whelp went on to carry out diversionary attacks on the Japanese-held Sakishima Islands while American forces laid siege to Okinawa. Although the Allied fleet was attacked by kamikaze pilots, *Whelp*, as a smaller ship, was not a target.[2]

After a refit in Melbourne for the ship and leave for the crew, the destroyer joined HMS *Wager* for escort duties with the battleship HMS *Duke of York,* carrying Admiral Fraser to Guam for talks with Fleet Admiral Nimitz of the US Navy. It was while he was in Guam that Philip heard of the bombing of Hiroshima on 9 August 1945.[3]

Whelp and *Wager* escorted the *Duke of York* and USS *Missouri*, the flagship of Admiral Halsey, commander of the South Pacific Area. The ships then spent several weeks in Tokyo Bay, where on 2 September 1945 the Instrument of Surrender was signed on *Missouri*.

The Queen and Duke honour the war dead during a service at the Field of Remembrance, St Margaret's, Westminster, in November 2002. (© Ian Lloyd)

Interviewed at the time of the fortieth anniversary in 1995, the Duke recalled being just 200 yards away from the historic event. 'You could see what was going on with a pair of binoculars,' he said, adding, 'it was a great relief.' As the flotilla headed for Hong Kong afterwards, the Prince realised in 'the most extraordinary sensation' that since hostilities had ended there was no need to darken the ships at night, by turning out the lights or closing all the scuttles. 'All these little things built up to suddenly feeling life was different.'

En route, *Whelp* picked up a number of British POWs who had been held by the Japanese. The ship's company made them tea, and the Duke's overwhelming memory is of how both the crew and the survivors 'just sat there, and both sides, our own and them, with just tears pouring down their cheeks'. The men were unable to speak and simply drank their tea.[4]

On 16 September Admiral Fraser accepted the Japanese forces' surrender in Hong Kong and Philip and his men took part in the VJ celebrations there. After these historic events, *Whelp* was decommissioned and Philip was given command of the ship for the return journey to Britain. They arrived at Portsmouth on 17 January 1946.

During his war at sea, Philip had seen active service in most of the oceans, taken part in the evacuation of Greece and Crete, had given backup when Canadian forces landed at Sicily, as well as during the Allied invasion of North Africa, witnessed the official surrender in the Far East and held a brief command. Not bad for a Royal Navy officer who wasn't even British at the time.

25

THE MOMENT THEY CLICKED

It was a watershed moment. Philip the 22-year-old naval hero watched and cheered as 17-year-old Elizabeth, dressed in a revealing costume, paraded on stage in that perennial Christmas favourite – a pantomime.

It doesn't sound terribly romantic but it was a far cry from their first memorable meeting at the Royal Naval College,

Dartmouth, in July 1939. Then Philip was a show-off 18-year-old cadet and Elizabeth, five years his junior, was very much a schoolgirl in her socks, classic little-girl shoes and unflattering beret. Now she was clearly blossoming into an attractive young woman with undoubtedly shapely legs to boot.

Six decades later their grandson, Prince William, would have a similar 'ker-ching' moment when he saw a skin-baring Kate Middleton sashay along a catwalk in a student fashion show at the University of St Andrews.

Philip very nearly didn't see the panto. He'd been confined to bed with flu at London's Claridge's Hotel but rallied in time to attend the third and final night of the show on 18 December 1943. That year's production was *Aladdin*, with Elizabeth as the principal boy and 13-year-old Margaret as Princess Roxanne.

An excited Elizabeth told her governess Marion Crawford: 'Who do you think is coming to see us act, Crawfie? Philip.' The Princess was flushed with excitement and Crawfie wrote, 'I have never known Lilibet more animated. There was a sparkle about her none of us had ever seen before. Many people remarked on it.'[1]

Philip sat on the front row alongside the King and Queen and his cousin Princess Marina. The King was more concerned than the Prince with his eldest daughter's costume, which he had personally inspected. 'Lilibet cannot possibly wear that,' he complained to Miss Crawford, 'The tunic is too short.'

The governess had the chance to give Philip the once-over from her position in the wings. 'He was greatly changed,' she noted. 'It was a grave and charming young man who sat there with nothing of the rather bumptious young boy I had first known about him.'[2]

Crawfie must have missed the bits when, according to his cousin Alexandra of Yugoslavia, Philip was 'nearly falling out of his seat with laughter' at such corny jokes as …

> Widow Twankey: *There's a large copper in the kitchen*
> Princess Elizabeth: *We'll soon get rid of him.*[3]

There was more laughter as Philip stayed for the weekend at Windsor Castle. He was back a week later with his cousin David Milford Haven to spend Christmas with the royal family.

Queen Alexandra recalled there was a party of nine seated for dinner on Christmas Eve and that 'Philip entertained the King with a half-comical account of the adventures on the *Wallace* off Sicily when three German aircraft dive-bombed her.'

Later they turned all the lights out in the drawing room and told ghost stories by the firelight. 'We settled ourselves to be frightened,' Margaret wrote, 'and we were NOT. Most disappointing.'[4] One might suspect Elizabeth and Philip enjoyed the ghostly blackout more than the complaining Princess did. Crawfie received an excited report from her older charge: 'We had a very gay time, with a film, dinner parties and dancing to the gramophone.' The King's private secretary, Alan 'Tommy' Lascelles, noted they 'frisked and capered away till nearly 1 a.m.'.[5] Even hard-to-please Margaret added, 'went mad and we danced and danced and danced … the best night of all'.[6]

In a thank-you letter to Queen Elizabeth, Philip hoped 'my behaviour did not get out of hand'. In another thank-you after another stay a few weeks later, he reflected on how much he loved 'the simple enjoyment of family pleasures and amusements', and the fact that the King and Queen's family gave him 'the feeling that I am welcome to share them'.[7] For the young man who had not had a house he could call home since the age of 9, the tight-knit royal family must have seemed as rock solid as Windsor Castle itself.

From now on, Philip and Elizabeth took a much greater interest in each other's lives and activities; as Marion Crawford noted, the Christmas of 1943 was a turning point for the young couple.

26

PATHWAY TO LOVE

For Elizabeth it was said to be love at first sight when she met Philip at Dartmouth Naval College shortly before the war. For much of the war their relationship could be described as cousinly, particularly as Philip had had an ongoing relationship with Osla Benning. Things began to intensify after the war when the Prince returned from the Far East and began a desk job at Corsham, Wiltshire. By the end of 1946 press and public were aware of the relationship.

THE CLUES ...

January–April 1940: Philip spent four months serving as a midshipman on HMS *Ramillies*. His captain, Vice Admiral Harold Tom Baillie-Grohman, noted a conversation he had with the Prince during their time at sea: Philip said, '"My Uncle Dickie has ideas for me; he thinks I could marry Princess Elizabeth." I was a bit taken aback, and, after a hesitation asked him: "Are you really fond of her?" "Oh yes, very," was the reply and "I write to her every week."'[1] At the time Philip was 18 and Elizabeth 14 in April.
Christmas 1940: Philip sends Elizabeth a Christmas card from Athens.
21 January 1941: Diarist Henry 'Chips' Channon noted after talking to Philip's aunt, Princess Nicholas of Greece: 'He is to be our Prince Consort, and that is why he is serving in our navy.'[2] Philip's response when quizzed about Channon's comment in 1971 was: 'It had been mentioned, presumably, that "he is eligible, he's the sort of person she might marry". I mean after all

… how many obviously eligible young men, other than people living in this country, were available? Inevitably I must have been on the list.'[3]

June 1941: In Cape Town, Philip's cousin Alexandra disturbed him writing a letter to Princess Elizabeth and teased him, 'but she's only a baby'. She thought he was angling for invitations to stay with her family.[4]

1943: Elizabeth sent her cousin Margaret Elphinstone a letter which says: 'It's so exciting. Mummy says that Philip can come and stay when he gets leave'. This probably refers to the December 1943 stay at Windsor.[5]

18 December 1943: Philip attended the pantomime *Aladdin* at Windsor Castle. He stayed the weekend and returned to spend Christmas with the royal family.

At Sandringham in January 1946 Queen Mary told her lady-in-waiting, Mabell, Countess of Airlie: 'They have been in love for the last eighteen months. In fact longer, I think. I believe she fell in love with him the first time he went down to Windsor'.[6] This dates the romance from Philip's two visits in December 1943.

March 1944: George II of Greece raised the subject of his cousin Philip's engagement to Elizabeth with her father. George VI felt his daughter was too young and wrote to his mother Queen Mary: 'We are going to tell George that P. had better not think any more about it at present'.[7]

Early August 1944: Mountbatten meets George VI to discuss Philip taking British citizenship and his possible marriage to Elizabeth.

10 August 1944: George VI writes to Mountbatten: 'I have come to the conclusion that we are going too fast', and asks Mountbatten to limit discussions to the question of citizenship only.[8]

24 August 1944: Lord Mountbatten met Philip and George II of Greece in Cairo in part to talk about Philip taking British citizenship and his possible marriage. 'Had very satisfactory discussions', noted Mountbatten in his journal.[9]

27 October 1944: Diarist 'Chips' Channon visited Princess Marina of Kent at Coppins. 'As I signed the visitors' book I noticed "Philip" written constantly. It is at Coppins that he sees Princess Elizabeth. I think she will marry him.'[10]

2 March 1945: Tommy Lascelles, private secretary to George VI, writes to the Home Office to find out 'what steps would have to be taken to enable Prince Philip of Greece … to become a British subject', adding, 'at an appropriate time'.[11]

October 1945: Prime Minister Clement Attlee suggested the question of Philip's naturalisation should be put off until the following year in case it had repercussions on relations with Greece, where civil war was raging and the restoration of the monarchy was as yet uncertain.[12]

1945: Philip's cousin Princess Alexandra of Greece lived near Windsor and 'used to see them holding hands, disengaging themselves sometimes until we came closer and they could see it was only us'.[13]

January 1946: George VI gave Philip a lift from London to Windsor for his reunion with Elizabeth on his return from the Far East.

1 April 1946: Philip is among a party of six accompanying Elizabeth to see *The Hasty Heart* at the Aldwych Theatre, London.[14]

Late April 1946: Philip tells his younger sister Sophie that 'he was thinking about getting engaged' and that 'Uncle Dickie was being helpful'.[15]

29 May 1946: Elizabeth and Philip were photographed together following the wedding of Elizabeth's cousin Andrew Elphinstone to Jean Hambro, although the newspapers didn't speculate on the relationship.

1946: John Dean, valet to Lord Mountbatten, 'had only one piece of evidence to go on' that an engagement was in the pipeline: 'Whenever Prince Philip brought a week-end bag, and I unpacked it, I always found a small photograph in a battered frame – a photograph of Princess Elizabeth.'[16]

12 June 1946: Philip apologised to Queen Elizabeth for his 'monumental cheek' in inviting himself to the palace. He told her a voice inside his head said, '"nothing ventured, nothing gained," – well I did venture and I gained a wonderful time.'[17]

5 September 1946: Philip was part of the royal party accompanying the King, Queen and the two princesses to the Braemar Games. It was the wettest gathering in memory and an audience of 20,000 received a thorough soaking in the open stands.

8 September 1946: The King, Queen and Princess Margaret drove to Crathie Church. Princess Elizabeth was confined her apartments with 'a slight cold' while Prince Philip walked the half-mile route to the kirk with Queen Elizabeth's brother Michael Bowes Lyon, past waiting crowds of onlookers and photographers.

9 September 1946: A rumour of an impending engagement between Elizabeth and Philip had been circulating in London, fuelled by a piece suggesting it in the London *Star*. The newspapers on the 9th reported that the King's private secretary, Tommy Lascelles, had announced from Buckingham Palace: 'Princess Elizabeth is not engaged to be married. The report published is not true.'

Then, as now, an official palace denial of an engagement is usually concrete proof that one is on the cards. Although the world and many outside the immediate family had no idea that in …

September 1946: The couple became unofficially engaged at Balmoral.

13 September 1946: Philip left Balmoral Castle after a three-week stay.

26 October 1946: 'It was my wedding which really put the cat amongst the pigeons,' recalled Patricia, Countess Mountbatten.

'The Princess was a bridesmaid, and Philip was an usher. The newsreel cameras captured him helping her to take off her coat and although none of us thought anything of it on the day, it was the first intimation that there might be something interesting between the two of them.'[18]

23 May 1947: Mountbatten noted in his diary, 'Saw [Queen] Elizabeth re Philip.' The following day he wrote: 'Philip and I talked about Lilibet.'[19]

9 July 1947: The engagement of Elizabeth and Philip was announced.

27

THE MYSTERY OF THEIR ENGAGEMENT

Despite living the most public of lives, the Queen and Prince Philip have managed to keep some parts of their shared history totally private. Their engagement is a case in point. It was publicly announced on 9 July 1947 but had taken place privately some ten months earlier when Philip was invited by Queen Elizabeth to stay at Balmoral for three weeks' shooting. Only Elizabeth and Philip know how their love affair moved up a decisive gear that previous summer.

It was on the Deeside royal estate, between mid August and early September 1946, that the deed was done. Philip himself let the cat out of the bag in an interview granted to his biographer Basil Boothroyd in 1971. 'There must have been a time when you decided you were going to marry Princess Elizabeth?' was the writer's no-nonsense opener. Philip's reply was as rambling as a day on the Cairngorms. 'I suppose one thing led to another,' he began cautiously, trying to be informative and annoyingly discreet in equal measure. 'I suppose I began to think about it seriously, oh let me think now, when I got back in '46 and went to Balmoral. It was probably then that we, that it became, you know, that we began to think about it seriously, and even talk about it.'[1]

We don't know if Elizabeth, as the more senior royal personage, followed in Queen Victoria's footsteps and suggested marriage to her suitor. Most biographies assume it was Philip who proposed. His cousin Princess Alexandra of Greece, whom one would assume was a reliable source, says of Balmoral 1946 in her biography of the Duke, 'Here at last Philip and Lilibet could be truly alone ... and Philip proposed.'[2] Alexandra then gives an account of the engagement location which Elizabeth revealed to her 'in an unguarded speech' which is more like a Mills & Boon novel than her usual formal style: 'beside some well-loved loch,' she recalled, 'the white clouds sailing overhead and a curlew crying out of sight'.[3]

We don't know who proposed, when they proposed or where they proposed, but we do know that the engagement ring only appeared in time for the official announcement and also that King George asked that an announcement should only be made after the King, Queen and two princesses returned from their mammoth tour of South Africa in early May 1947.

Philip's suggestion of a 1946 Balmoral engagement is, however, backed up by a letter he wrote to Queen Elizabeth in September after he left the estate. In it he pondered if he deserved 'all the good things which have happened to me', especially 'to have fallen in love completely and unreservedly'. Clearly euphoric and in love, he added: 'Naturally there is one circumstance which has done more for me than anything else in my life.' Only their official biographies will dot the 'i's and cross the 't's.

28

PHILIP FLUNKS AN EXAM

Benjamin Disraeli memorably said: 'Everyone likes flattery; and when you come to Royalty you should lay it on with a trowel.' How else would Prince Charles have managed to study at Trinity College, Cambridge, having notched up two A-levels – a B in History and a C in French? Then there's the similar elevation of his grandfather, George VI, who finished bottom of the class in exams at the Royal Naval Academy at Osborne but ended up as a midshipman and also did a year at Cambridge University.

Philip happily bucked the trend. 'He sought no special favours and, indeed, found them insulting,' recalled Eileen Parker, ex-wife of his friend Mike Parker. One example she cited was of Philip's commanding officer on HMS *Whelp* who addressed him as 'Sir', much to his embarrassment.[1]

A more significant case occurred when Philip was stationed in Malta and sat the exam that would result in his promotion to lieutenant commander. It involved a detailed knowledge of gunnery, torpedoes and anti-submarine warfare. After he'd done the papers, Mike Parker was called to the office of the commander-in-chief, Admiral Sir Arthur Power. Here he found the admiral walking up and down clutching two of the papers in which Philip hadn't done so well. An examiner that, according to Parker, was a polo player with a jealous streak when it came to Philip, had marked him low on anti-sub. 'This bloody man has failed Prince Philip,' fumed the commander-in-chief.[2] His instinct was to waive the two papers but wanted to check with the equerry first. Parker said Prince Philip would never agree to a cover-up. Sure enough, when he reported back to his boss, Philip said: 'If they try to fix it, I will resign.'[3] In the end he resat the papers and passed with flying colours, and he was offered the command of HMS *Magpie*.

Despite such a creditable attitude, very occasionally Philip pulled rank in his later navy days, even after his marriage. Once, on shore leave in the South of France, he drove a group of friends on a picnic expedition into nearby Italy. Reaching the border crossing they realised that one of the party had forgotten her passport. Eileen Parker remembered: 'Prince Philip drew up slowly by the customs patrol and gave them ample time to study his face closely.' Recognition dawned and they were waved through 'in a flurry of pompous obeisance'. As he drove them off, Philip chuckled: 'There are some compensations in this job, after all.'[4]

29

AN UNWELCOME WELCOME

'They were bloody to him,' recalled Earl Mountbatten's son-in-law John Brabourne, 'They didn't like him, they didn't trust him and it showed.'[1]

The 'him' Brabourne referred to was the man Princess Elizabeth had fallen in love with. The 'them' were senior courtiers as well as aristocratic friends of the royal family. For a short time the damning words would even apply to George VI and Queen Elizabeth themselves.

It was no secret at court that Elizabeth's mother wanted her to marry a British aristocrat. 'We always joked that Queen Elizabeth had produced a cricket eleven of names she hoped the Princess would fall for,' recalled former assistant private secretary, Edward Ford. 'They were all Eton men and most of them were the heirs to dukedoms – Hugh Euston [Grafton], Johnny Dalkieth [Buccleuch], Sonny Blandford [Marlborough] and so on. The only batsman missing off her list was Prince Philip.'[2] To be fair to Queen Elizabeth, when the official engagement of Elizabeth and Philip was about to be announced, she did manage to joke to her old friend Arthur Penn: 'I say, Arthur, how annoyed the Grenadiers will be!'[3] – a reference to the guards regiment half her cricket team had served with.

The future Queen Mother wasn't the only royal lady who had reservations about Philip. Princess Margaret felt, and told her friends, that Philip wasn't good enough for her sister.[4] Even as late as 1978 the historian Sir Roy Strong was told by a royal friend that, 'HRH and Prince Philip didn't hit it off – all those jokes about the navy irritated her.'[5]

The King's reservations were less about Philip than about his eldest daughter's youth and the lack of opportunity she'd had to meet possible suitors thanks to the war and her royal duties. An early marriage would also deprive the King of the daughter he had so much in common with, as one eyewitness observed. Mabell, Countess of Airlie, was lady-in-waiting to Queen Mary as well as a close confidante. She felt George VI had a 'secret dread' about Elizabeth marrying so young since he would lose 'his constant companion in shooting, walking, riding – in fact in everything'.[6]

Making mischief in the background were three sets of aristocratic friends who all disliked Philip intensely. 'Lords Salisbury, Eldon and Stanley think him no gentleman,' wrote Princess

Elizabeth's private secretary, Jock Colville, in August 1947, adding sardonically, 'and in a sense they are right.'[7]

Half a century later Peter Ashmore, appointed an equerry to the King in 1946 and thus an eyewitness to Philip's arrival at court, recalled:

> The old guard found him hard to swallow. The Eldons and the Salisburys, who were close friends of the King and Queen, ganged up against him and made it plain that they hoped they were not going to let their daughter marry this chap. None of the aristocrats and Old Etonians round the table were in favour of him.[8]

Edward Ford remembered Philip had 'no retiring graces and wasn't in the least afraid to tell the King's friend Lord Salisbury, what he felt.'

It wasn't just the King's friends who had reservations, but his senior courtiers too. Edward Ford recalled some felt 'this rough diamond, will he treat the Princess with the sensitivity she deserves?'[9] They were clearly unaware that the fact that Philip didn't treat Elizabeth with 'the sensitivity she deserves' was one of the personality traits that attracted her to him in the first place.

The King's private secretary, Tommy Lascelles, was even more damning in private. Writing to royal biographer Harold Nicolson, he revealed that both the King and Queen 'felt he was rough, ill-tempered, uneducated and would probably not be faithful'.[10] Another courtier thought the royal household 'feared him because he was new-broomish and they were set in their ways. He was innovative even then and no respecter of the status quo.'[11]

Another eyewitness to the negative reaction to Philip was the Princess's cousin Margaret Elphinstone, who noted that many of his critics in royal circles felt he was 'a foreign interloper out for the goodies'.[12] The use of the word 'foreign' is interesting since, although Philip served in the British Navy throughout the Second World War and was a descendant of Queen Victoria, he was widely perceived by those close to the King and Queen as Germanic. The three critical lords, Salisbury, Eldon and Stanley, 'profess to see in him a Teutonic strain', and one referred to him as 'Charlie Kraut'.[13] Queen Elizabeth, who had lost a brother Fergus Bowes Lyon during the First World War and who remained vehemently anti-German throughout her long life, was said years later, in private, to have dubbed her son-in-law 'the Hun' and felt he ran the royal estates 'like a Junker'.[14] Princess Margaret picked up on the foreign slurs, asking her governess Marion Crawford, 'Crawfie, do you like Philip?' When Miss Crawford replied, 'very much', the Princess insisted, 'But he's not English. Would it make a difference?'[15]

Chief among the mischief-makers was Queen Elizabeth's younger brother, David Bowes Lyon, who tried to influence her to block the match. The Prince's childhood friend Gina Wernher thought Bowes Lyon 'a vicious little fellow … who had it in for Philip right from the start'.[16]

Bowes Lyon, like the other critics, was no fan of Philip's uncle, Dickie Mountbatten. 'I'm sure they thought he'd be a very bad influence on Philip,' recalled Mountbatten's eldest daughter Patricia, 'and that Philip might be a chip off the old block.'[17] In later life the Queen Mother reflected airily, 'We always took Dickie with a pinch of salt.'[18]

It wasn't just the royal circle that had reservations about Philip's background. An opinion poll after he had taken British citizenship revealed that 40 per cent of participants objected to the royal marriage on the grounds that he was 'foreign'. There was confusion about whether his antecedents were Greek, Danish, German or British.[19]

The combined anti-Philip brigade failed in their efforts to hinder the match, partly due to Princess Elizabeth's determination for it to succeed but also partly because her father grew to admire his future son-in-law. 'I like Philip,' the King wrote to his mother Queen Mary as early as 1944. 'He is intelligent, has a good sense of humour & thinks about things in the right way.'[20] On Philip's visits to Balmoral after the war, the King taught him how to shoot and the sport bonded the two men. The only fly in the ointment was Philip's occasionally irreverent moments. Since he lacked a kilt, the King lent him some of his own father's collection. Unfortunately George V was a shorter man than Philip so the young man appeared in something resembling a tartan miniskirt and performed a mock curtsey to the sovereign, who promptly exploded with rage.

A sign of the trust and affection the King had for Philip is evident in a reassuring comment he made to him during one of these pre-engagement visits. 'Always come to me if there is anything bothering you with the family,'[21] said George, which suggests he realised that Philip was not having an easy time of it. It was a single comment that would hit the spiteful friends and courtiers (as well as Queen Elizabeth's entire cricket team) for six.

30

QUIPS, GAFFES AND BANTER: THE DUKE'S MEMORABLE CLANGERS 21–30

UPSETTING THE HOME NATIONS

21 **Dunblane, Scotland:** Shortly after the Dunblane school massacre in 1996, *'If a cricketer suddenly decided to go into a school and batter a lot of people to death with a cricket bat, are you going to ban cricket bats?'*

22 **Oban, Scotland:** To a driving instructor in Scotland during a 1995 visit, *'How do you keep your natives off the booze long enough to get them through the test?'*

23 **Northern Ireland:** When a farmer's wife flew to London to attend a charity event in Chelsea at the height of the Troubles, she was startled when Philip said to the Ulsterwoman next in line, *'So you managed to get here without getting your knickers blown off!'*

24 **Stornoway, Scotland:** To an armed female police officer on the Isle of Lewis: *'You look like a suicide bomber.'*

25 **Lockerbie, Scotland:** Meeting local residents after Pan Am Flight 103 exploded over the town in 1993 killing 250 people, *'People say after a fire it's water damage that's the worst. We're still drying out Windsor Castle.'*

26 **Scotland:** Talking to employees of a Scottish fish farm, *'Oh! You're the people ruining the rivers.'*

27 **Scotland:** On being made chancellor of Edinburgh University in 1953, '*Only a Scotsman can really survive a Scottish education.*'

28 **Sheffield, England:** During a visit to Fir Vale Comprehensive School, which had once had a poor academic reputation, he was introduced to parents, '*Were you here in the bad old days? ... That's why you can't read and write then!*'

29 **Reading, England:** Meeting pupils at Queen Anne's School, Reading, in their blood-red school uniforms, '*It makes you all look like Dracula's daughters!*'

30 **London:** Opening City Hall in 2002 he declared, '*The problem with London is the tourists. They cause the congestion. If we could just stop the tourism, we could stop the congestion.*'

31

PHILIP THE JEWELLERY DESIGNER

It was the early summer of 1947 and shoppers in Old Bond Street never gave a second glance to the elderly lady heading into the jeweller's Philip Antrobus, whose showroom was a Mecca for London's elite. The lady was Philip's mother, Princess Alice, who took on the role of a regal middleman in a cloak-and-dagger operation to secure an engagement ring for Princess Elizabeth.

It was Alice's brother, Lord Mountbatten, who had suggested the retailer to Philip, who wanted somewhere that had not previously associated with the royal family for this top-secret mission. With press interest in a possible royal engagement already at fever pitch, 'Philip dare not show his face at jewellers', for fear of being recognized,' as Alice wrote to Mountbatten.[1]

Philip wanted to design the ring himself and his mother offered to give him the diamonds from a tiara she owned. Obtaining it wasn't a straightforward process since her jewels had been deposited in a Paris branch of the National Westminster Bank by Philip's father following his wife's mental collapse in 1930. Philip's father had been dead for two and a half years by this time and it fell to his son and three surviving daughters to sign for their release.[2]

Philip designed a platinum ring featuring eleven diamonds, a central solitaire stone of 3 carats, with five smaller stones set in each shoulder. The ring was made by George Taubl and the stones set by Harry Marchant.[3] After the engagement was officially announced the jeweller told the press he had had no idea for whom the ring was intended. Although we have no idea of Philip's reaction to it, Princess Alice declared it 'a great success'.[4]

The husband-to-be also designed a broad bracelet, measuring 3.7 x 17.8cm in a geometric pattern as a wedding gift for his bride. Once again it was made using diamonds from Alice's tiara and set in platinum. The Queen usually wears it over her white gloves at ceremonial events including state banquets and the State Opening of Parliament.

Philip isn't the first royal prince to design jewellery for his wife. Prince Albert also created a wedding present for Queen Victoria, made up of a large oblong sapphire surrounded by twelve round diamonds. He gave it to her the day before the marriage ceremony and she chose to wear it on her wedding dress. After her death it was worn by three royal consorts – Alexandra, Mary and Elizabeth – and has been worn countless times by the present Queen.

Albert went on to create many pieces for Victoria, often with nature, particularly flowers, as a theme – from an enamel and emerald necklace that was a wedding present in 1842 to the bracelet made up of gold leaves which was a gift to mark the twelfth anniversary of their engagement.[5]

Philip also used flowers in his own anniversary gift for his wife. To mark their five years of marriage he created a jewelled gold bracelet which he asked Boucheron to make. It romantically features interlocking 'E's and 'P's and includes two small sapphire crosses, a ruby cross and two ruby- and diamond-studded flowers with fluted pearls. The central medallion depicts Philip's naval badge set in diamonds.[6] He gave it to Elizabeth in November 1952 during the first year of her reign and it is a poignant reminder of the promising naval career he had to forsake the previous year in order to assume full-time royal duties.

Jewellery design was to continue in the next two generations. In 1986 Prince Andrew designed a ring made up of an oval ruby surrounded by ten diamond drops, set in 18-carat white and yellow gold for his engagement to Sarah Ferguson.

In November 2017, Prince Harry showed he had inherited his grandfather's design skills by giving Meghan Markle an engagement ring he had created himself featuring a large central diamond with two smaller ones. He described it in a TV interview on the day: 'The ring is – is obviously yellow gold because that's her favourite and the main stone itself I sourced from Botswana.' Again mirroring his grandfather seventy years earlier, he used diamonds that had belonged to his mother, though for an altogether more emotional reason: 'The little diamonds either side are from my mother's jewellery collection to make sure that she's with us on this – on this crazy journey together.'

32

AN END TO HIS VICES

SMOKING

Philip gave up smoking at the request of Princess Elizabeth. Her father, paternal uncles and even her grandmother Queen Mary were all regular smokers. In a startling photograph from 1945 Princess Margaret, aged 15, was photographed smoking with her father at a time when it was illegal for anyone under 18 to purchase tobacco.[1]

The Prince took to smoking during his wartime service with the navy, often getting through a case of cigarettes a day.[2] Both his mother and maternal grandmother were heavy smokers and his cousin Lady Pamela Hicks recalls running upstairs as a girl to retrieve Grandmama's cigarettes and even splitting them in half to try to stop her smoking so much.[3]

Biographers usually maintain Philip smoked his last cigarette on the night before his wedding and never had one again. Certainly he had no problem going cold turkey, though the date is uncertain. His cousin Alexandra maintained: 'So determined and disciplined is Philip … that precisely seven months before he married I remember he deliberately gave up smoking and he never relapsed.'[4]

DRINKING

Queen Alexandra also provides us with the only anecdote we have of Philip drunk. In the summer of 1938, aged 17, he holidayed in Venice with his cousin and her mother Princess Aspasia of

Greece. One of Kurt Hahn's rules at Gordonstoun was that pupils had to promise abstinence from alcohol, so as a youth Philip only drank the occasional glass of champagne at family weddings. Now with schooldays behind him he was free to experiment.

Lord and Lady Melchett gave a party at one of the fishermen's tavernas on the Venetian island of Torcello. 'Almost before we knew what was happening the Italian wine had gone to my cousin's head,' she wrote years later. 'He began to make us all laugh by dancing around the terrace like a young faun … Then, fired by our general enjoyment of his antics, he began swinging from the pergola.' Not knowing his own strength, the squiffy Prince broke the pergola, brought down the vine growing on it and ended up disappearing in the greenery. The outraged owner and his daughters 'and a rueful, suddenly sobered Philip cleaned up the mess'. Happily for the teenager, the Melchetts obligingly paid for the damage.[5]

Alexandra also claims it was the 'probably' the first and only time Philip got drunk.

33

PHIL THE DISH

Many friends and associates have testified how extraordinarily attractive Prince Philip was in his heyday:

Oh come to my arms,
You bundle of charms,
Philip Mountbatten RN.

A ditty doing the rounds of upper-crust London in the 1940s, recalled by a cousin of the Queen.

Philip's stunning good looks and action-man image attracted crushes galore from post-war socialites. This shot of him jumping from his water-skis at Marmaris in Turkey in 1951 shows what they had all missed out on. (Hulton Deutsch / Getty)

We were all in love with him.

The same relation.

He is extraordinarily handsome.

Henry 'Chips' Channon, diary entry on 21 January 1941, after meeting the 19-year-old Philip.

Philip, with a golden beard, hit feminine hearts, first in Melbourne and then in Sydney, with terrific impact.

Philip's cousin, Princess Alexandra of Greece, recalling his 1944 shore leave in Australia.

You couldn't have a more good-looking son-in-law.

Queen Ingrid of Denmark, in a letter to Queen Elizabeth, October 1947.

Good-looking? He was astronomical!

Lady Gina Kennard, lifelong friend.

He's very handsome. He has inherited the good looks of both sides of the family.

Queen Mary, whose ice-cold personality clearly melted; she knitted him pullovers and scarves during the Second World War.

[He] has the looks of a typical Prince of a Hans Andersen fairy tale.

Olga Franklin, in a 1944 interview with Philip for the *Newcastle Journal*.

This absolute Greek God – he looked stunning.

Lady Pamela Hicks, cousin, recalls Philip in his youth.

Look how good-looking Grandpa is there. He's an absolute stud. Those glasses, slicked-back hair …

Prince Harry, grandson, looking at family videos of Prince Philip in the 1950s.

Prince Philip, so handsome and cheerful. [He and the Queen] A truly romantic couple, star quality in excelsis.

Noël Coward, November 1953.

She was dazzled by him when she was a little girl, and she found when he was older, he was still very amusing, he was still very enthusiastic – he had the kind of charisma that dazzled people.

Lady Pamela Hicks on Princess Elizabeth's adoration of Philip.

She was mad about him.

Family friend on the same topic.

He was willing to go to any lengths to raise money for the first charity he was involved with, the National Playing Fields Association. In the early 1950s he accepted a cheque for the NPFA from 5,000 girl campers at Skegness, who sang 'All the Nice Girls Love a Sailor'.

Oooh. It's not many women who actually get to kiss a Duke.

Charlady Mrs Eileen Barton, who rushed up and planted a kiss on Philip's cheek as he left a drug addiction centre in Chelsea in July 1969.

34

PRE-WEDDING JITTERS?

Once the public engagement was announced, Philip, like Diana Spencer and Catherine Middleton decades later, was subject to intense media interest. In a letter to her biographer Betty Shew, Princess Elizabeth recalls Philip once driving her in his MG sportscar to London. They were followed by a photographer – which, she said with understatement, was 'disappointing'.

Philip's cousin Alexandra remembered later: 'I did not see Philip before the wedding, but we privately knew he was getting "worked up", and no wonder.'[1]

As one biographer puts it, 'Philip now began a strained and unnerving period',[2] during which he had to get used to being trailed not only by half of Fleet Street but also by an ever-present police officer appointed on the day after the engagement. Philip protested to Scotland Yard in vain. Round-the-clock protection was another slice of unwanted royal life he just had to stomach.

While the police tried to keep a discreet presence around Philip, the photographers were out in force for Philip's official stag night, which was celebrated at London's Dorchester Hotel. It was organised by George Norfolk, captain of Philip's old ship HMS *Whelp*, and the guest list was made up of captains and first lieutenants of the 27th Destroyer Flotilla which had ended up in Japan at the very end of the war. Guest of honour was Philip's uncle, who had recently been created Earl Mountbatten of Burma. The stag do was a useful diversion, for 'the day before his wedding Philip was so touchy and jittery' that best man David Milford Haven 'had to exercise every ounce of tact and diplomacy' to get him through his last bachelor day.[3]

Things improved once Philip was reunited with his old navy pals. Chief among them, Mike Parker recalled it as 'a very happy occasion. It was an evening of comrades. Philip was an orphan of sorts and we were family.'[4] The 'family' started quietly enough with a glass of sherry each, followed by champagne with dinner before some of them moved on to beer, which was when things ended up a bit riotous. When photographers managed to get into the room they were received cordially enough until one of the eleven naval chums decided they should turn the tables. Seizing the cameras, they took photos of the snappers in their macs and trilbies before taking out the flashbulbs and smashing them against the wall, 'uttering blood-curling war whoops as they exploded,'[5] and yelling, 'Now it's our turn to have the last laugh.'[6] A relatively sober bridegroom left at 12.15 a.m. saying, 'Sorry I must go. I have an early morning date!'[7]

At Kensington Palace the following morning, valet John Dean woke Philip up at 7 a.m. and found him none the worse for his late-night revels: 'He woke at once and was plainly in great form, extremely cheerful and in no way nervous.'[8]

The bridegroom gave a far less assured performance for his cousin, Patricia Knatchbull, who was also staying at Kensington Palace. 'After breakfast, we were alone together and I always remember him saying: "I'm either being very brave or very foolish!" Naturally I reassured him that he was doing exactly the right thing, as one would.'[9] In another interview she added: 'He was apprehensive. He was uncertain – not about marrying Princess Elizabeth, but about what the marriage would mean for him. He was giving up a great deal … Everything was going to change for him.'[10]

35

PHILIP'S AUSTERITY WEDDING

Winston Churchill called it 'a flash of colour on the hard road we have to travel'. Had he been prime minister at the time he would no doubt have given the razzmatazz of a royal wedding his fullest blessing. As it was, dour Clement Attlee and his Labour Party were running the country and they greeted the idea of a lavish spectacle with less enthusiasm.

George VI, mindful of the suffering his country had endured in six years of warfare and was now enduring in post-war austerity, also erred on the side of caution. Attlee vetoed a public holiday as 'unwise', and the King agreed there would be no souvenirs produced or stands and decorations along the processional route.

Not everyone was happy with all this negativity. 'Chips' Channon wrote in his diary: 'Someone in the Government apparently advised simplicity, misjudging the English love of pageantry and show. Now it is too late and an opportunity missed.'[1]

The King's decision to replace court dress with day dress appealed to Philip, who would always dress the part but was never comfortable with too much ostentation. He wore his usual naval uniform with the addition of the stars of the Order of the Garter and the Greek Order of the Redeemer, and carried his maternal grandfather's ceremonial sword. To avoid any confusion with his best man's naval uniform, the latter's larger cap was marked with ink inside since it would have embarrassingly dropped over the groom's ears if he picked up the wrong one.

The guests also watched the pennies. 'Anyone fortunate enough to have a new dress drew all eyes,' recalled Queen

The look of love: Elizabeth and Philip pose for photos on their
wedding day, 20 November 1947. Winston Churchill said the
marriage brought 'a flash of colour' to brighten the post-war gloom.
(Author's collection)

Mary's lady-in-waiting.[2] Even royalty failed to sparkle: 'I always remember Princess Juliana of the Netherlands looking round at all the jewellery and exclaiming "but it's all so dirty", remembered one of the bridesmaids.[3]

On his wedding day Philip breakfasted on just coffee and toast, though he did top up with a gin and tonic to steady his nerves before he left for the abbey. He emerged five minutes early, saw a policeman shake his head, and retreated until the required moment. Before leaving, he shook hands with Miss Pye, his grandmother's maid of fifty years, whom he had dubbed 'Piecrust' as a child.

Philip's earlier nervousness was dispelled by the time he reached Westminster Abbey. 'Princess Elizabeth looked well, shy and attractive,' noted the ubiquitous Channon, 'and Prince Philip as if he were thoroughly enjoying himself.'[4]

The ceremony was witnessed by a who's who of European royalty. 'It was a tremendous meeting place,' remembered Princess Margaret, adding cheekily, 'People who had been starving in little garrets all over Europe, suddenly reappeared.' The kings of Norway, Denmark and Iraq, to name but three; others had lost their thrones but still kept their place in the pecking order. One was about to join the exiled royals club: King Michael of Romania, who lost his throne on his return but at least found love in London in the shape of Princess Anne of Bourbon-Parma.

Missing from the guest list were the Duke and Duchess of Windsor, eleven years after his abdication to marry her – an omission which so annoyed his sister, the Princess Royal, that she failed to attend the wedding, claiming incapacity through a heavy cold. Philip's side was noticeably depleted thanks to the absence of his three sisters, who were cold-shouldered by the palace and not invited because it was so soon after the war. 'They minded terribly,' recalled their cousin Lady Pamela Hicks.

'I mean it's not as it they were stormtroopers!'[5] Their mother, Princess Alice, sent them a twenty-two-page account of the day in a letter, and their cousin the Duchess of Kent volunteered to travel to Germany to give them her account of the day.

Philip's side of the abbey was boosted with the presence of his navy pals, as well as villagers from Corsham where he was currently lecturing, and also his fellow skittles players from his local, the Methuen Arms.

Millions of others, without seats in the abbey, watched a film of the ceremony which was shown in cinemas from the following day. Copies were flown to the USA for distribution there, and in Allied-occupied Berlin it was shown seven days a week in a packed cinema. Even the fledgling television service, with reception limited in those days to the greater London area, showed the film. A TV camera had also been positioned at the palace to show the bride's procession leaving for the abbey.

Afterwards, 150 guests sat down to enjoy an 'austerity' wedding breakfast. Instead of the ten courses that had fed previous bridal parties, Elizabeth and Philip's guests were given fish, partridge shot on the royal estates and ice cream. Thankfully royal menus were traditionally written in French, which sounded more tempting: 'Filet de Sole Mountbatten', 'Perdreau en Casserole' and 'Bombe Glacée de Princesse Elizabeth'. With the influx of twenty-eight royal guests staying at Buckingham Palace, the Royal Household had also applied to Westminster Food Office for extra rations.

Prince Philip's lack of a place to call home was noticeable when it came to decorating the wedding cake. Since it was a four-tiered, 9ft-tall edifice weighing in at 500lb (226kg), there was plenty of room for the three craftsmen to create the couple's life histories in sugar-craft. The only problem was there was not too much to say about Philip in comparison to Elizabeth. Having iced her various royal homes, it was decided to add Philip's athletic pursuits to make up for the lack of bricks and mortar in his life. He did much better on the third tier where, alongside the bride's various hobbies, they added the groom's war record.

36

WEDDING PRESENTS

If Lieutenant Philip Mountbatten needed reminding he was the less important member of the bridal couple he would have only had to rummage through the 2,583 presents received from well-wishers in the run-up to wedding on 20 November 1947. The vast majority of them were sent with the Princess in mind – from a leather saddle to prints of Windsor Castle and Elizabeth's 'E' cypher was stamped, carved, engraved or embroidered on a plethora of gifts sent by the public.

Only a dozen or so could be said to be aimed solely at Philip, headed by his mother's gift of the flattering painting of her by society artist Philip de László. A Mr Long-Brown sent a framed aqua-tint of Cheam, the Duke's English prep school, while his German school at Salem sent an album, and Kurt Hahn, his headmaster at Gordonstoun, sent 'a history and journal of the school's activities'.

Friends and colleagues from his navy years also remembered him. The former captain of the Royal Naval College at Dartmouth sent a fishing rod. His shipmates from HMS *Whelp* collected for a silver salver, and the officers of the 27th Destroyer Flotilla, with which *Whelp* served, sent a mahogany shield featuring all the ships' badges. His closest friend, Lieutenant Mike Parker, also sent two watercolour prints of *Whelp*.

Another friend, the photographer Baron Nahum, presented a framed colour photograph of the Duke, while a Mr Eustace Boucas sent a miniature of Philip as a baby. The groom's modest pile of gifts also included a shaving set in a crocodile case from a Mr A.C. Kingham and six pairs of shoes from the Boot Manufacturers' Association of Northampton.

Of course, the Duke could share many of the 'joint' presents, from the cinema provided by his uncle Earl Mountbatten to the two gold saris sent by the Maharajah of Sangli. There was also part of the holy carpet from the Great Mosque at Mecca that was now under glass and doubling as a supper tray, or the equally surprising gift from two children – Jill and Jeremy Cotton – a dartboard.

As for the bride's presents, some of the gifts say a lot about how the members of the public perceived Elizabeth. They obviously felt they knew her almost as a daughter or sister, and the range of intimate gifts reflected this, from stockings – sixteen pairs of silk ones and over a hundred nylons – to a hand-knitted bed jacket; and from handmade lingerie to a pale blue garter decorated with old lace.

Like any couple, they received presents for the home. Some were described as 'gifts of sumptuous utility', including an upright and a cylinder vacuum cleaner from Hoover Ltd, a 'compact personal weighing machine' from Salter & Co., a 'Thermega' electrically heated blanket, an automatic potato peeler and a television set, and – like every other couple in Britain – two toast racks, albeit solid silver ones.

The wedding was only two years after the end of the Second World War. Ukrainian prisoners of war still in a camp at Haddington in Scotland sent a traditionally decorated hand-made box and, in another touching gesture, 'Latvian displaced persons in Germany' posted Elizabeth some handmade evening shoes. It was known as the 'austerity wedding' and hence there were gifts such as 10lb of icing sugar sent by Pamela Mungomery in Australia, four dozen tins of salmon from America, and 500 cases of tinned pineapples 'to be distributed as the Princess desires' from the government of Queensland.

Among the Hepplewhite chairs and diamond brooches were some gifts that were odd, to say the least. A Ms J. Wilson sent 'a hand-dressed doll tea cosy and twelve egg cosies'. Then there was a small bust of Queen Victoria made in biscuit in 1891, 'a large collection of household dusters' from a Miss Clara Walsh, a book entitled *Mazdaznan Science of Dietetics*, another one called *Free Negro Labor and Property Holding in Virginia 1830–1860*, an ostrich egg and a live Siamese kitten. An equally live – though presumably not for long – turkey was sent by air from America by little Julie Aloro to the Princess 'because she lives in England and they have nothing to eat in Europe'. Finally, a tad precipitately, gift 2528 was 'two hand-knitted cot covers'.

37

HONEYMOON HYSTERIA

'The level of adulation, you wouldn't believe it,' Philip once recalled about his and Elizabeth's early married years.

The newly created Duke of Edinburgh had his first real taste of it on his honeymoon or at least the first week of it when he and the Princess stayed at Broadlands, the mansion near Romsey, Hampshire, which belonged to the Mountbattens.

The newly-weds arrived at Winchester Station on the royal train. The waiting royal limousine blocked the view and the vast crowd on the road outside groaned until the car was backed up to allow a glimpse of the pair. Also present were Elizabeth's dresser and confidante Margaret 'Bobo' MacDonald and Philip's valet John Dean, who were in charge of the suitcases – fifteen for Elizabeth, two for Philip. They were accompanied by loyal footman Cyril Dickman and protection officer Albert Perkins with the furled umbrella he used to fend off encroaching reporters or photographers. Last, but certainly no means least, in the party was Elizabeth's corgi Susan.

The couple kept the lights on inside the car for the 1.5-mile drive through the city, probably thinking that was to be their final act of public acknowledgement for a week. Unfortunately this wasn't the case and the Broadlands estate was circled by eager crowds and hopeful photographers. John Dean recalled: 'sightseers refused to leave the young couple alone … hiding in trees and long grass to spy on them as they came walking, riding or jeeping by'.[1] The Broadlands phonelines were jammed with thousands of calls from well-wishers from as far away as America, and a second detective had to man the switchboard to vet them.

For those who couldn't make it to Romsey, enterprising journalists strove to find every morsel of information from staff and locals. One report covers the arrival of the couple inside the mansion. Written in a style that makes Barbara Cartland read like Tolstoy, we are told Elizabeth's 'proud slim shoulders drooped a little as Philip's arm went round her at the bend of the stairway. She leaned against him looking up with a grateful shy smile.' Arriving at their bedroom overlooking the river Test, the Princess apparently exclaimed: 'Oh how lovely it is in here.' It's not surprising it was 'lovely' since the same reporter tells us that housekeeper Mrs Monks had at least twenty times 'smoothed the pale pink crepe-de-chine sheets and two pillow cases appliquéd with a white satin leaf motif'.[2]

Not everyone would be snuggling up in crepe-de-chine sheets. Inspector Perkins was in an attic, making up a couch to spend the night on.

Lord Mountbatten's valet and right-hand man, Charles Smith, who had known Philip since he was young, thoughtfully set up a romantic scene in the dining room. Instead of the main table he used a small, circular one placed in front of a log fire, where they had a dinner of potato soup, roast chicken and ice cream by candlelight.[3]

Intrusion from press and public alike reached a crescendo three days later when the couple attended Sunday worship at Romsey Abbey. Nearly all Romsey's 7,000 citizens plus 3,000 visitors in cars and coaches arrived from as far afield as the coast and London to see the Edinburghs; police reserves were brought in to control them.[4] Crowds surged into the grounds of Romsey Abbey to see Elizabeth and Philip greeted by Canon W.B. Corban. Some climbed on gravestones while others brought their own ladders, chairs and even a sideboard. Afterwards they queued for hours just to sit in the seats that had been occupied by the royal couple.[5]

Four days into his marriage, Philip had discovered what life in the royal goldfish bowl was going to be like.

38

PHILIP AND A ROYAL MISTRESS

It is the late spring of 1946 and 25-year-old Philip is sipping cocktails in the *belle époque* grandeur of the Café de Paris in Monte Carlo, when he is joined by an elegant middle-aged woman for one of the oddest meetings of his life.

The woman is the Comtesse Andrée de la Bigne and for well over a decade she was the mistress of Philip's father, Prince Andrew of Greece. Also present at the meeting is Philip's old navy friend Mike Parker, who would relate the event more than half a century later to two of Philip's biographers: 'It was like a scene from a film. We realised it must be her at once. She made a proper entrance. She was elegant. She wore blue glasses.'[1] Not only was she very striking, but she seemed totally at home. As she entered she smiled at the doorman and said, 'Evenin' Charles,' recalled Parker, who also noted that she and Philip 'hit it off at from the first'.[2] Mike diplomatically left the two to talk about Philip's father and for Andrée to arrange to hand over Prince Andrew's possessions to his son.

Although she'd been the older Prince's mistress for well over a decade, the Comtesse wasn't mentioned in his will. His widow, Princess Alice, in a kind-hearted gesture, gave her his car and any of his possessions she wanted.[3] Alice had naively hoped to revive her marriage to Andrew and was told by one of his staff that the Comtesse was 'an adventuress, feathering her own nest'. This seems likely, since he died virtually penniless and, according to Philip's grandmother Princess Victoria, she had 'sucked him dry etc, as such women generally do'. Princess Alice was less acerbic and wrote to Philip in January 1946 that Andrée was 'the friend who looked after Papa so touchingly to the end'. The details of 'the end' were sent to Andrew's widow by his mistress.[4]

It is assumed that she was the Andrée de la Bigne born in 1903, who acted under the name Andrée Lafayette opposite Arthur Edmund Carewe as Swengali in the 1923 Hollywood film *Trilby* and several other early films.[5] Described on her arrival in America as 'an actress of ability' and 'one of the most beautiful girls in France',[6] she had a short-lived marriage to an American actor called Arthur May Constant and died in Calvados, France, in 1989.

De la Bigne may have inherited her skills as a paramour from her great-grandmother, Comtesse Valtesse de la Bigne (1848–1910), who was mistress to the Emperor Napoleon III as well as a sizeable chunk of the art world, including painters Édouard Manet, Édouard Detaille, Gustave Corbet and Eugène Boudin. In her will Valtesse thoughtfully left her sumptuous, roomy and much-used brass bed – which had been created in 1877 by another artist – to the French nation for permanent display.[7]

39

A WORKING ROYAL

In the lead-up to his marriage, Philip made his first two public speeches. It is a pretty safe bet he wouldn't have been asked to make either if he hadn't been about to wed the heiress presumptive.

On 5 July 1947, five days before the official engagement was announced, Philip returned to his alma mater, Cheam School, to celebrate its tercentenary. Rapidly promoted to being its most famous alumnus, he told the assembled great and good, 'We recent old boys were just young enough to be killed. I was one of the lucky ones.'

Those who were not so lucky were remembered on 1 November when Philip unveiled the war memorial at Corsham, Wiltshire, where he was an instructor at the nearby Petty Officers' School. In his speech he used the past as a lesson for the future: 'It is wrong to accept that another war is inevitable. It is only by each one of us actively working for peace all the time that we can reduce its chances … We hold a sacred trust.'[1]

After his marriage, Philip worked first in a desk job at the Admiralty before taking a staff course at the Naval Staff College,

Greenwich, so it wasn't until 2 March 1948 that he was able to undertake his first solo royal engagement. As patron of the London Federation of Boys' Clubs he watched boxing matches between youths aged between 14 and 18 in the Royal Albert Hall.

The class system was clearly still rigidly in place with Philip, charity executives and the audience all dressed in black tie watching working-class lads knock seven bells out of each other. Afterwards the Duke entered the ring to present prizes to the victors. Here he displayed two characteristics that would remain with him for the following seven decades of engagements. Firstly, he had already mastered his technique of standing with his hands behind his back. Secondly, we see him deliver a dull but worthy speech before going off-piste with a quip about 'a lot of people who got their faces bent many years ago' now being back wielding the towels for the boys. It was a style neither his father-in-law George VI nor, in fact, any of his new in-laws had tried.

40

QUIPS, GAFFES AND BANTER: THE DUKE'S MEMORABLE CLANGERS 31–40

ON THE MONARCHY

31 During an interview for Scottish TV he explained his outspoken contribution to the family firm, '*The monarchy functions because occasionally you've got to stick your neck out … The idea that you don't do anything on the off chance*

you might be criticised [means] you'd end up living like a cabbage and it's pointless. You've got to stick up for something you believe in.'

32 While undertaking royal duties he once revealed how he copes with the lengthier ones, *'I never pass up a chance to go to the loo or take a poo.'*

33 Arriving in Brazil for a state visit in 1968, *'The man who invented the red carpet needed his head examined.'*

34 Being interviewed by Jeremy Paxman about royal life, *'Any bloody fool can lay a wreath at the thingamy.'*

35 His view on his daughter Princess Anne, *'If it doesn't fart or eat hay, she isn't interested.'*

36 After he'd viewed Andrew and Fergie's designs for their new home at Sunninghill Park, *'It looks like a tart's bedroom.'*

37 On being asked about Prince Charles succeeding to the throne, *'Are you asking me if the Queen is going to die?'*

38 A 1962 comment about the cuisine at Buckingham Palace, *'I never see any home cooking – all I get is fancy stuff.'*

39 In 2008, Philip met former BP chief Lord Browne who had recently resigned after details of his private life were exposed in a Sunday newspaper, *'I gather you've had some problems since we last met,'* said the Duke, adding, *'Don't worry, there's a lot of that in my family.'*

40 Asked by a schoolchild if he ever got nervous meeting heads of state, *'Well, it's surprising how you grow out of it.'*

41

PHILIP AND CHARLES: GOOD COP OR BAD COP?

In 1994 the publication of *The Prince of Wales: A Biography* highlighted the often-volatile relationship between father and son. The fact that the book was authorised by Charles and the author Jonathan Dimbleby was given access to the Prince's journals, letters and, crucially, to his inner circle, only made the allegations all the more devastating for the Queen and Prince Philip.

Subsequent interviews with Philip as well as palace-backed books and profiles of the Duke have, in the main, only reinforced the negative image of two very different personalities. So much so that their shared passions, hobbies and intellectual pursuits as well as Philip's positive role in Charles's childhood have all but been wiped from history.

BAD COP

Prince Charles has rarely voiced criticism of his father in public, although aged 20 he gave an intriguing comment in an interview in June 1969 to mark his forthcoming Investiture as Prince of Wales. Asked by the BBC's Cliff Michelmore if Prince Philip was 'a tough disciplinarian' and if he, Charles, had been told 'to sit down and shut up' by his father, Charles replied: 'The whole time, yes,' before adding filially, 'I think he has had quite a strong influence on me particularly in my younger days.'[1]

Jonathan Dimbleby's official biography of the Prince of Wales was serialised in the *Sunday Times*. The first extract, which condemned the Prince's relationship with his parents, was published on 16 October 1994, the day before the Queen and Duke arrived in Moscow for their state visit to Russia, the most historic and politically significant royal tour since their visit to China in 1986.

The unfortunate timing disappointed courtiers but the content caused widespread dismay and is said to have greatly hurt Charles's parents. Dimbleby asserted that, unlike Princess Anne, 'the Prince was timid and passive and easily cowed by the forceful personality of his father', who 'easily drew tears to the child's eye'. Philip, it was said, had no idea how sensitive his eldest son was and the latter 'used to curl up … he just shrank'.[2]

A decade later Philip's friend and biographer Gyles Brandreth asserted in his 2005 book *Charles and Camilla: Portrait of a Love Affair* that the Queen and Prince Philip were 'appalled' after reading such claims and the Duke of Edinburgh even branded his son 'bloody stupid'.

Brandreth went on to say that the Prince's decision to talk voluntarily about family matters to a journalist and to allow access to private journals and correspondence 'seemed, to his parents, sheer foolishness'. The author added that the Queen and the Duke of Edinburgh were also 'hurt by what their son had to say about them as parents' and that while they may not be perfect, 'they had meant well'.[3]

Prince Philip's only comment on the matter to Brandreth was, 'We did our best'.[4]

The difference in the characters of the two princes is clear in how they both responded to the challenges of education at Gordonstoun School on Scotland's dramatic Moray coast. While Philip thrived on the Spartan regime and he-man tutelage in the pre-war school, the altogether more sensitive Charles hated his father's alma mater, infamously dubbed 'Colditz in

kilts'. Of course, the Duke had been a relatively unknown foreign prince when he attended the newly opened school in the
mid 1930s. Charles, on the other hand, was Prince of Wales
and the future king, and according to Jonathan Dimbleby 'was
picked on maliciously, cruelly and without respite'.[5]

The younger Prince was punched on the rugby field, had slip-
pers thrown at him while he was in bed, was hit with pillows
and occasionally, surreptitiously, punched in the dark. 'Last
night was hell, literal hell', he wrote home, but his father's 'reaction was to write bracing letters of admonition' urging Charles
'to be strong and resourceful'.[6] To be fair, the Queen and Duke
couldn't really withdraw the Prince from his educational night-
mare without causing embarrassment to Gordonstoun and
risking the inevitable media circus. The stiff-upper-lip, grin-
and-bear-it attitude was second nature for the royal parents but
in this case failed to help their sensitive eldest son.

Given the furore generated by the Dimbleby biography's critical approach to Philip's parenting skills, it would have been
expected that the subject of Charles would be strictly a taboo
one in any interview with the Duke. In May 1999 when asked
by Gyles Brandreth, for a *Sunday Telegraph* profile, about his
similarities with his eldest son in mannerisms, interests and so
on, Philip interjected, 'Yes but with one great difference. He's a
Romantic and I'm a pragmatist. That means we do see things
differently.' After a pause the Duke added ruefully, 'And because
I don't see things as a Romantic would, I'm unfeeling.'[7]

A further low point in father–son relations came in 2001
when journalist Graham Turner was allowed to interview
Philip's staff and confidants for a mostly on-the-record profile
of the Prince to mark his forthcoming eightieth birthday. The
impression given to Turner was that Charles 'is quite frightened

of his father'. The most damning sentence in the piece was that Philip 'now regards Charles as precious, extravagant and lacking the dedication and discipline he will need if he is to make a good king'.[8] A deeply irate Philip immediately disowned the comments and both rang and wrote to his son apologising and denying that he considered him unworthy to be king. Senior aides revealed that Charles accepted the apology and that 'the Prince accepts that if these things were said, then they were without the authorisation of his father'.[9]

GOOD COP

Father and son have often been seen as alike due to their similar mannerisms, impeccable style and hands-behind-the-back stance. Charles once joked about the latter when he addressed the Master Tailors' Benevolent Association annual dinner in February 1971. He told the guests that it was sometimes thought that he and his father both stood with their hands behind their backs as if it were some hereditary or genetic trait. 'The answer is, we both have the same tailor … He makes the sleeves so tight, we can't get our hands out in front.'[10] It's not on record what their shared tailor, Edward Watson, thought about the quip.

Their military service followed a similar path. From training at the Royal Naval College, Dartmouth, Philip served twelve years with the Royal Navy including commanding HMS *Magpie*. Charles did a six-week course at Dartmouth and his six-year career in the navy ended with his command of the mine-hunter HMS *Bronington*. Both princes trained to fly helicopters and piloted various types of aircraft. In 1962 Philip carried out a two-month flying tour of South America alongside his co-pilot Peter Middleton, the Duchess of Cambridge's paternal grandfather. The Duke gave up flying in August 1997 after accumulating 5,986 hours as a pilot in fifty-nine types of aircraft in forty-four years. Charles's flying career ended igno-miniously three years earlier after he crash-landed a BAe 146 aircraft of the Queen's Flight in the Hebrides.

At Gordonstoun both princes were imbued with one of the school's founding principles of service to the community in order to develop a sense of social responsibility and compassion to others. The lessons learned motivated Philip to develop his Duke of Edinburgh's Award Scheme and Charles to launch the Prince's Trust, both of which help young people to develop skills that will benefit them personally and society in general.

Both princes take a deep interest in spiritual matters. Philip launched St George's House, based at Windsor – an organisation dedicated to the exploration of faith and philosophy. His letters to the Dean of Windsor regarding Professor Sir Fred Hoyle's lecture 'Evolution from Space' was published in book form as *A Windsor Correspondence* in 1984. Five years later the Prince and the dean produced *Survival or Extinction: A Christian Attitude to the Environment.* When it comes to religion, Charles has a similarly enquiring mind and has studied Islam and Judaism, and attended Catholic masses. As king he will be Supreme Governor of the Church of England. Regarding this role, the former Archbishop of Canterbury, George Carey, said, 'He is an individual who wants to chart new territory, and that will be very interesting indeed … He is very outspoken.'[11]

Their views on architecture have at times mirrored each other. Biographer Tim Heald was given access to a memo about a proposed addition to an existing building in which the writer criticises architects for promoting their own aesthetics rather than sympathy with the original building. It begins:

Their statement is exactly the one which allowed so many lovely country houses to be ruined during the late 19th century with monstrous Victorian additions at different level, different scales and everything else … who ever heard of anyone making a modern addition to a van Dyck or a Rembrandt?

The phrase 'monstrous Victorian additions' – so similar to his criticism of the proposed National Gallery extension as 'a monstrous carbuncle' – suggests it was penned by Charles. In fact this was Philip's reaction to the proposed new King George VI Memorial Chapel at St George's Chapel, written in June 1967.[12]

A love of sport has also been a strong bond between father and son. As a child Charles was taught to shoot and fish by Philip, and the Duke took Charles and Anne sailing in his 12m yacht *Bloodhound*, which Philip recalls as 'good times, happy days'.[13] The sport they are inevitably linked with is polo. Charles, so shy and timid as a child, turned into a demon once he was in the saddle. He was 'eager to emulate his father's dash, he was an intrepid player, if a rough horseman, not afraid to gallop and reckless with his own safety'. For once a rather proud Philip 'approved of his son's attitude'.[14]

42

OL' BLUE EYES

Hollywood and royalty has been a potent mix for generations and one that's often an advantage for both sides – social cachet for the film stars and singers and for royalty a boost for their charities whenever a celebrity came on board.

Sometimes the relationship was purely fun. The entertainer Danny Kaye was a firm favourite with the young Elizabeth and

Philip. In the late 1940s they invited him to a buffet supper at Clarence House, where they were joined by the King (another huge fan) and Queen Elizabeth, whom he sat next to and 'kept in convulsions of laughter'.[1] Kaye was often a weekend guest at Coppins, the Buckinghamshire home of Philip's cousin, the widowed Duchess of Kent. The two then drove over to Windlesham Moor, the Edinburghs' country home, where valet John Dean recalled, 'it was amusing to watch him capering around Princess Elizabeth on the lawns.'[2]

For Elizabeth's twenty-third birthday in April 1949, the Edinburghs went to see Laurence Olivier and Vivien Leigh in *The School for Scandal* at the New Theatre. Afterwards the Oliviers joined the Princess and Duke for supper and dancing at the Café de Paris.

A chance to brush shoulders with the glamorous young royal couple proved irresistible for other stars too. On 10 December 1951 Philip hosted a midnight matinée at the London Coliseum in aid of the National Playing Fields Association (NFPA), of which he was president. Among the performers were Noël Coward, Orson Welles and newly-wed couple Tony Curtis and Janet Leigh. Heading the guest list was a couple almost as famous as the Edinburghs and just as glamorous – Frank Sinatra and wife Ava Gardner, who came over from America and gave their services for free. Photos of the occasion show Philip smiling broadly throughout the night. Behind the scenes, Sinatra was less happy, berating the orchestra and shouting at the press, due in part to the theft of an estimated £6,000 worth of gems belonging to Miss Gardner from their suite at the Washington Hotel in London's Curzon Street during their stay.[3]

Sinatra had been invited by Philip to meet at Clarence House the previous year in order to ask the singer to partake in the fundraiser. So taken was the latter with the cause that he donated all the royalties of a forthcoming record to the NPFA and even sent over sports gear from the USA to give to children using the playing fields.

Philip wasn't the only royal figure to bond with Sinatra. Princess Margaret was a huge fan and collected his records. In 2006 a two-page handwritten note written by the Princess in March 1971 inviting the singer to Kensington Palace was sold for £1,500 in London. In it she writes, 'We would love to dine with you and perhaps it would amuse you to see our ancient dwelling which we have brought up to date.'[4] The fact she also asked him to 'brush up' on his song 'Out of This World' suggests Ol' Blue Eyes was going to have to sing for his supper.[5]

Sinatra said of HRH: 'Princess Margaret is just as hep wide-awake as any American girl, maybe more so. She is up on all the latest records and movies, and has a lot of wit and charm too … She is the best ambassador England ever had.'[6]

43

TWO DUKES AND THE KING OF JAZZ

It's not generally known that the Duke has been a lifelong fan of jazz.

Until its demise, he was patron of the Jazz Development Trust, founded in 1998 by legendary saxophonist John Dankworth to encourage interest in, and performance of, jazz. The 1947 book *Royal Wedding* by palace-approved biographer Betty Spencer Shew says the Duke was fond of 'Duke Ellington's records, of which his favourite is "Take the 'A' Train".'[1]

Prince Philip would cross paths with both the song and his fellow Duke on several occasions. Ellington and his orchestra played at the 1958 Leeds Festival, with Philip in the audience. Afterwards the Prince told Ellington he was sorry he'd missed the opening number, 'Take the "A" Train', as it was one of his favourites. That evening Ellington was introduced to the Queen, who had been at another event earlier and she said, 'I was so sorry I couldn't come to any of your concerts, but my husband tells me he thoroughly enjoyed himself when he listened to you.'[2]

Ellington was so bowled over by meeting the young and attractive Elizabeth that he promised 'something musical will come from this'. He subsequently composed a suite of six songs which he dedicated to the Queen. He recorded them at his own expense and had just one record made, which he sent to the Queen as a present. *The Queen's Suite* was only played in public in 1976, two years after Ellington's death.

American lyricist Don George, famed for penning 'The Yellow Rose of Texas', was a close friend of Ellington's. In his 1981 biography of the bandleader, George recounts a meeting between Philip and the jazz Duke after a concert in aid of the Equity Actors' Benevolent Fund in London. The Prince apparently said, 'My God, Duke, when have you slept last?' Ellington replied, 'I don't know. I think I slept about three or four months ago.' The Prince then enthused, 'The band sounds great, and it's always a pleasure seeing you,' adding, 'Why don't we all go back to the palace and put some eggs on? We can have a jam session.' Ellington agreed: 'Let's go, baby!'[3] Unfortunately there is nothing to corroborate the story either in the Court Circular or in other biographies of Ellington.

Don George may have confused it with another charity fundraiser, the Royal Variety Performance of 26 November 1973, in aid of the Entertainment Artistes' Benevolent Fund, attended by the Queen and the Duke. Ellington, who by now was suffering from terminal lung cancer and would die the following May, once again played Philip's special song thanks to a request from the palace. Afterwards the bandleader told the press that Philip complained that 'he would have liked more – but I played all his favourites. He also ticked me off for because he said I didn't play the full version of Take the A Train.'[4]

Prince Philip wasn't the first British royal to be enamoured with Duke. The Queen told the bandleader during their 1958 meeting that her father, George VI, had had a collection of his LPs. The King's younger brother, Prince George, Duke of Kent, met him at a party hosted by Lord Beaverbrook in London in 1933 and asked him to play 'Swampy River' while George leaned against the piano. Later the two Dukes played four-hand duets together.[5]

Kent's older brother, the Prince of Wales, later Duke of Windsor, also performed at the Beaverbrook party, taking to the drums to accompany the pianist Leslie 'Hutch' Hutchinson (who, legend has it, played in more ways than one with Philip's aunt, Edwina Mountbatten). Ellington later recalled, 'We expected some Little Lord Fauntleroy stuff, but he really gave out some low-down Charleston.'[6] When the Prince was in the north-west he made a point of seeing Ellington in concert in Liverpool and earned plaudits in the local press for sitting in the back of the theatre in the cheap seats when he could have insisted on a front-row view.

Jazz and the House of Windsor first met in 1919 when the Original Dixieland Jazz Band played for King George V, who apparently cried out in delight at one of their songs, 'Tiger Rag'.[7] In August of that year a jazz band played at a Buckingham Palace garden party thrown by the King for his household and their families as a thank-you for their hard work during the Great War. The band performed in the amphitheatre where the palace lake had been drained early on in the conflict.[8]

George VI invited jazz bands back to the palace several times during his reign. His favourite performers were Sidney Bechet – George was taken with his composition 'Characteristic Blues' – and legendary trumpeter Louis Armstrong. Armstrong, dubbed the 'King of Jazz', wowed the King of England and, at a 1932 palace jam, cheerily dedicated '(I'll Be Glad when You're Dead,) You Rascal, You!' to the monarch with the words 'This one's for you Rex.'[9]

Princess Margaret was another huge jazz fan and saw Armstrong perform at London's Empress Hall in 1956. 'Satchmo' later told the British press, 'Your Princess Margaret is one hip chick.'

Ten years after playing for the 'hip chick', Armstrong serenaded her brother-in-law at a Hollywood dinner party during Philip's charity fundraising trip of 1966. To the tune of his hit song 'Hello Dolly', 'Satchmo' improvised:

Hello Philip, well hello Philip,
We've looked forward to this night and here you are;
You're looking droll, Princey, you're tophole, Princey,
In this room that's filled with glitter, you're the brightest star.
I say old chap, you're super, a real showbiz trouper.
'Cos you're heading the Palace right today.
Say! I love your style, Philip,
You're wowing them in the British Isles, Philip,
For you we stand and shout hooray, Buckingham is the greatest house to play;
A long and lovely happy stay to you.

Then to wild applause the singer yelled: 'Regards to the missus, with love and kisses.'

At the end of the night the gowned and dinner-jacketed stars at the Hilton Hotel – including Dean Martin, Jack Lemmon,

Shirley MacLaine, Kirk Douglas and Burt Lancaster and Gregory Peck – reprised the Armstrong song, changing the lyrics to: 'Cheerio Philip. Time to go Philip. It was so nice to be with you tonight.'

The Duke's verdict on the evening: 'Fabulous!'

44

THE THURSDAY CLUB

It's been labelled everything from 'mildly louche' to a venue for 'rip-roaring stag parties' which, rumour has it, were 'not always stag'.[1] The Thursday Club was an all-male weekly lunch group founded by Philip and various contacts. If anything untoward did occur, there is no firm evidence and the worst that can be claimed is that it was an excuse for a macho booze-up which, given its time frame of the late 1940s to mid 1950s, was certain to have been completely un-PC.

For Philip, in his pressure-cooker world of huge media interest, a constant security presence and living with his in-laws for the first two years of marriage, it was a safety valve to let off steam and mix with like-minded men. His decision to throw off the shackles of royalty – if only for a lunchtime – didn't go down well with courtiers. Eileen Parker, wife of his equerry Mike, claimed, 'One of the main subjects of friction between Prince Philip and the Old Guard at Buckingham Palace concerned his apparent desire to continue bachelor friendships.'[2]

One such bachelor was the society photographer Baron Nahum who worked under the name 'Baron' and who later employed Antony Armstrong-Jones as an assistant, thus paving the way for him to meet Princess Margaret. Baron entered the royal orbit via a meeting with Dickie Mountbatten in Malta and went on to photograph the Duke and Duchess of Kent's children before taking Elizabeth and Philip's official wedding photos in 1947.

'Hardly known as a model of sexual propriety',[3] Baron was one of the founders of the Thursday Club, which met on the third floor of Wheeler's Restaurant in Old Compton Street, Soho. Famous names attending were the actors David Niven, Peter Ustinov and James Robertson Justice, as well as harmonica-playing Larry Adler, the artist Felix Topolski whom Philip asked to paint a 200ft mural of the Coronation, and Kim Philby before he was outed as a Soviet spy. Oddly enough, given Philip's wariness of the media, many distinguished journalists were also members, including Arthur Christiansen, editor of the *Daily Express*, and his counterpart at the *Daily Mail*, Frank Owen. The only aristocrats among them were Lord Glenavy, who achieved fame in the 1970s as the stammering panellist Patrick Campbell on *Call My Bluff*, and Philip's cousin David Milford Haven. The latter let the Prince down badly by selling his story of the royal wedding to a newspaper and the Thursday Club let its feelings be known by naming him 'C*** of the Week' at its next meeting.[4]

One thing the men had in common was the necessary wealth to allow them to end the working week on a Thursday since most of them wouldn't have been fit for anything other than a weekend in the country after leaving. 'Thursday night was a lost cause if you happened to be the wife or girlfriend of any of the members,' recalled Milford Haven's former squeeze.[5]

The format was the same each week: a set-price lunch (usually steak), plenty of house white wine and vintage port, before the men began speeches or indulged in practical jokes. One of them involving Philip centred around Baron's wish to photograph the bird in a cuckoo clock which had one of the fastest movements anyone had known. Poised ready at 1.29 for the creature to spring into action on the half-hour, it wasn't 'cuck-ooo' that galvanised Baron but three smoke bombs thrown in his direction. Unfortunately, the loud bangs sent a landslide of soot down the chimney as well as a posse of policemen racing upstairs to find a blackened Prince sitting by the fireplace surrounded by cronies laughing their heads off.

It was the laughter that Mike Parker recalled in his later years. 'We had fun at those lunches … but nothing louche or lewd. I can assure you.' Philip, he said, 'had an instinct for preservation' and 'he was always correct'.[6] There's no evidence he did what most of the speakers did to wake up a dozing, sozzled, gathering, which was to take their trousers off.

So valuable was the group to Philip that he allowed them to organise a black-tie stag do at the Belfry Club, now a private dining venue owned by Anton Mossiman, on 14 November 1947, five days before his official one. Topolski illustrated the menu for their 'Distant Country Member Lieutenant Philip Mountbatten, who is to be married on 20 November 1947'. The twenty-five men dined on foie gras, turtle soup, mixed grill and crepes Suzette.

It's hard to imagine the Prince's in-laws were happy at his association with the high life of 1940s and 1950s London. The Queen's cousin Princess Alexandra of Kent quizzed Eileen Parker about some of Philip's friends after meeting them at the Dorchester Hotel and agreed with the equerry's wife that a few of them were 'distinctly odd'. As for the Queen herself, who seems to have indulged her husband's need for a lads-only break, she apparently referred to the Thursday crew as 'Philip's funny friends!'[7]

45

FIRST HOME

Fire devastated Windsor Castle on 20 November 1992, which happened to be the Queen and Duke's forty-fifth wedding anniversary, but it is largely forgotten that fire had also destroyed the first home they were due to occupy after their marriage in 1947.

Sunninghill Park was purchased by the Crown Estate in 1944 and with its 700 acres adjoining Ascot Racecourse it was thought a handily placed country residence for the equine-loving Elizabeth and her husband. It had been occupied by the RAF during the war and needed extensive renovation. An offer to give the building to Windsor Rural District Council to be converted into flats was hastily withdrawn when the King decided to grant it to the couple as a Grace and Favour home in August 1947. It was made clear that in those days of austerity only a few rooms would be renovated and decorated by the end of the year.[1]

Meanwhile, the council obligingly accepted the monarch's offer to convert twelve huts in the park for housing and grovellingly announced that if Princess Elizabeth came to live at Sunninghill Park she could be assured she would have the esteem and affection of the whole district.[2]

As with the Windsor Castle fire, it was while the building was being renovated that fire took hold in the early hours of 30 August. The alarm was raised just after midnight and fire engines from five locations managed to control it by 1.45 a.m. but by then half the building had been destroyed and nearly all the roof burned. Like the castle fire which was started by a spotlight left too near a curtain, the Sunninghill one was accidentally started by workmen. The day after the fire police blamed a casually discarded cigarette end that had lain unnoticed in the newly timbered library.[3]

In the end, the Edinburghs moved into Windlesham Moor, which had belonged to the widow of financier Philip Hill. At the end of January wedding presents, including tables, chairs, antique furniture and glassware, were removed from public display at St James's Palace and taken by lorry to the Surrey home. The couple moved in on 30 January 1948 and one of the first acts of the dog-loving pair was to pass on a live Siamese cat sent to them as a wedding present by a fan to the cook at Windlesham.[4]

46

PRINCESS ANNE: THE SON HE NEVER HAD

Visitors to the Duke's private library at Buckingham Palace have often been struck that among the array of family photos on display the only one featuring his children was 'a big misty, romantic Seventies portrait of Princess Anne'.[1]

Asked in 1971 by his biographer Basil Boothroyd if he saw his own heredity coming out in his children, Philip joked, 'Yes, all the worst parts.' He went on to give three examples of why Charles was similar to the Queen, but Anne he felt had much of his own 'abrupt directness and practicality'.[2] The Princess herself referred to their much-referenced similarities when approached for an interview by Philip's biographer Tim Heald. 'It's impossible to judge a portrait of oneself,' she wrote to Heald, 'and almost as difficult to judge one of a close member of one's family – especially if you're supposed to be exactly like them.'[3]

The signs of their close bond were propitious from the moment she arrived at 11.50 a.m. on 15 August 1950. That same day Philip learned he was promoted to the rank of lieutenant commander in the Royal Navy. In a letter to his grandmother, the Dowager Marchioness of Milford Haven, Philip proudly announced, 'It's the sweetest girl.'

While much has been written about the Queen and Duke's remote parenting skills, particularly with their eldest children, key evidence suggests otherwise. Mike Parker remembered that no matter how busy the royal parents were they always set aside time for Charles and Anne. The Princess herself recalled that Philip was always careful to be with the children at bedtime and often read them stories. 'Nanny', she says, 'was always *Nanny*, never some sort of surrogate parent.'[4] Having said that, Philip's strong personality clearly daunted the sensitive Charles, whereas it had little impact on the more resilient Anne. She has always been a chip off the old block. As one of Philip's staff commented, 'She won't take any nonsense.'[5] She also responded to the way her parents allowed her and her brothers to pursue their own roles within the family firm: 'We've all been allowed to find our own way and we were always encouraged to discuss problems.'[6]

The two share a wry sense of humour. At the wedding breakfast following her wedding to Mark Phillips in 1973, Philip began his father-of-the-bride speech with 'Unaccustomed as I am …' before pausing for laughter and continuing, 'to speaking at breakfast'.[7]

Four months later Anne and Mark were almost kidnapped at gunpoint by Ian Ball, a fanatical loner who shot three people during the attack. The Princess typically kept her cool throughout the ordeal and afterwards phoned her parents, who were on a visit to Indonesia. Philip dealt with the phone call at 5 a.m.

On parade: the Duke followed by the Princess Royal attends the 2008 Trooping the Colour ceremony. (© Ian Lloyd)

local time and later proudly remarked: 'If the man had succeeded in abducting Anne, she'd have given him the hell of a time while in captivity.'[8]

The shared banter extends to their work life too. When Anne took over as president of the Fédération Équestre Internationale after Philip had held the same post for twenty years, she joked, 'He keeps being quoted at me and I've told them that if I hear his name mentioned once more I will go!'[9] Even when they occasionally disagree it is done by Anne with 'just the right smidgen of eye-rolling exasperation'. Otherwise 'she talks about him … with real affection'. The only difference of opinion Tim Heald could uncover concerned 'the arcane matter of equine veterinary practice', in which they held differing views so 'the matter was rapidly dropped'.[10]

Anne of course 'works like a Trojan', as the Queen's cousin Margaret Rhodes once commented. For a time she and her father topped the list of most engagements carried out each year. These days it's Anne and Charles who vie for the number one spot. So impressed was Philip with his daughter's work ethic that it was he who lobbied for her to have the title Princess Royal for years before she was finally granted it in 1987. They also support each other in personal matters. Philip was saddened when her marriage to Mark Phillips ended and was by her side to give her away at her later marriage to her mother's former equerry, Tim Laurence. Biographer Gyles Brandreth claims the Queen and Duke 'worry about her' and adds a 2004 comment from Philip that 'things aren't easy for Anne'.[11]

In return Anne has never missed an opportunity to praise her father and mother as well as her upbringing: 'Judging by some families, I think we are all on pretty good speaking terms after all this time and that's no mean achievement.'[12]

47

'THE WHOLE WORLD HAD DROPPED ON HIS SHOULDERS'

For four years from July 1949 until just before the Coronation, Philip had his own home at Clarence House and, more importantly for him, was head of it.

He and Elizabeth had selected the décor, recruited a relatively small household by royal standards and dined with the senior members of the team at lunchtime. Mike Parker recalled the Princess felt so relaxed 'you could hear her singing around the house'.[1] 'I suppose I naturally fulfilled the principal position,' Philip later reflected on those early years. 'People would come to me and ask me what to do. In 1952 the whole thing changed very, very considerably.'[2]

That change memorably occurred on 6 February 1952 when Elizabeth and Philip were on a short visit to Kenya en route to Australia. At the time the couple were at Treetops Hotel, a wooden structure in the top of a tall tree at the foothills of the Aberdare Mountains where the two of them were able to watch elephants, buffalo and rhinos gather at the nearby waterhole. At some point during their overnight stay Elizabeth's father, George VI, died in his sleep at Sandringham. The royal party had returned to Sagana Lodge, a wedding present to the couple from the people of Kenya, before they were given the news. These days the couple would have known within minutes, but it took several hours for the news to reach them. Mike Parker had been told by a reporter there were rumours from London that the King had died. He turned on the radio at the lodge and the

BBC World Service was playing doleful music, which helped confirm the story. It was Parker who informed the Duke and would later recall that 'at that moment Prince Philip looked as if the whole world had dropped on his shoulders'.[3] After breaking the news to Elizabeth, Philip retreated to a sofa and could be seen slumped behind a copy of *The Times*.

That moment would, in the words of one his biographers, mark his 'near-extinction as an individual under the grinding constitutional millstone'.[4] Just as the establishment had done its best to alienate him in the run-up to his engagement in 1947, now once more the palace old guard and key politicians closed ranks against him, making sure he wouldn't have a say in the running of the monarchy.

In the space of a year he had given up a promising career in the Royal Navy which could, as many of his contemporaries believed, have resulted in him reaching First Sea Lord by merit rather than position. In return he embarked on full-term royal duties during which this proudest of men would forever have to walk three paces behind his wife, live in homes not of his choosing but inherited by the new sovereign, and owing his parliamentary allowance to his wife's position rather than through a job. On top of this, senior courtiers were suspicious of him. 'He was very badly treated by the Queen's then private secretaries, Tommy Lascelles and Michael Adeane … They decided to shut him out and they succeeded.'[5] Half a century on, he commented with resignation rather than rancour, 'I was told "Keep out" and that was that.'[6]

Even twenty years into the reign, by the time both men had retired, Philip still felt this position as consort was unfairly limited in comparison with his female predecessors in the role. 'Because she's the Sovereign, everybody turns to her,' he explained to writer Basil Boothroyd. 'If you have a King and Queen, there are certain things people automatically go to the

Queen about. But if the Queen is also the *Queen* they go to her about everything.' Not only did this add to his wife's workload, but 'it's frightfully difficult to persuade them not to go to the Queen, but to come to me'.[7] As Mike Parker noted back in 1952, 'there were a lot more of them than there were of us'.[8]

It wasn't just the royal household that excluded Philip but also the prime minister, Winston Churchill. 'Prince Philip was totally excluded,' recalled Lady Pamela Hicks. 'Churchill really made him feel totally apart from the whole thing.'[9] Churchill had suspected that Philip would be a puppet consort with his uncle Mountbatten pulling the strings. The war hero never got over Mountbatten's involvement in Indian independence and once rather dramatically told the Earl what he had done to the subcontinent had 'slapped him across the face with a whip'.[10]

Harold Macmillan, the third prime minister of Elizabeth's reign, detailed Churchill's antagonism towards the Duke in his diary. Just a month into the new reign, Macmillan's wife Dorothy ('D') lunched with the prime minister ('C') and his wife Clemmie ('Mrs C'): 'C was in a vile temper. Mrs C confirmed to D afterwards that it was "Philip". I think he is much distressed at the situation developing at the palace.'[11] 'The situation' relates to the row over the name of the new dynasty (see Chapter 48: 'That Damned Fool Edinburgh'). In his diary three days previously, Macmillan recorded: 'It is still more probable that the Mountbattens are exercising their influence pretty strongly,' something Macmillan felt 'might prove very dangerous'.[12]

Originally Philip suggested to Elizabeth that they could continue living at Clarence House and use Buckingham Palace as an office, something the new Queen was happy about. When the old guard informed Churchill of this, he would have none of it. Having entered Parliament in the reign of Elizabeth's great-great-grandmother, Churchill regarded the palace as a potent symbol of the monarchy and declared: 'To the Palace they must go!' Mike Parker was present when the family drove the short distance across the Mall in the spring of 1953 and recalled, 'there wasn't a dry eye in the car'.

This drastic change for the family deeply affected the Prince. Just two days after the funeral of George VI, Philip's eldest sister Margarita visited him and noted, 'He was in a black depression and could hardly be got to stir from his room.' He told her, 'you can guess what's going to happen now',[13] presumably referring to the impact the King's death would have on their lives. In November of that first year of the new reign, photographer Cecil Beaton witnessed the Opening of Parliament by the Queen and was struck by how Philip 'looked extremely ill, his eyes hollow, his complexion green and his pale hair beginning to thin'. Beaton may have been right about the effect the strain was having on the Duke but history has disagreed with his prediction: 'I doubt he will live long.'[14]

Other relations noticed Philip's depression. Ex-King Peter of Yugoslavia, married to Philip's cousin Alexandra, told her after lunching at Buckingham Palace: 'You could feel it all underneath … I don't know how long he can last … bottled up like that.' Alexandra herself wrote, 'the extreme nervous tension of those days was bound to have an effect. Shortly after moving into Buckingham Palace, he came in to breakfast one morning looking so yellow that Elizabeth insisted on calling the doctor. Philip had jaundice.'[15] The disease is often brought on by stress and depression.

On the positive side, Philip did try to carve out a role, or as he put it, 'I tried to find useful things to do.' He started with their new home, trying to update some of the arcane traditions at Buckingham Palace. 'I did my best. I introduced a Footman Training Programme. The old boys here hadn't had anything quite like it before … We had an Organisation and Methods Review. I tried to make improvements –

The Duke in reflective mood in Windsor Great Park in May 2011. Over the years, Philip would often brood about his role and the future of the monarchy. (© Ian Lloyd)

without unhinging things.'[16] Mike Parker, who assisted him in the reforms, explained: 'We explored the whole palace', treading on a number of toes as they did so. 'We met with a fair amount of resistance. But I think we made a few improvements, dragged some of them into the twentieth century.'[17] The Queen made Philip Ranger of Windsor Great Park, to protect and maintain the 2,020-hectare (5,000-acre) parkland around the castle. He was also asked to manage the two private estates of Balmoral and Sandringham which she had inherited from her father.

He devised a programme of royal engagements and duties that also benefited the Queen, since it enabled him to go to places and meet people she didn't have the opportunity to do. As Mike Parker pointed out, he was able to give her 'the low-down on absolutely anything'.[18]

Last but not least, although constitutionally he was more or less non-existent, he was still very much head of the family unit, as his cousin Pamela Hicks noted:

> they were still able, with these two small children, to have a family group where he could be the *pater familias* and have authority. He was very, very accepting. But she was very careful to let him take part in things and relied on his enormously.

Her reliance on him and his support would make the reign of Elizabeth II almost a joint one. As Countess Mountbatten commented, 'Prince Philip has always been there for the Queen in so many, many ways. I don't think for one moment she could have done all she has done without having had him there.'[19]

48

'THAT DAMNED FOOL EDINBURGH'

Two days after the funeral of King George VI, the late King's mother Queen Mary received an unexpected visit from Prince Ernst August of Hanover at Marlborough House, her London residence. The Prince broke the news to her that he'd been at a dinner party hosted by Philip's uncle Earl Mountbatten at his Broadlands estate in Hampshire. The meal had taken place just two days after the King's death and the host, rather insensitively, boasted that 'now the House of Mountbatten reigns'.

For the supremely ambitious Earl it was a dream come true that his surname, which Philip had taken in 1947, would be the name of the new royal dynasty. As a great-grandson of Queen Victoria he would have been aware that while Victoria belonged to the House of Hanover, her successor Edward VII reigned as first king of the House of Saxe-Coburg-Gotha, which was his father, Prince Albert's, homeland. This triple-barrelled German name proved increasingly embarrassing to Edward's son George V during the First World War, and in 1917 he changed the name of his dynasty to the soundly British House of Windsor. Now, if history repeated itself, Elizabeth would be the last of the House of Windsor and Prince Charles would be the first king of the House of Mountbatten.

The 84-year-old Dowager Queen spent a sleepless night after Ernst's visit and the following day summoned Jock Colville to visit her. Colville, a former private secretary to Princess Elizabeth, now held the same position to the prime minister,

In 1952 the Queen was persuaded by her advisers to announce that the name of the royal dynasty would continue to be known as the House of Windsor. Shortly before the birth of Prince Andrew, shown here in his first photoshoot in the summer of 1960, the Queen righted this snub to her husband and decreed that her descendants would take the name Mountbatten-Windsor (see Chapter 98). (©Keystone / Stringer / Getty)

Winston Churchill. Declaring that her husband had changed the name in perpetuity, the new Queen's grandmother fumed, 'What the devil does that damned fool Edinburgh think that the family name has to do with him?'[1]

Colville relayed the Queen Mary's concerns to Churchill, who 'went through the roof'.[2] At a Cabinet meeting later in the day a consensus was reached that the existing name should be maintained and that the Queen must be informed.

Philip himself had only used the name Mountbatten for a matter of months in 1947 between his naturalisation as a British citizen and his marriage in November when he was given the title of Duke of Edinburgh; he had no particular ambition to use it as the name of the new dynasty. Instead he suggested Windsor and Edinburgh, to which one again Churchill gave a 'firm, negative, answer'.[3]

On 9 April the Queen issued a proclamation declaring her 'Will and Pleasure that She and Her Children shall be styled and known as the House and Family of Windsor'.

Philip was said to be 'devastated'[4] and famously said, 'I am the only man in the country not allowed to give his name to his children. I am a bloody amoeba.'[5] This quote has appeared in nearly every account of his life, apart from one. In an unpublished volume by respected historian Tim Heald, Philip had read and annotated the manuscript himself. When he reached the 'bloody amoeba' phrase he scribbled a typically blunt comment in the margin: 'Rubbish.'[6]

49

AND TO CROWN IT ALL ...

If proof were needed that Philip's role as consort lacked the prestige and significance of a queen consort, it came on 2 June 1953. That day in Westminster Abbey his wife was crowned and anointed as Her Majesty Queen Elizabeth II, while he had not much more than a walk-on part in the proceedings.

One of the peculiarities of Britain's monarchical system is that the female consort not only gets to be queen but she is entitled to be crowned alongside her husband. Like the king, she has a specially woven purple velvet train, and a consort's crown that is made afresh for each incumbent. In theory, if a king marries after his accession his wife could have her own coronation ceremony. This was the case with Henry VIII's second wife, Anne Boleyn, who was crowned in 1533, though his wives three to six didn't have one each due to death, divorce, execution and the vast cost of putting on such an elaborate show on a regular basis.

Reflecting his harsh treatment from courtiers and the government since the Queen's accession, for Philip the period up to and including the Coronation was also full of slights and injustices …

1   **Idle Philip:** Philip chaired the committee which also included the Archbishop of Canterbury and the prime minister. He almost certainly wouldn't have known at the time the words of a senior palace official who suggested it to Churchill since the Duke 'is insupportable when idle' and it would give him a responsible job – i.e. keep him out of mischief.[1]

2   **The real organiser:** Bernard Marmaduke Fitzalan-Howard, 16th Duke of Norfolk, rather than Philip was in overall charge of the Coronation, and had organised the Coronation and funeral of George VI. The reason for this was that he was Earl Marshal of England, a title going back to the twelfth century. Since 1672 it was officially made a hereditary position for the Howard family. So, regardless of talent, brains (even as a duke he had been unable to get a place at Oxford University), personality or personal wishes, the Duke of Norfolk had to oversee the most lavish spectacle so far seen in twentieth-century Britain. Even more absurd, as the premier Catholic layman in England he was overseeing a purely Anglican ceremony during which the Queen made an oath to protect and maintain the Church of England.

3   **Blown out of the water:** As an innovator, Philip asked Geoffrey Fisher, Archbishop of Canterbury, if some features

relevant to the world of 1953 could be introduced to the ceremony. He was given the ecclesiastical brush-off.

4 **Ban the Prince?** In fact, the archbishop would have liked Philip excluded from the planning process altogether, writing, 'There must be no association of him in any way with the process and rite of the Coronation.'[2]

5 **No-fly zone:** Prime Minister Winston Churchill opposed Philip's use of a helicopter, then regarded as a security risk, in order to visit British and Commonwealth troops. 'In the run-up to the Coronation … it was just more practical but it caused a ruckus,' Philip recalled half a century later, still rankled by the fuss. 'I didn't go through the proper channels. There was a lot of pettifogging bureaucracy.'[3]

6 **Struggling with the telly:** The Queen, the palace, Churchill, the archbishop and Philip's Coronation Committee all rejected the idea of the BBC covering the Coronation live. It was leaked to the press that it wouldn't be shown live and opinion polls showed that 78 per cent of people wanted it televised. Eventually Philip persuaded the Queen of its merits and the palace backed down.

7 **Walk on by:** Another opinion poll backed Philip processing with the Queen through the abbey. In the event he sat with the royal dukes of Gloucester and Kent and watched his wife make a stately entrance on her own, followed by her maids of honour.

8 **Second best:** Philip was not the first person to pay homage to the newly crowned sovereign – that role went to the Archbishop of Canterbury, followed by Philip, then the other royal dukes. However, he did have one significant moment: the Queen had insisted that Philip should be by her side for Holy Communion.

9 **Not quite the ticket:** Philip's three surviving sisters, Margarita, Theodore and Sophie, lobbied hard to be

The coronet and robe of a royal duke, worn by Philip during the 1953 coronation. On the far right is the cocked hat of an Admiral of the Fleet, which he wore during the carriage procession to and from Westminster Abbey. (© Ian Lloyd)

included in the guest list, having been excluded from the wedding in 1947. They were allowed to attend with their husbands but just two of their children each and no other German relations could attend. Also banned was the Duke of Windsor at the suggestion of Elizabeth. According to Archbishop Fisher, 'The Queen would be less willing than anyone to have him there.' A former monarch witnessing the anointing of a new one just didn't sit well.[4]

10 **Snap unhappy:** Philip would have liked his old Thursday Club pal Baron Nahum to take the official photographs, but the Queen Mother lobbied and succeeded in getting Cecil Beaton. Anne Glenconner, one of the maids of honour, recalled: 'Cecil Beaton was in a stew, hopping up and down, and … the Duke of Edinburgh – he was an amateur photographer – kept on saying: "no you've got to be there".' Tired of Philip arranging the group, 'in the end Cecil Beaton said: "Look I'm taking the photographs you know, I think I'd better get on with it."'[5]

11 **Just joking:** Elizabeth had the route of her procession inside the abbey marked out on the palace ballroom floor so she could practise with her maids of honour carrying knotted bed sheets to imitate her 6.5m (21.3ft) train. Philip couldn't resist making fun of the whole procedure until the Queen finally snapped and said: 'Don't be silly. Come back here and do it again properly.'[6]

12 **Ruler of the Queen's Navy:** One 'error' that nobody had thought of in advance met with Philip's approval. On the day of the Coronation he rode with the Queen in the Gold State Coach in the uniform of an Admiral of the Fleet. However, when it came to designing and producing the many official Coronation souvenirs, Philip had yet to be appointed, so all the merchandise shows him wearing the uniform of a commodore. This delighted him, according

to Queen Alexandra of Yugoslavia: 'My cousin took secret pleasure, I believe, in being historically linked in this way with the highest naval rank he had actually earned.'[7]

50

QUIPS, GAFFES AND BANTER: THE DUKE'S MEMORABLE CLANGERS 41–50

WOMEN

41 Lady Longford: The biographer of both Elizabeth II and Victoria recalled a friend of hers sent her part of a hat from Paris, fixed with some flowers and feathers on it for her to wear at a palace garden party. Philip took one look at it and exclaimed: '*Where did that come from?*' She told him and he said: '*Oh, I see. It's do-it-yourself hat.*'

42 When a woman in a reception line told Philip she was a solicitor he replied, '*I thought it was against the law these days for women to solicit,*' before roaring with laughter and walking away, leaving her red with embarrassment.

43 On a visit to Kent in 2012 he couldn't help but notice Hannah Jackson, a 25-year-old blonde lady wearing a red dress with a zip right down the front. He pointed it out to a nearby policeman: '*I could get arrested if I unzipped that dress.*'

44 To a fashion writer in 1993, '*You're not wearing mink knickers, are you?*'

45 One of his earlier quips: *'How does a girl get a mink? The same way a mink gets a mink.'*

46 Another one even he couldn't get way with these days: *'When a man opens a car door for his wife, it's either a new car or a new wife.'*

47 To some scantily clad female singers in the musical *Chicago* at the Adelphi Theatre, London, 1999, *'Where on earth do you keep your microphones?'*

48 In a 1961 speech to the Scottish WI, *'British women can't cook.'*

49 To a group of women clerics at a 2012 Lambeth Palace reception comprising a nun, Rev. Canon Dr Frances Ward and the Dean of St Edmundsbury Cathedral, *'So this is the female section. Are you all gathered here for protection?'*

50 Discussing tartan with Annabel Goldie, former Scottish Tory leader, *'That's a nice tie … Do you have any knickers in that material?'*

51

DON'T CALL ME ALBERT!

Prince Philip has never liked the oft-made comparison between himself and the last male consort, Prince Albert. Asked by one of his biographers about the example of his great-great-grandfather, Philip gave the exasperated reply, 'Oh, yes. The Prince Consort', before pausing and then explaining the difference in the nature of their two roles. 'The Prince Consort's position was quite different. Queen Victoria was an executive sovereign … The Prince Consort was effectively Victoria's private secretary.

But after Victoria the monarchy changed. It became an institution. I had to fit in with the institution.'[1]

Those that know Philip tend to shy away from the comparison. Michael Mann, Dean of Windsor, once said, 'He has never tried to be a Prince Albert.' Royal biographer Elizabeth Longford didn't 'believe the Duke of Edinburgh likes being compared too much to Albert because he's got his own ideas'.[2] Having said that, there is also the daunting challenge of Albert's legacy. In just twenty-one years between his marriage and death, the Prince managed to combine his role as private secretary with an avalanche of achievements as patron of the arts, enthusiastic supporter for industry, technology and design, social reform activist and the mastermind behind the 1851 Great Exhibition, the first international trade fair, which attracted 6 million visitors, a third of the population of Britain at the time. For Philip, who always hated being compared to any successful man, Albert was the ultimate threat from the grave.

There are nevertheless some inevitable comparisons …

Both men were abandoned by their mothers for poignant reasons. Philip's mother was sectioned for her mental health when Philip was 9, and he wouldn't see her properly again until he was 16. Although both of Albert's parents had extra-marital affairs, when his mother, Princess Louise, fell in love with her husband's equerry she was banished from court and Albert never saw her again from the age of 5. She died of cancer in 1831 when he was 11. After turbulent childhoods both men found love and stability in their marriages.

Both men were impoverished, by royal standards. Philip had more or less only the clothes he stood up in when he returned from the war; a guest at a palace garden party noticed how worn his uniform was. Albert was lambasted by the press and the establishment, with a popular song claiming he was in it for the money: 'He comes to take for "better or for worse" / England's fat queen and England's fatter purse.'

Both men had pushy uncles. King Leopold I of the Belgians, uncle to both Victoria and Albert, masterminded their union just as Lord 'Dickie' Mountbatten encouraged Philip's union with Elizabeth.

Both men had run-ins with leading politicians. Albert had a long and bitter conflict was Lord Palmerston, foreign secretary from 1846 to 1855, while, as we have seen, Philip and Prime Minister Winston Churchill clashed over the name of the new royal dynasty, moving the Queen and Duke to Buckingham Palace, and Philip's aim to pilot his own aircraft.

Both had issues with their eldest son and heir. Albert Edward, Prince of Wales, rebelled against Albert's punishing schedule for his education and ended up a pleasure-loving copy of Victoria's 'disreputable uncles'. Pragmatic, bullish Philip has rarely seen eye to eye with the more sensitive Charles. On the other hand, Albert venerated his eldest daughter Vicky, who was similar to him in her drive to learn and her liberal political views; similarly, Princess Anne is a carbon copy of her father.

Both carried out careful household management at Buckingham Palace and Windsor. Albert was appalled that candles throughout the palaces were replaced each day whether they had been used or not, and insisted each should be used as long as practical. He also cut staff wages and reduced jobs, something Philip did by installing dishwashers to replace the army of palace servants used to wash kitchenware, and replaced the antiquated telephone system with an intercom. Curiously, the archaic habit of powdering footmen's wigs survived Albert's reforms and continued until Philip abolished the practice.

In 1951 Philip was asked to preside over a meeting of the British Association for the Advancement of Science, a role that Albert held in 1859. Keen to make an impact, Philip read

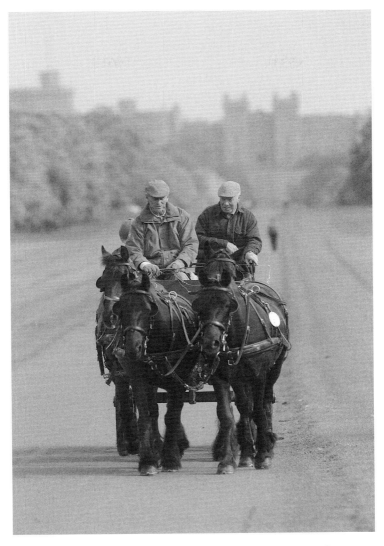

Both Prince Albert and Philip were given the title Ranger of Windsor Great Park. Here, Philip, an expert four-in-hand carriage driver, enjoys an early morning practice on the Long Walk, with Windsor Castle in the background. (© Ian Lloyd)

everything he could on his illustrious forebear and said in his speech: 'I am proud to pay tribute to this man who saw so clearly the part science was to play in the future of this country.'

Both men have a lasting legacy. Albert's Great Exhibition passed into folklore and its Crystal Palace venue, relocated in south London, lasted until it burned to the ground in 1936. Philip's name will forever be associated with the Duke of Edinburgh's Award Scheme founded in 1956.

52

MOTHER-IN-LAW TROUBLE

As we've seen, Philip didn't tick too many boxes for Queen Elizabeth. She and her circle were suspicious of the impoverished Greek prince from a broken home, with a posse of neo-Nazi relations and an oddball education at Gordonstoun. His habit of roaring into the Buckingham Palace quadrangle in his MG sportscar, wind-blown and open shirted, might have attracted Princess Elizabeth but did little to entrance her mother. Elizabeth Snr preferred camp, witty, omega males, from Cecil Beaton to Noël Coward: men who were unthreatening, deferential and, above all, entertaining.

Philip was none of the above. 'Queen Elizabeth found Philip cold and lacking in our kind of sense of humour,' recalled one lady-in-waiting. 'He wasn't able to see the ridiculous things, and that is perhaps rather Germanic. And he didn't set out to charm her.'[1] To be fair to Philip, the list of royal party games was an acquired taste. His parents-in-law had a fondness for charades, an adult version of hide and seek called 'Murder', passing the matchbox via your nose (with which even austere Queen Mary joined in) and one they labelled 'Parada' where guests imitated high-kicking Polish soldiers and marched past the King to military music.

Even if he wasn't the type to lead the usual conga round the royal apartments at the end of a party, Philip was far from being a wallflower at these gatherings. Despite his relative youth he was unafraid to make his opinions known. After one such outburst in early December 1946, the 25-year-old wrote to Queen Elizabeth apologising for getting carried away and starting 'a rather heated discussion'. It was on politics, a subject area in which Philip's views were leftist and the Queen's were conservative with a large and small 'c'. According to her official biographer, Philip 'had by now come to the conclusion that trying to shift her from her instinctive conservatism was unproductive'.[2] With the announcement of his engagement to the Princess still half a year away, Philip no doubt felt it expedient to hope his future mother-in-law had not found him 'violently argumentative and an opponent of socialism', and to forgive him 'if I did say anything I ought not to have said'.[3]

Just before the engagement was announced, Queen Elizabeth wrote to a few confidantes to let them know first. Her letters wax lyrical about her daughter's intended, but to the King's private secretary, Tommy Lascelles, who shared her misgivings about Philip, she was more downbeat. 'One can only pray', she wrote, 'that she has made the right decision, I *think* she has – but he is untried as yet.'[4]

Four and a half years later the relationship between the two was to be tested following the death of the King, when Queen Elizabeth lost her power base and her forthright and opinionated son-in-law took her place as consort. Three weeks after the accession the new Queen was talking to assistant private secretary Martin Charteris when her mother's limousine glided into view and the weary Elizabeth said: 'Here comes the problem!'[5] The problem, according to another courtier, was that 'she was no longer the boss'. One of her family blamed astrology: 'She was a Leo and like all Leos she didn't enjoy being number two.'[6] Although she had the added boost of an additional 'queen' in her new title of Queen Elizabeth the Queen Mother, to differentiate her from her daughter, she also lost a certain amount of status, particularly when she moved to Clarence House, or, as she called it, that 'horrid little house'.

To compensate her mother for the loss of the King and her status and to motivate her to bring her undeniable charisma back onto the royal stage, the Queen ordered a dispatch box to be made for her mother to receive at least some royal papers in. She also made her a Counsellor of State, the first dowager queen to hold this office. This meant she was the quasi-monarch during Elizabeth and Philip's early, lengthy overseas visits, including the six-month Coronation tour of 1953–54.

Philip, with that 'new-broomish' attitude the courtiers feared, wanted to change anything he thought could do with it. Courtiers and politicians opposed him left, right and centre, but his chief opponent was his mother-in-law.

Even twenty years into the present reign, when Philip decided to re-landscape the approach to Sandringham House, it was made clear the Queen Mother preferred it as it was and so that's how it stayed.[7] The Queen Mother would go on to oppose nearly every significant change: the opening of Buckingham Palace to the public, the Queen having to pay tax, the scrapping of the royal yacht *Britannia* and the disappearance of the royal flight.

Although she failed to stop this march of progress, she did have the occasional triumph. When the Court Circular was slightly modernised in the 1990s she objected and got her own way. So while an entry for the monarch might read: 'Tony Blair had an audience of the Queen,' those for her mother were still written like the King James Bible: 'Major X had the honour of being received by Queen Elizabeth the Queen Mother,' and official Clarence House letters always thanked correspondents for their letters that 'I laid before Queen Elizabeth' rather than handed to her.

Maintaining Queen Elizabeth in the Edwardian luxury to which she'd been accustomed didn't come cheap, and while the naturally frugal Philip and Elizabeth privately despaired at the huge bills generated down the Mall at Clarence House, the Queen readily paid off a vast number of them. Whether it was settling the invoices for her mother's ever-expanding wardrobe or her considerable number of racehorses, the only negativity shown by the Queen was to scribble an exasperated: 'Oh dear Mummy!' across them.

Mother-in-law and son-in-law maintained an uneasy truce as the decades passed. They had to, in part, since they were often under the same roof, especially during her six-week Christmas and New Year stay at Sandringham. Even in her later years the Queen Mother referred to him as 'the Hun' occasionally, even if he was in the room,[8] which guests found rather awkward as it was difficult to know how playful she was being. Honest to the point of rudeness, Prince Philip 'privately regarded her showgirl performances for public consumption as somewhat phoney'.[9]

On the other hand the Queen Mother loyally defended Philip to the outside world. When biographer Tim Heald asked her: 'What nationality do you think of Prince Philip as being?' there was no mention of the Hun, or Johnny Foreigner but a suitably patriotic: 'Oh he's an English gentleman.' She also showed Heald a sketch of Philip by Pietro Annigoni, which she had on display at Clarence House, proudly describing it as the best portrait of him ever done.[10]

While one might expect her to have been supportive in her comments to a royal biographer, it is interesting to note she

Philip, as Chancellor of the University of Cambridge, greets the Queen Mother on her visit to Girton College, 9 June 1993. (© Ian Lloyd)

once directly intervened in a Fleet Street attack on Philip. When legendary *Daily Express* journalist Jean Rook tore into Philip in one of her most excoriating pieces, the Queen Mother asked her close friend Woodrow Wyatt to intercede. In a letter of May 1990 she asks him to take up the topic with Lord Stevens, proprietor of the *Express*.[11] Wyatt saw Stevens the next day and while the newspaperman argued that there were no good members of the royal family apart from the Queen, he agreed that Rook had gone over the top and that he would have a word with her. Wyatt then went on to write a supportive piece on Philip in his own *News of the World* column a few days later. In June he met the Queen Mother again and 'she thanked me for defending Prince Philip when he couldn't reply himself'.[12]

As she continued to defy the years and to carry on appearing in public even into her hundred and second year, Philip, like all of her relations, seemed to regard her with veneration and with the growing feeling that 'she's eternal'. It certainly must have seemed the case when she was able to attend his own eightieth birthday Thanksgiving Service in June 2001. Over the half-century of her widowhood, Philip never forgot one particularly touching gesture. Whenever they met, he would kiss her on either cheek, kiss her hand and then bow to her. It was a balletic performance and one that showed his respect not just for his mother-in-law but for an anointed queen.

53

WHAT HAVE YOU COME AS?

'Poor darlings, they have never had any fun yet,' wrote George VI in his journal on VE Day, reflecting on Elizabeth and Margaret's five-year virtual incarceration at Windsor for the duration of the Second World War.[1]

Like most of their generation they then fully embraced the post-war world of nightclubs, restaurants and private parties and, once he'd returned from the Far East in early 1946, Philip also threw himself into a hectic social life.

Like the young Victoria and Albert, the couple relished fancy-dress parties, even if, unlike Victoria and Albert they didn't bother to coordinate their costumes. In May 1948 they turned up at Coppins, the Buckinghamshire home of the widowed Duchess of Kent, dressed as a Spanish infanta and a policeman. A fellow guest, Henry 'Chips' Channon, spotted Elizabeth 'in black lace, with a large comb and mantilla', dancing every dance until 5 a.m. despite being over three months pregnant with Charles. Prince Philip, says Channon, 'was the success of the ball, and was wildly gay with his policeman's hat and handcuffs. He leapt about and jumped into the air as he greeted everybody … His charm is colossal.' The two joined in the riotous hokey-cokey at 3 a.m.[2]

The following summer the pair were once again in costume for a party at 14 Prince's Gate, London, the American ambassador's residence. This time Elizabeth was dressed as a maid with a black frock, white apron and white cap, and Philip as a butler. Meanwhile Margaret, never one to hide her light under a bushel, went as a good-time girl from the Folies Bergère. Her outfit consisted of a low-cut red and black dress with a huge red bow at the front, black fishnet stockings, high heels and a red feathers in her hair.[3] She was a close friend (very close indeed if you believe the rumours) of the ambassador's daughter Sharman Douglas. The two of them, plus the Princess's lady-in-waiting and three others, danced a memorable can-can. In Hollywood two days later, the actor Danny Kaye had to deny he'd taught the Princess how to high kick her way across the room, though he conceded he might have given 'a couple of pointers' to Sharman Douglas but Margaret wasn't present.[4]

It's noticeable that the Edinburghs were cautious in their choice of outfits at the Prince's Gate do. Among the 300 guests who danced to Maurice Winnick's band until 5 a.m. were a polar bear, a rajah, a scarlet devil (not Margaret), several people in pyjamas and – in those buttoned-up times – 'several men wearing open-neck shirts'.[5]

Margaret went on to wear fancy dress at the drop of a hat and appeared as a memorable Mae West and Sophie Tucker in her later years. The Queen dressed as the Queen of Swaziland at Prince William's 'Out of Africa' twenty-first birthday party at Windsor but Philip appears to have hung up his butler's apron and handcuffs for good.

54

EDINBURGH GREEN

Buckingham Palace, with its white and gold décor, can resemble the Ritz Hotel with Rembrandts and Vermeers thrown in, so it's unsurprising that when he joined the family firm the down-to-earth Philip devised his own muted colour scheme. He produced an official livery colour in dark green. Named 'Edinburgh green', it was worn as the staff livery at the royal couple's Clarence House residence. At the 1953 Coronation, the Duke's page wore the green and silver uniform.

It was also his colour of choice for his private cars. In 1954 he bought an Aston Martin Lagonda 3l drophead coupé, one of only twenty produced. The bodywork was in Edinburgh green with dove grey leather upholstery. It was made to his specification, with an extra vanity mirror for the Queen and a radio telephone.

The Lagonda was taken on board the royal yacht *Britannia* for Philip's use when he opened the 1956 Melbourne Olympic Games. In November 1959 he used it to drive the Queen to Luton Hoo, the Bedfordshire mansion of Sir Harold Wernher, where the couple traditionally spent their wedding anniversary. With Philip at the wheel, and the six-months pregnant monarch in the passenger seat, they made their first trip on a British motorway, joining the newly opened M1 at St Albans and leaving it 15 miles later. The *Guardian* was able to report, 'for much of the way, the Duke kept to the inside "slow" lane, cruising at about 50mph, but occasionally he pulled out to overtake lorries'.[1]

In the 1960s and 1970s the Queen owned two Rovers for private use, both in Edinburgh green: a 1963 Rover 3.5l saloon and a 1971 Rover P5B 3.5l saloon.[2]

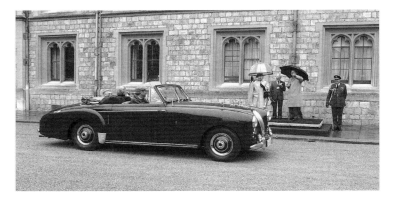

The Queen and Duke acknowledge the owners of a 1954 Lagonda
with its distinctive shade of Edinburgh Green, once owned by
Prince Philip, during a parade of Aston Martins at Windsor in 2005.
(© Ian Lloyd)

The then Princess Elizabeth helped promote her husband's
colour of choice in 1951 in her capacity as patron of the British
Colour Council. The now defunct BCC was an official body
that indexed named colours used by government, industry and
so on. Before the royal couple made their first official visit to
Canada and the USA in the autumn of 1951 it was announced
that the Princess had chosen Edinburgh green and Elizabethan
rose as their colours of choice to commemorate the tour.
Diplomatically, it was made clear that Edinburgh green is the
colour of the silver spruce, native to North America.[3]

55

THE RUMOURS

From the day he married, rumours of Philip's alleged infidelity have surfaced time and again and, together with his predilection for gaffes, will no doubt be on the shortlist of topics covered by biographers, journalists and documentary makers for years to come.

Certainly the Duke has been enormously attractive to women over the years thanks to his matinée idol looks, as well as his wit, charm, sparkling eyes and the obvious kudos of his being the first gentleman in the land. Biographer Graham Turner was told by a courtier in 2001 that 'all the girls in his office have to be 36-24-36'. Another former member of the household recalled: 'If an attractive girl comes into a room or there's a particularly pretty girl wearing something striking in a line-up he'll say "Mm!" very appreciatively, though not in a way that makes you feel embarrassment for the Queen.'[1]

Investigative journalists have tried for decades to unearth the tiniest morsels of fact about the Duke's supposed dalliances and, in the absence of any concrete evidence, have had to resort to printing conjecture and nudge-wink gossip. No one has ever admitted, on or off the record, to either an affair with the Prince or being his natural offspring from a liaison. In 1995 a German newspaper thought it had the scoop of the decade when it gleefully reported that Philip had twenty-four illegitimate children and that this had been confirmed by Buckingham Palace. Sadly for the Teutonic news hounds it turned out they'd confused 'illegitimate children' with 'godchildren'.[2]

It doesn't help Philip's defence that half of Europe's kings and consorts have bed-hopped more times than they've had a state dinner, suggesting faithlessness is a royal norm. Both Albert II of Monaco and ex-King Albert II of Belgium have admitted to fathering illegitimate children, and a BBC radio documentary claimed Philip's near-contemporary and fellow consort, Prince Bernhard of the Netherlands, also had children out of wedlock.[3] If we are to believe a recent biography, the award for regal she-nanigans well and truly belongs to Juan Carlos I of Spain who, the book claims, has had 5,000 lovers.[4]

In this country, generations of Elizabeth and Philip's forefathers have philandered for Britain. Take the Queen's great-grandfather, Edward VII, dubbed 'Edward the Caresser', who it has been claimed had several illegitimate children, including Sonia Keppel, grandmother of Camilla, Duchess of Cornwall.

The contenders …

'THESE THREE OLD CHESTNUTS'

1 **Hélène Cordet, actor and cabaret singer (1917–96):** Rumours of a relationship between the Prince and showgirl date back to the late 1940s when the Italian press, noticing Hélène was not invited to the royal wedding although her mother had been, speculated that Princess Elizabeth had banned her from the ceremony. It was noticed that a teen-aged Philip had both given Hélène away and been best man at her first wedding and that he was godfather to her son and daughter and paid for their education. In actual fact Hélène was an old family friend. Her mother, Anna Foufounis, was the wealthy widow of a Greek royalist who had befriended Philip's family in Paris in 1920s. In her autobiography *Born*

Bewildered, she protested her innocence of a relationship with the Prince but fanned the flames by revealing that, when she turned on the TV to watch a programme about a circus she noticed Philip in the audience. 'For a moment', she wrote, 'I went back years and got quite hot under the collar.'[5]

2   **Daphne du Maurier, writer and playwright (1907–89):** The Cornwall-based author of *Rebecca* and *Jamaica Inn* was married to Lieutenant Colonel Sir Frederick 'Boy' Browning, dubbed the 'father of the British airborne forces' and later treasurer to the Duke of Edinburgh. Maurier was an occasional guest at royal events but found the visits a strain. She hated every minute of their stay at Balmoral in 1953, writing: 'I felt as if I was sitting on the edge of a chair all the time, not sure what I should do.'[6] The author's official biographer Margaret Forster described a possible romance with Philip as pure fantasy.[7]

3   **Anna Massey, actor (1937–2011):** Born into an acting dynasty – her father was Hollywood actor Raymond Massey and her brother was the actor Daniel Massey – Anna was also the niece of Vincent Massey, Governor-General of Canada. She spoke of the Philip rumour in a 1991 interview: 'I don't know how it started as I only met the Duke once at my uncle's and have never met him since.'[8]

According to journalist Fiammetta Rocco, 'The palace is happy for what it calls "these three old chestnuts" to be repeated but draws the line at commenting on fresh additions.'

OTHER STARS

4   **Pat Kirkwood, British stage actor, singer, dancer (1921–2007):** A huge star of the late 1940s and early 1950s, Kirkwood

was the first woman to have her own series on the BBC. Theatre critic Ken Tynan described her legs as 'the seventh wonder of the world' but today she is largely remembered for a single meeting she had with the Duke of Edinburgh. Late one night in October 1948, when Princess Elizabeth was eight months pregnant with Prince Charles, Philip escaped the claustrophobic atmosphere of Buckingham Palace and joined his photographer friend Baron for a night on the town. At 11.30 p.m. they picked up Kirkwood from the London Hippodrome where she was starring in the revue *Starlight Roof*. The group headed for the Mayfair club Les Ambassadeurs before going on to the Milroy Club, where Philip whirled Kirkwood round the dance floor watched by diners who rushed upstairs to watch them and who were treated to the Duke pulling funny faces at them. The star later recalled: 'we danced for about two hours, waltzes, sambas, the lot. I admit that if he hadn't been married, I might have developed a crush on him. But despite all those rumours we did not have an affair.'[9] News of the Prince's indiscreet night out appeared in the newspapers and, according to Kirkwood, Philip was rapped over the knuckles for the escapade by his father-in-law, the King, and told not to repeat it.

5   **Merle Oberon, Hollywood star (1911–79):** Prince Philip attended a dinner party at Oberons' house in Mexico City in October 1968 while attending that year's Olympic Games. Jody Jacobs, a society editor of the *Los Angeles Times*, was present and later recalled Christina Ford, married to Henry Ford, suggesting to the Prince they all go for a swim in the host's pool. Philip apparently blanched and said: 'Uh, uh. I think it's time for me to leave.'[10] According to biographer Charles Higham, Philip stayed with Oberon and her husband several times, and on one visit hosted a party for her on the royal yacht *Britannia*. Higham also claims

the actress attended a private dinner party at Buckingham Palace hosted by the Queen and Duke,[11] and, while she was recovering from heart surgery they sent their wishes for a speedy recovery.[12] All the surviving accounts we have point to a friendship rather than a relationship.

6   **Katie Boyle, actress and television personality (1926–2018):** One biographer claimed the Prince and Boyle, best known for presenting the Eurovision Song Contest on four occasions, were having a tryst when she received a message that her husband would shortly be home, forcing Philip to beat a hasty retreat via the back door. Describing the rumour as 'hateful', she declared: 'an affair. It's ludicrous, pure fabrication.'[13]

THE ARISTOCRATS

7   **Penelope Knatchbull, Countess Mountbatten of Burma (1953–):** The rumour-mongers have had a field day dissecting Philip's relationship with the woman we first knew as Penny Romsey, then Brabourne, now Mountbatten. For several decades the two have enjoyed a close friendship and have regularly been snapped in cosy situations – carriage driving side by side, whizzing through the grounds of Windsor Castle on his mini-motorcycle with Penny clinging on to his jacket, driving together through the grounds of Wood Farm with Penny at the wheel, and so on. Again there has never been proof of a relationship, other than a platonic one, and the Queen likes Penny so much the two women have in recent years arrived together at church at West Newton, on the Sandringham estate, in the Queen's car. They have been photographed by the Queen's side at the Royal Windsor Horse Show and in 2004 the Queen, Duke, Penny and husband Norton Knatchbull went as a group to watch *Anything Goes* at the Theatre Royal, Drury Lane.

Philip and Penny Romsey (now Penelope Knatchbull, Countess Mountbatten of Burma) watch the carriage-driving competition during the Royal Windsor Horse Show, 11 May 2013. (© Ian Lloyd)

8 **Alexandra Anastasia 'Sacha' Hamilton, Duchess of Abercorn (1946–2018):** Sacha was the daughter of Philip's lifelong friend Gina Wernher and sister of Natalia Grosvenor, Duchess of Westminster. She was once photographed holding hands with him on the Greek island of Eleuthera. She says a love of the writings of the Swiss psychiatrist Carl Jung first brought them together and they had 'riveting conversations'. She went on to rubbish talk of anything more salacious: 'It was a passionate friendship, but the passion was in the ideas … I did not go to bed with him. It probably looked like it to the world … but it didn't

happen. He isn't like that … He needed a playmate and someone to share his intellectual pursuits.'[14]

❦

Other noble names linked with the Duke in a way he wishes they weren't include the late Jane, Countess of Westmorland, whose husband David was the Queen's Master of the Horse from 1978 to 1991, the Italian Countess Bonnie Frescobaldi and, most startling of all (though equally uncorroborated), HRH Princess Alexandra, the Queen's favourite cousin.

❦

Only a handful of people have gone on record claiming the Duke has had affairs, and none of them is closely involved with either Prince Philip or his alleged girlfriends. Royal writer Sarah Bradford, Viscountess Bangor, told Philip's biographer Gyles Brandreth: 'There is no doubt in my mind at all. The Duke of Edinburgh has had affairs – yes full blown affairs and more than one! … The women he goes for are always younger than him, usually beautiful and highly aristocratic.'[15] In her 1996 biography of the Queen she mentions 'Philip's obvious flirtations and his affairs'.[16] Finally in 2009 she appeared to backtrack when she admitted to a journalist, 'quite honestly what real evidence is there?'[17]

A less connected source was the Hollywood legend Lauren Bacall who claimed that fellow actors David Niven and Douglas Fairbanks Jnr helped cover the Duke's supposed relationships. 'Philip always had women,' declared Bacall, 'and they covered for him, and pretended that his women were their women.' Fairbanks Jnr was a close friend of Philip's cousin Princess Marina, Duchess of Kent, but neither man had more than an occasional meeting with the Duke.

In 1996 a tabloid headline trumpeted 'Philip's 27 Trysts with Beauty'. This story was based on an interview with former footman Norman Barson, who was based at the Edinburghs' Windlesham Moor home for much of 1948. He claimed that the Prince would regularly drive a 'young, slim, pretty, well-spoken' woman, who was not the Princess, to Windlesham in his MG sportscar. Despite the fact that 'she looked lovingly in his eyes', and after they had left 'the staff would find cushions strewn around the floor' together with newspapers and magazines, Barson admitted, 'I never saw them kiss or canoodle.' The footman also claimed the couple left via the servants' door and Philip would say: 'Don't forget, Norman, you haven't seen me.'[18] No one else has come forward to corroborate the story and it conflicts with the memories of John Gibson, also a footman to the couple during the early years of their marriage: 'I just don't believe all that stuff about him having other women ... He never gave me a feeling other than he was devoted to [the Queen].'[19]

Those friends, relations and courtiers whom one would imagine really would know the truth of any such liaisons have always resolutely defended the Prince to the media and to biographers. Former private secretary Sir Martin Charteris, who at times could be disarmingly frank about the Queen and Duke's personalities in interviews, especially off the record, was unequivocal when he spoke to writer Anne de Courcey at the time of the royal Golden Wedding in 1997: 'I simply don't know of anyone who has claimed to be his mistress or to have had a particular close relationship ... If anybody had enjoyed such a relationship, do you think for one minute we wouldn't have heard about it?'[20]

The late Countess Mountbatten was also 'absolutely certain' that her cousin had been faithful. 'He would never behave badly ... He has always loved the Queen ... He wouldn't want to do anything to hurt her.'[21] Philip's straight-talking Aussie friend Mike Parker, who accompanied the Duke to private parties and the Thursday Club lunches, would definitely have known the truth. He was adamant: 'Philip has been one hundred percent faithful to the Queen. No ifs, no buts. Take it from me, I know.'[22]

The only uncertain voice among the inner circle belonged to the Queen's cousin Margaret Rhodes who, when asked about the rumours by Gyles Brandreth, 'was less certain. "I don't know," she said to me, brow furrowed, staring in to a coffee cup, "I just don't know."'[23] Interestingly, when the present author interviewed Mrs Rhodes at her home in Windsor Great Park for a feature on the Queen's eightieth birthday, she visibly jolted at the mention of the Brandreth quote and said: 'Oh don't mention that, and please don't repeat it,' suggesting she regretted musing aloud on the sensitive topic.[24]

So what effect have more than seven decades of scurrilous allegations had on the Prince?

Gyles Brandreth neatly sums it up when he writes: 'Publicly he brushes it off. Privately he broods. He knows what people say.'[25]

The Duke made light of it to Countess Mountbatten when he said: 'when I see the tabloids I think I might as well have done it.'[26] He was equally flippant when directly questioned about it for the first time by journalist Fiammetta Rocco in 1992. 'Have you ever stopped to think that for the last 40 years, I have never moved anywhere without a policeman accompanying me? So how the hell could I get away with anything like that?' Perhaps concerned what her palace-backed feature for the *Independent* would unearth, a few days later Ms Rocco received a hand-delivered letter threatening legal action if she took the matter any further.[27]

The suggestion that he broods on the subject is borne out by the story of him showing Brandreth a ten-page photocopy from the Australian magazine *Woman's Day*. Under the headline 'Prince Philip's Torrid Sex Life' was an article based on extracts

from a new book by Nicholas Davies which 'they daren't publish in Britain'.[28]

By the time he was interviewed by Jeremy Paxman in 2006,
Philip seemed resigned and more downbeat about the subject.
'As far as I'm concerned,' he told Paxman, almost wailing, 'every
time I talk to a woman, they say I've been to bed with her – as
if they had no say in the matter.' The Prince elaborated: 'I mean
I like carriage driving. And they go and say "Oh so and so is his
'driving companion'." By the end of the interview he is almost
bellicose: 'Well, I'm bloody flattered at my age that some girl is
interested in me. It's absolutely cuckoo!'[29]

As for the Queen, as far as we can gauge, she is unperturbed by
the Duke's fondness for female company. 'The Queen doesn't
mind when he flirts,' claims Lady Pamela Hicks. 'He flirts with
everyone and she knows it means absolutely nothing.'[30] She
has never felt threatened by the pretty women included in the
Balmoral and Sandringham house parties: 'The Queen is toler-
ant, she just says: "Philip likes to have them around."'[31] According
to the late Sacha Abercorn, the Queen was always aware he had
an eye for the ladies: 'she gives him a lot of lee-way. Her father
told her, "Remember he's a sailor. They come in on the tide."'[32]

Not only is there a lack of concrete evidence to suggest the
Prince did have affairs, but there are several lesser-known
anecdotes that give the impression he never would. One of his
supposed girlfriends told biographer Graham Turner that he
has 'never done anything remotely improper with me', and,
moreover, 'I know of at least one woman who tried extremely
hard to seduce him, but even she didn't succeed'.[33]

The diarist James Lees-Milne recorded that decades earlier
an aristocratic friend of an aristocratic friend 'swore that when
in her teens she used to lie in the same bed with Prince Philip,

a bolster in between them. They would talk for hours. She was much in love with him. He would not transgress the bolster.'[34]

If we believe the above then Mike Parker was right when he forcefully maintained that when it came to infidelities, 'that bloke was totally in control of himself ... That man is so straight and loyal, I don't think he could ever seriously contemplate it.'[35] Perhaps, like the knights of old, the Duke of Edinburgh was governed by a chivalric code of conduct, more concerned with honour and morality than sex. Though there again ...

56

TOURS DE FORCE

In his sixty-five years as a royal consort, Prince Philip has made 637 solo tours to 143 countries. If these statistics weren't mind-bogglingly impressive on their own, on top of this he also accompanied the Queen on her state and Commonwealth visits to 117 countries. Many of these joint visits were repeat ones – sixteen to Australia, twenty-two to Canada, six to Jamaica, ten to New Zealand and so on.

While recent overseas royal tours by the Queen's grandchildren rarely last more than a week, Elizabeth and Philip's early ones were mammoth undertakings. During the 1950s the Duke made three landmark tours, each lasting for several months ...

TOTAL ADORATION – THE CORONATION TOUR 1953/54

At the end of the Coronation year of 1953, the royal couple undertook a five-and-a-half-month tour of Commonwealth states including Bermuda, Jamaica, Aden, Uganda, Malta, Gibraltar, Ceylon, Australia and New Zealand as well as a handful of island territories.

The statistics are jaw-dropping. With Philip by her side, the Queen heard 276 speeches and 508 renditions of 'God Save the Queen'. She made 102 speeches, shook 13,213 hands, witnessed 6,700 curtsies, and recycled her Coronation dress three times to open parliament in Australia, New Zealand and Ceylon.[1]

At one point in New Zealand, the Duke managed to carry out thirty-six hours of engagements with just five hours' sleep because of the tragic Tangiwai rail disaster. On Christmas Eve 1953, the Whangaehu River bridge collapsed sending the Wellington-to-Auckland express passenger train crashing into the river and killing 151 people. Philip flew to the central North Island at 5 a.m. on 31 December to attend a mass funeral service for twenty-one of the victims before resuming the planned itinerary.[2]

An estimated three-quarters of the populations of both Australia and New Zealand are thought to have seen the royal couple, if only as a blurred flash in a motorcade. Few today can recall the impact this most glamorous of couples had on the world of the early 1950s. The overseas tours of Princess Diana and the Duchess of Cambridge both received saturation coverage by the media and guaranteed crowds of fans, but theirs was nothing compared to the early ones of the Queen and Philip. 'The level of adulation you wouldn't believe it,' recalled the Duke half a century later. 'It could have been corroding. It would have been very easy to play to the gallery, but I took a conscious decision not to do that. Safer not to be too popular. You can't fall too far.'[3]

THE 'ROYAL SPLIT' TOUR 1956/57

Philip's second lengthy tour of the decade lasted from October 1956 until the following February. It began with an invitation for him to open the 1956 Melbourne Olympic Games and ended up stretching into a four-month, 40,000-mile tour of the far-flung outposts of the old empire. Using the Royal Yacht *Britannia* as a base, the Duke visited the Falkland Islands and Tristan da Cunha, via Ceylon, Malaya, New Zealand and Papua New Guinea. En route, he became the first member of the Royal Family to cross the Antarctic Circle.

A second reason for the tour was Philip's increasing frustration with court life. Four years after the accession, he was still being treated with suspicion by the old guard and he keenly felt the suffocating atmosphere around the young Queen. As one approved biographer put it: 'Buckingham Palace was a place from which he needed to take a rest.' [4]

Others have regarded it as an extended stag party, with Philip surrounded at sea by an all-male guest list headed by Mike Parker, the artist Edward Seago (who helped improved the Prince's watercolour skills) and veteran Antarctic explorer Sir Raymond Priestley.

At one point it was widely assumed the tour would be called off after the start of the Suez Crisis, when English and French paratroopers dropped into Egypt to try to stop the President Nasser's seizure of the Suez Canal. Since *Britannia* was designed as a hospital ship during times of war, her services might have been needed, but after a few days American intervention resolved the Suez Crisis.

More damaging to Philip's reputation were the rumours of a rift between the Queen and Duke. It began when Mike Parker's wife Eileen sued for divorce while her husband was on the final leg of the tour. This led to speculation in the American press that all was not well within the royal marriage. *The Baltimore Sun* claimed London was awash with rumours that Philip was having an affair with an unnamed woman in a flat belonging to a court photographer. Legendary broadcaster Alastair Cooke commented that: 'Not since the first rumours of a romance between the former King Edward VIII and the then Mrs Simpson have Americans gobbled up the London dispatches so avidly.'[5]

The story grew in strength as journalists commented that Philip was away for his ninth wedding anniversary (although he did send Elizabeth a bouquet of white roses and a photo he'd taken of two iguanas embracing), as well as spending Christmas without his wife and two young children and that he had added on another ten days to the final stop at Gibraltar.[6]

Palace press secretary Richard Colville issued a statement to the American press: 'It is quite untrue that there is any rift between the Queen and Duke', which promptly lit the media's blue touch paper on both sides of the Atlantic. Fleet Street flew its finest news teams out to meet the royal yacht. 'When we reached the Rock,' said Parker, 'the world's press was waiting. It was not a pretty sight.' The very soon to be ex-equerry added that Philip was 'very hurt, terribly hurt, very angry,'[7] about the ill-founded rumours and Parker's honourable resignation which deprived him of one of the few faces he trusted at the palace.

Prime Minister Harold Macmillan helped bring a positive end to the 'rift' story. On the day after Philip's return he told his Cabinet that he had proposed to the Queen that the Duke should be given 'the style and dignity of a Prince of the United Kingdom' and that she had gladly agreed.[8]

DODGING DAME MARGOT FONTEYN'S GUN-RUNNERS

The Duke's third tour of the 1950s was scandal free but just as eventful as the first two. At ninety-nine days, it was the shortest of the three tours though still pretty lengthy, with Philip flying a total of 19,700 miles with another 16,300 miles at sea, once again on *Britannia*.

The tour began in India in 1959 – the first British royal visit since Independence and a precursor to the Queen's state visit in 1961 – and on to Singapore, Sarawak, Borneo, Hong Kong, the South Pacific and finally the Bahamas. In one of his speeches in the Far East the Duke said: 'I have had very little experience of self-government. In fact I am one of the most governed people in the world,' a joke with more than a grain of truth in it, and perhaps a clue to why he was escaping palace life for yet another sizeable chunk of time.

As with the 1953 tour, Philip was feted and clearly adored, particularly in India. The 25-mile journey from Mumbai to an atomic energy plant and a dairy colony was lined with dense crowds and forced his car to slow down several times, delaying his programme by fifty-five minutes.[9] He may not have played to the gallery on the 1953/54 tour but he certainly bathed in the adulation on this one and sat on the folded hood of the car, wearing a felt hat to protect him from the sun, and waving to either side in full Queen Mother mode.

Being the sole focus of attention seems to have agreed with him and in Madras enthusiastic crowds garlanded him so much that he joked he 'could not see out!' In the Solomon and Gilbert Islands he was carried ashore in a canoe shoulder high, given a 6ft string of shell money on Malaita Island (the local currency for the purchase of brides) and presented with a loin cloth in Santa Cruz.

Two unforeseen adventures occurred during the later stages. Sailing from Hong Kong to the Solomon Islands, *Britannia* was buffeted by stormy seas as she tried to avoid Tropical Storm Sally. A more serious incident was the news that a band of revolutionary soldiers from Cuba was being sent by Fidel Castro to liberate Panama. They were expected to arrive the same day Philip was due to be entertained at a dinner hosted by President de la Guardia. However, the invasion was delayed and the Duke had sailed down the Panama Canal and was Caribbean bound when the armed rebels landed two days later. One of the leaders was Dr Roberto Arias, the husband of prima ballerina Dame Margot Fonteyn, who had arrived at the Panamanian coast with rebels, guns and his wife aboard his yacht. Fonteyn's part in what British Defence Minister John Profumo dubbed a 'slap dash comedy' only came to light with the release of government documents relating to the coup in 2010.

British ambassador in Panama Sir Ian Henderson telegraphed Whitehall that:

> She knew that her husband was gun-running, she knew that he was accompanied by rebels and at one point she used her yacht to decoy government boats and aircraft away from the direction her husband was taking. I do not regard her conduct as fitting in any British subject, let alone one who has been highly honoured by Her Majesty the Queen.

Although she was thrown into jail overnight, Dame Margot seems to have graced Panama's most luxurious gaol. Henderson noted:

> She had been allotted the prison's 'presidential suite', reserved for political prisoners of high standing … and the English-speaking 2nd Lieutenant detailed to look after her was careful to provide fresh flowers for her dressing table.[10]

This was to be the last of Philip's mammoth solo tours. Perhaps cheeky newspaper headlines such as 'The Duke Visits Britain' on his return from the 1959 sojourn made him wary of booking *Britannia* for another multi-nation voyage.

The second tour had resulted in him becoming a prince on his return. The third one led to a larger family as, nine months and nineteen days after his return, Philip became a father for the third time with the birth of Prince Andrew.

57

THE DAY THE QUEEN SPORTED A BEARD

It was probably the most awkward meeting they ever had. After four months apart during which rumours of a royal break-up were rife, the Queen and Prince Philip were reunited at a military airbase in Portugal prior to a three-day state visit.

Both parties must have felt nervous, but making it worse were the massive thunderstorms lashing the Iberian peninsula. Philip, on board the royal yacht, had already docked at Setúbal, 48km (30 miles) south of Lisbon. So squally were the conditions that ten small boats moored alongside *Britannia* sank overnight. Meanwhile there was talk of Elizabeth's Viking aircraft having to land as far away as Gibraltar.

In the end, the Queen's flight landed more or less on time at Montijo military airfield, on the opposite side of the river Tagus from Lisbon.

Philip, bronzed and clean-shaven after growing a bushy auburn beard during his time away, bounded up the steps of his wife's aircraft. Running into the arms of the Queen, he found he was the victim of a practical joke. To ease any tensions there might be after all the media rumours of a royal separation, Elizabeth had set up a prank. Having been amused at seeing her hirsute husband's photograph in nearly every newspaper, she coerced her lady-in-waiting, and all the other members of the household on board, to don a false beard to accompany her own bushy auburn bristles. The Duke roared with laughter, the Queen said: 'Goodness what a wonderful tan,' and all was back to normal.[1]

Sadly the reaction was never photographed as the blinds were kept firmly lowered at the back of the aircraft, but the photos of them descending the steps minutes later show them both beaming with happiness. Philip had also given some thought about what to wear and his tie was dotted with love hearts.

The couple drove to the royal yacht for a forty-eight-hour reunion before beginning the Portuguese state visits. As they drove along southwards several eyewitnesses noticed the Queen and Duke were holding hands in the car and again as they boarded *Britannia*.

58

WHEN IS A PRINCE NOT A PRINCE?

Throughout the first five years of her reign the Queen tried repeatedly to find a suitable title for Philip, perhaps as compensation for everything he had given up – his Greek royal status, his Greek Orthodox religion and his promising career in the navy.

In May 1954 she wrote to Winston Churchill expressing a wish that Philip should be given the title Prince of the Commonwealth. Churchill didn't think it an impressive enough title and wondered about reviving Albert's title of Prince Consort. When he broached the subject with Cabinet colleagues, the foreign secretary, Anthony Eden, came up with his own suggestion of Prince of the Realm.[1] The Queen requested the prime minister to sound out Commonwealth prime ministers at their forthcoming meeting. All but Canada's prime minister Louis St Laurent supported the idea. In the end Philip himself aborted it, telling the Queen he didn't want to change his title.

A solution of sorts emerged in 1957 when newspapers commented that Philip wasn't actually a British prince, since the style HRH bestowed on him by George VI in the run-up to the 1947 wedding didn't, as some believed, automatically make him a prince. When it came to registering Prince Charles's birth, the King deleted the word 'prince' from the draft and decided the entry for the father's surname should read: 'His Royal Highness Philip, Duke of Edinburgh'.[2] In fact the royal son-in-law had a whole variety of titles following his naturalisation as a British citizen. The most peculiar one he held was for twenty-four hours on the eve of his wedding. The King had already made him a Knight of the Garter and Letters Patent signed by George on 19 November made Philip a Royal Highness. The next day, on the morning of the wedding, more Letters Patent bestowed the Dukedom of Edinburgh on – wait for it ... 'Lieutenant His Royal Highness Sir Philip Mountbatten, K.G., R.N.'. How he must have chuckled over that one.[3]

Meanwhile, the Queen was still worrying about her husband's lack of a worthy title. Shortly before leaving office in 1955 Churchill suggested to her that Philip could be declared 'His Royal Highness the Prince'. The matter dragged on through the premiership of Anthony Eden to that of Harold Macmillan who in 1957 agreed with the palace that Philip should henceforth be known as 'His Royal Highness, The Prince Philip, Duke of Edinburgh'. Interestingly he was given 'The', a capitalised definite article, which was normally only used by the monarch's children. Letters Patent were issued on 22 February 1957 finally making Philip a British prince.

59

SPECIAL BREW

Each place setting at a state banquet has three glasses positioned ready for red and white wines and champagne. When Prince Philip attended them there was also a tumbler for his favourite tipple – Double Diamond beer. The Duke drank a small bottle of it each evening and was more than disappointed when Carlsberg UK ceased production of it in the early 1990s.

During the Queen's state visit to Italy in 2000, he refused the country's finest wines, declaring: 'I don't care what kind it is, just get me a beer!' Four years later, leaving a reception in Liverpool, the Duke helped himself to two cans of brown ale 'for the onward journey', tucking them into his inside jacket pocket.

In December 1995 Prince Philip visited Samuel Allsopp Brewery, the original brewers of Double Diamond, during a visit to Burton-on-Trent, Staffordshire. A unique 'Royal Diamond' beer was created for the occasion and given to the royal visitor. Finally in January 2016, he was notified of a new version of the discontinued beer. His private secretary wrote back on behalf of the Duke, requesting a sample of the new Dual Diamond – 'It was very nice of you to suggest that Prince Philip might like to try Dual Diamond beer' – and asking brewer Mick Machin to courier some to Buckingham Palace.

Raising a toast of beer rather than champagne, Philip at a ceremony to mark his retirement as Chancellor of the University of Cambridge in 2011. (© Ian Lloyd)

STIRRED NOT SHAKEN

For those James Bond-style black-tie receptions, the Duke enjoys his own 'Prince Philip Martini' recipe:

Lace the cocktail glass with Vermouth by stirring a slice of lemon and a small amount of Vermouth in ice and then discarding the liquid.
Add a triple measure of gin to some ice.
Leave for ten minutes to chill it.
Pour the liquid, not the ice, into the cocktail glass.

60

QUIPS, GAFFES AND BANTER: THE DUKE'S MEMORABLE CLANGERS 51–60

RACISM

51 At a palace reception for British Indians in 2009 before the Indian president's state visit he spotted businessman Atul Patel's name badge, *'There's a lot of your family in tonight!'*
52 Pointing to a dodgy-looking fuse box during a visit to Glasgow in 1998, *'That looks as though it was put in by an Indian.'* (He later explained, 'I meant to say cowboys.')
53 To multi-ethnic group Diversity, winners of 2009 *Britain's Got Talent, 'Are you all one family?'*

54 To black politician Lord Taylor of Warwick in 1999, *'And what exotic part of the world do you come from?'*

55 In 2010, after President Obama, on a 2010 UK visit, told the Duke he had just breakfasted with leaders of the UK, China and Russia, *'Can you tell the difference between them?'*

CELEBRITIES

56 Film stars: Oscar-winner Cate Blanchett sat next to the Duke at a Buckingham Palace lunch and was surprised when he said, *'I hear you're an actor? Well, I was given a DVD player for Christmas and I can't work out whether I put the green cord in or the red cord.'* The baffled guest replied, 'Sir, it's really not my expertise,' while thinking, 'He's invited me to lunch to tell me about his DVD player.'

57 Madonna: At the 2002 premiere of *Die Another Day,* the Duke met the iconic star who sang the theme for the Bond movie, *'Are we going to need ear plugs?'*

58 Film stars: Actor Ray Winstone was filming in Windsor when a Range Rover screeched to a halt and the Duke wound down the window and asked what they were all up to. Winstone replied: 'We're making a film, sir, with Sir Tom Courtenay and Sir Michael Caine. Would you like to meet them?' The Prince gave a firm, *'No'* and drove off.

59 Newsreader: Michael Buerk once told the Duke he had heard all about the Duke of Edinburgh's Award Scheme and was hit back with *'That's more than you know about anything else then'.*

60 Tom Jones: A comment at a small-business lunch after someone argued that it is difficult to get rich in Britain, *'What about Tom Jones? He's made a million and he's a bloody awful singer.'*

61

THE DUKEBOX

A shared love of the outdoors and nearly everything equine would bond Philip and Elizabeth from the start. Their interest in music was more hit and miss.

The Princess was taught to play the piano by Mabel Lander, who was herself a pupil of the Polish maestro Theodor Leschetizky. 'Lilibet was naturally musical,' recalled her governess Marion Crawford, and she 'loved lessons, but hated to practise'. Unlike her sister Margaret she didn't read music well, but did have the ability to pick up a tune by ear and improvise.[1]

Sports-mad Philip, on the other hand, never played an instrument. He did, however, have some interest in classical music. Royal correspondent Betty Spencer Shew, whose book on Elizabeth and Philip's wedding was written with background information supplied by the Princess herself, claimed, 'I know that one of his favourite pieces is the "Valse Triste" by Sibelius.'[2] Mrs Shew goes on to describe Elizabeth's clear soprano singing voice which the accredited journalist had heard herself in the corridors of Buckingham Palace. The two princesses had enjoyed singing lessons at the home of the Countess of Cavan in Prince's Gate and Crawfie had formed a madrigal society at Windsor during the war years. Philip, on the other hand, 'enjoys listening to singing but by his own confession, he is no singer'. Asked if he sang baritone, bass or tenor he retorted with an early example of brusqueness: 'no idea', followed by 'off-key'.[3]

During their courting days and early married life the couple relished the new wave of American musicals that enlivened the gloom of post-war Britain in the late 1940s, particularly

Oklahoma! They saw the latter at the Drury Lane Theatre many times, including a special visit on 4 August 1947 when the engaged couple joined the King and Queen and Princess Margaret to celebrate Queen Elizabeth's forty-seventh birthday. A week earlier they'd been at the Coliseum Theatre with Princess Margaret to see *Annie Get Your Gun*, preferring to sit in the stalls rather than the royal box.[4]

Behind closed palace doors the couple spent hours playing records on Elizabeth's wind-up gramophone. They shared a mutual love for the songs of Bing Crosby but the song most likely to be heard was 'People Will Say We're in Love' from *Oklahoma!* which had rapidly become 'their song'.

62

THE QUEEN RAISES PHILIP'S SIX-BAR LIMIT

History was made on 26 February 1957 when it was announced the Duke of Edinburgh would join the elite group of two other royals who were entitled to a full verse of the National Anthem.

For some reason it was the Ministry of Defence rather than the palace that declared that, in accordance with the wishes of the Queen, 'the full version of the National Anthem will in future be played whenever a Royal salute is given for His Royal Highness, the Prince Philip, Duke of Edinburgh.'

An MOD spokesman said that up until then only the Queen Mother and the Queen herself were entitled to the full version and that non-queenly royals had to make do with a six-bar version. Later the same day, Philip was given the full unabridged version during a lunch hosted by the Lord Mayor of London at Mansion House to mark the Duke's return from his four-month tour of the Commonwealth and Antarctica.

When it comes to the National Anthem, the Queen has strict views on the appropriate number of verses. In 2000 Reg Wilcock, long-time deputy steward to the Queen Mother, died at Clarence House and was allowed a funeral service at the Chapel Royal, St James's Palace. Senior courtiers turned down various funerary requests from Wilcock's partner (and fellow steward) William Tallon, so Tallon contacted the Queen directly. She granted them all, including the playing of the National Anthem, though adding the proviso: 'Only the first verse.'[1]

Having said that, both the Queen and Duke have been ser-enaded with a variety of unorthodox versions – from the band in Canada that accidentally played 'Roll out the Barrel', to the calypso version composed for New Labour's super-cool opening of the Millennium Dome by the Queen. Performed at eighteen minutes past midnight, it was her first National Anthem of the twenty-first century.

Half a century after his musical promotion, Philip was caught unawares during a state luncheon on the royal tour of Latvia in 2006. As the chords of the anthem died away, the Duke started to sit down and was mid-squat when the enthusiastic local choir started on the second verse. He remained standing at the end, wisely as it turned out, since the good folk of Riga gave the hardly ever heard third verse. With the Queen well and truly saved, Philip was heard to loudly mutter, 'Is that all?'

63

THE D OF E AWARDS

It all began at Brown's Hotel in London's Mayfair in the autumn of 1954. Kurt Hahn, the legendary founder of Gordonstoun School on Scotland's north-east coast, summoned a former pupil to tea and gave him what amounted to an ultimatum. 'My boy,' declared Hahn, 'I want you to start an awards scheme!' The 'boy' launched a pilot scheme in 1956 and the organisation bearing his name still flourishes six and a half decades later.

The aim was to fill the gap for boys between leaving school at 15 and entering National Service at 18, with self-improvement exercises familiar to Gordonstoun alumni, including sport and service to the community. It sounds like plain sailing but in the beginning the scheme was surprisingly controversial and treated with suspicion. The Scout movement regarded it as a rival, while the Welsh and Scots thought it an English nationalist organisation. The Conservative government of the time hated it. In 2011 Philip's former private secretary, Brigadier Sir Miles Hunt-Davis, recalled: 'There were comments made. "What is this man trying to form – a sort of youth organisation?" And I'm not sure someone didn't say a Hitler youth organisation.'

The Duke was initially reluctant to get too involved. 'I said, "Look, I can't start it, but if you put together a committee of the great and good, I would be perfectly happy to chair it," which is what happened.' The first director was Sir John Hunt, leader of the 1953 expedition that conquered Mount Everest and therefore an ideal choice. The Prince didn't even want the award to be named after him. 'That was strictly against my better judgement. I tried to avoid it but I was eventually overridden.'

The award – Bronze, progressing to Silver and ultimately Gold – was initially available only to boys aged between 14 and 18, but there was great demand for a similar scheme for girls and this was launched in September 1958. By 1980 the upper age limit had been extended to 24 and the award took on its current four-section format: Service, Adventurous Journey, Skills and Physical Recreation.

Its rapid gain in popularity surprised even the Duke. 'When the first trial of the award was launched in 1956, no one had any idea quite what would happen,' he recalled. 'In the event it was an instant success, and the award has been growing and expanding worldwide ever since.' Since its inception nearly 7 million young people in the UK have taken part in the scheme.

TIMELINE

1956   The award scheme was launched as a pilot scheme.

1957   By the end of the first year 7,000 boys had started the programme and 1,000 had achieved an award.

1958   A programme for girls was launched.

1980   Upper age limit extended from 18 to 24.

1986   Prince Edward achieved his Gold Award at the age of 22 (he has since taken over his father's role in the organisation).

1988   The International Award Association was founded. Forty-eight countries were involved – some run under their own names, e.g. in Uganda it is the Source of the Nile Award.

2001   The Duke stood down as chairman of Trustees at the age of 80 but remained as patron.

2013   The Duke's daughter-in-law, Sophie, Countess of Wessex, became global ambassador for the international arm.

2016   The award scheme's Diamond Jubilee year. The Countess of Wessex completed a 450-mile cycle ride from

Edinburgh to Buckingham Palace, raising £180,000 for the scheme.

In the UK since 1956 over 3.1 million awards have been achieved and over 6.7 million have been started (as of 31 March 2020).

64

SARTORIAL STAR

Prince Philip has been a regular favourite of fashion pundits for decades. In the late 1960s American fashion writers voted him the best-dressed man of the year, way ahead of his celebrity flower-power rivals. Half a lifetime later the 94-year-old Prince was named most stylish man in the royal family by *GQ* magazine in January 2016, coming a creditable twelfth in the best-dressed list, some twenty-six places higher than his grandson Prince Harry.

When it comes to clothes, style, fashion, or whatever you want to call it, Philip's is a rags-to-riches story, or as near to it as royalty can aspire.

According to John Dean, who was his valet in the late 1940s and early 1950s, the only clothing the young Philip was interested in, before his marriage, was his uniforms: 'he had three, and looked very smart in them'. They were paid for by his grandmother on an account at Gieves and Hawkes, where all naval officers went for their uniforms. Apart from them the only suit he owned was a grey lounge suit, preferring 'to knock around in blazer and flannels', though once he was a regular guest at the royal homes of George VI he added evening wear and a shooting suit 'with knickerbocker trousers'.[1]

Dapper chap: the Duke at Tattenham Corner station, after
disembarking from the royal train, for the 1996 Epsom Derby.
(© Ian Lloyd)

Dean soon 'realised that his civilian wardrobe was, in fact, scantier than that of many a bank clerk'. On his visits to London to stay with the Mountbattens, he never brought spare clothes and at the end of the day Dean was obliged to wash and iron Philip's solitary shirt and wash, and often darn, his socks.[2]

Philip may have seemed blasé about his clothes to Dean but when it came to staying with his royal soon-to-be in-laws he could be acutely embarrassed about his meagre wardrobe. One of his naval chums, Admiral Sir William O'Brien, later recalled 'Philip saying that he was rather ashamed at the look on the face of the footman who was laying out his clothes at Balmoral and Sandringham'.[3]

According to assistant private secretary Edward Ford, the problem was sensitively sorted out by the Princess's father: 'I think the King sent him to his tailor and more or less kitted him out.'[4] Philip was allowed to borrow kilts at Balmoral, and footman John Gibson recalls the Prince having to borrow a bow tie before coming down to dinner during his first Christmas at Sandringham in 1946. He even wore his late father's heavily repaired clothes.[5] While his lack of a suitable wardrobe led to raised eyebrows from condescending courtiers and valets, some in royal circles found Philip's frugality and his unwillingness to lavish money on clothes a positive character trait. Queen Mary's lady-in-waiting and close friend Lady Airlie met Philip at a palace garden party the day after his engagement was announced. She liked the fact he was wearing, in her words, a 'shabby' uniform with 'the usual after-the-war look' and 'not having got a new one for the occasion as many men would have done, to make an impression'.[6]

Marriage into the royal family meant he had to invest in clothes to suit every occasion, from white tie for a state banquet to a top hat and tails for Royal Ascot. He used Hawes and Curtis as his tailor, bought his shirts from Harrods, his shoes

Holding his Lock & Co. top hat on the way to Royal Ascot, June 2011. (© Ian Lloyd)

from Lobb of St James's Street and his hats from Lock & Co. His socks were a self-supporting design called 'Tenover' patented by Freddie Smith, once a page to George VI.[7] Later he added Johns and Pegg, makers of suits, blazers and sports coats, to his list, as well as another Savile Row bespoke tailor, Kent, Haste and Lachter, for shirts and suits. North of the border he used Kinloch Anderson for kilts and anything else tartan, as well as Lyle and Scott for his sweaters.

One impressive item he didn't have to buy was his Order of the Garter robes. Mr Ravenscroft of the royal robemakers Ede and Ravenscroft arrived at Clarence House bearing the robe that had belonged to the King's great-uncle, the Duke of Connaught.[8] Philip wasn't the only one to wear a garter cast-off; Princess Elizabeth wore the robe belonging to her late grandfather the Earl of Strathmore, while Queen Elizabeth's had an even more impressive pedigree having previously been worn by Queen Victoria.

The Queen's accession in 1952 also brought with it whole new wardrobe requirements for her consort since Philip was catapulted to the top of the three armed forces. He became Admiral of the Fleet, Field Marshal, and Marshal of the Royal Air Force in the same promotion. He once said one of the reasons he tried not to overeat was to avoid the necessity of having to have another set of armed forces uniforms made. Like the Queen, he was to become adept at quick changing. During a visit to Wales in 1954 one onlooker noted that he nipped into Cardiff Town Hall in his Welsh Guards uniform and emerged less than five minutes later in his blue suit.

As we've seen, Prince Philip joined the royal firm as something of an outsider. He was never a typical British aristocrat and this has been reflected in his attitude to fashion. One of the Queen's longest-serving aides noted:

one small thing is his suits. If you're part of the crowd who've been through Eton and the Guards, there's a certain kind of suit you're expected to wear. It's a pinstripe with a white line. I know of only two people who wear

pinstriped suits with a blue or red line and one of them is
Prince Philip.

The same man also pointed out that while many aristocrats
wear their handkerchiefs draped out of their top pocket in a
slightly foppish manner, the Duke's is ramrod straight across.[9]
Another maverick choice of suit was one of his favourites from
early in the Queen's reign which has been woven with hundreds
of tiny letter 'P's making up the discreet pattern.

Like the Queen, he has never been a slave to fashion but kept
faith with his early well-tailored look. Other members of the
family, notably his brother-in-law Lord Snowdon, threw themselves into the sartorially awful 1960s and 1970s with abandon.
Tony was once spotted in the Deeside village of Ballater, near
to Balmoral, wearing tweed knickerbockers, long leather boots
and a brown velvet anorak – well, it was 1965.[10] Four years later
the Earl designed his own uniform for his role as Constable

Philip's suit with a pinstripe made up of the letter 'P'. (© Ian Lloyd)

of Carnarvon Castle for the Investiture of the Prince of Wales in 1969. He greeted the Queen and Duke on the castle steps dressed in a hunting green zip-up tunic with belt of corded black silk. Apparently the Queen had a job keeping her face straight and the press dubbed him 'Buttons'.

Princess Anne, who has turned sartorial recycling into an art form, once said: 'A good suit goes on for ever. If it is properly made and has a classic look, you can wear it ad infinitum. The economy was bred into me.' It is clearly something she has inherited from her father. His former pilot, Geoff Williams, recalled: 'He wore a pair of shoes that looked sixty years old, and suits with patches. His valet was always telling him that he needed more shirts and he'd reply that he had enough already.'[11]

65

ROYAL VARIETY: NOT ALWAYS THE SPICE OF LIFE

Several years ago the Queen was sitting for a portrait at Buckingham Palace. The anxious young artist apologised for making her keep the same rigid pose for over an hour. 'Don't worry,' said the monarch reassuringly, 'I'm used to it. I've had to sit through the Royal Variety Performance nearly every year.'

On 3 November 1947 the London Palladium was the venue for Philip's first and Elizabeth's third Royal Variety Performance,

A souvenir article on the Royal Variety Performance 1987. (© Ian Lloyd)

held two and a half weeks before their wedding. Top of the bill that year were Laurel and Hardy, making a rare UK appearance, and standing out from the usual homegrown talent of Gracie Fields, Tommy Trinder and the Crazy Gang. The 26-year-old Lieutenant Mountbatten would have discovered that every year the royals have to sit through a variety of oddball acts. In 1947 they were 'entertained' by the likes of Borrah Minevitch's Harmonica Rascals, James Currie's Water Spectacle and Cynthia & Gladys with Indian Clubs. King George VI, who was a huge fan of variety, told the organisers, 'we haven't laughed so much for years'.

Philip didn't see another Variety Performance until 3 November 1952 when, as Queen and consort, the royal couple had little choice in the matter. He was to remain a stalwart, if prickly, supporter of the show over the following six decades.

Tailoring the acts to amuse the royal guests has always been one of the aims. In 1952 comedian Tony Hancock had the Duke falling off his seat with his sketch featuring a lieutenant commander in the Royal Navy.

A regular ducal highlight was the all-female dance troupe. The Tiller Girls always met with his approval and in 1967 he was also keen to see the high-kicking Parisian Bluebell Girls open the show. Unfortunately, a delay in his return flight from Canada meant he was just too late to see them. 'Have I missed the Bluebells?' he asked the Queen as he took his seat, though he was in time to see another bevy of agile girls perform with the Romanian Dance Company.

On 10 November 1969 during the traditional meet and greet at the end of the show the Duke uttered one of his most famous put-downs, telling full-throated singer Tom Jones his songs were 'hideous', followed up with 'What do you gargle with? Pebbles?' Twelve years earlier he had politely asked legendary opera singer Mario Lanza: 'I hear you are on a European tour at the moment; I hope it's proving successful.' Lanza replied, 'If you call five thousand dollars a night successful, yes,' adding, 'what's your story?' Prince Philip replied, 'Oh my story is about as interesting as my voice,' and moved on.[1] Not all the stars fared so badly. Sophie Tucker, 'Last of the Red Hot Mommas', recalled, 'The Queen and Prince Philip were wonderful to me. We had some good laughs together.'

At most theatres the flower-bedecked royal box usually offers an ideal vantage point from which to scrutinise the cast. At the London Palladium the couple were able to see who was waiting to come on in the wings as well as the cue cards listing the acts. Occasionally though, their seats were too close for comfort. When Elton John topped the bill on 26 November 2001, he played more or less underneath the royal box with his back to them. 'I wish he'd turn the microphone to one side,' grumbled the Queen. 'I wish he'd turn the microphone off!' retorted her consort.[2]

Over the years they have also relied on each other to work out who's who. The performance on 1 December 1997 coincided with their Golden Wedding, and Sir Trevor MacDonald read out a fulsome and moving tribute to the Queen and Duke from Nelson Mandela. In the royal box Philip misheard the greeting and asked his wife, 'Who's it from?' The Queen muttered, *sotto voce*, 'Mandela.' Turning to the Benevolent Fund executives, the Duke said: 'he could have told us himself. We saw him last Thursday.'

After the 1997 Golden Wedding tribute the Duke once again threw a spanner in the works. Back in the 1940s it was well known that the young lovers had been to see *Oklahoma!* time and again and that 'People Will Say We're in Love' was rumoured to be their song. Half a century later, to mark the royal couple's anniversary, legendary Broadway star Barbara Cook – who had played Ado Annie in *Oklahoma!* as early as 1951 – was flown over especially to duet the number with Michael Ball. Later, in the line-up of stars, the Duke shook hands with Ball and said: 'You were the chap that sang that special song weren't you? Well I've never heard it in my life.'

Growing hard of hearing, the Duke had once complained he found the Yiddisher Bronx accent of comedian Jackie Mason impossible to follow, complaining: 'I didn't understand a word he said.' On 3 December 2007 he missed the introduction of the British musician Seal. 'Who's that then?' he asked the Queen. 'Seal,' she whispered back. 'What … Steel?' persisted her husband. 'No, Seal,' hissed the monarch. None the wiser, the Duke was heard to mutter, 'Bloody silly name.'[3]

Impresario Lord Bernard Delfont who organised the show for many years once compared producing it to 'being in a car crash and only suffering from shock'. When it came to the royal guests, two issues were always paramount in his mind: timing and taste. Whenever the shows ran over, polite notes were sent from Buckingham Palace asking him to try to ensure the Queen could leave on time in future.

Taste was even more hazardous for the production team. Self-regulation and a bit of intimidation usually helped. In the mid 1980s Max Bygraves was persuaded to drop a joke about Princess Michael of Kent and two years later Stephen Fry and Hugh Laurie cut out a four-letter word and a joke about sex so as not to embarrass the Queen.

Nudity was another issue to worry about. When the Kwa Zulu African song and dance company were due to appear in the show on 10 November 1975 Delfont was unsure whether the women in the company should appear topless as they did in their West End show. He took the precautionary measure of contacting the palace to check out the royal reaction. Back came the reply, 'The Queen has seen topless ladies before.'

Her Majesty may have seen topless ladies but she got more than she bargained for on 26 November 2001 when The Full Monty topped the bill. The idea was for the five actors to strip down until they were just about to whip off their G-strings, at which point the lights would be switched from the stage on to the auditorium and the dazzled audience would be spared any blushes. Unfortunately the lights failed and five naked and embarrassed men were left floundering at the footlights. The Queen remained deadpan and, turning to her hosts, asked, 'Is that it then?' which they were not sure was a reference to the end of the show or what she'd just witnessed. Noticing their concern, the Duke had the final word: 'Don't worry, we've been to Papua New Guinea. She's used to it.'[4]

On 19 November 2012, the day before their sixty-fifth wedding anniversary, the Queen and Duke attended their final Royal Variety Performance, held for once at the Royal Albert Hall. It was the Queen's thirty-ninth attendance at the show and the Prince's twenty-seventh.

66

MAN OF FAITH

Religion is in his genes. After all, his mother, Princess Alice, founded a nursing order of nuns, the Christian Sisterhood of Martha and Mary, and his great-aunt, the Grand Duchess Elizabeth Feodorovna of Russia, was abbess of a religious order and was canonised as a Holy Martyr by the Russian Orthodox Church.

Prince Philip was baptised in the Greek Orthodox rite at St George's Church in the Old Fortress in Corfu. His faith, along with his nationality, was changed in the run-up to his marriage. The Archbishop of Canterbury, Geoffrey Fisher, wrote to George VI to point out that the Greek Church, 'though on the closest and most friendly terms with us, is not able to enter into full communion with us'.[1] Lieutenant Mountbatten agreed to 'have his position regularised' and the service was conducted privately at Lambeth Palace, the archbishop's official residence.

Philip, always a regular churchgoer, attends a service at St Margaret's, Westminster, in 1997. (© Ian Lloyd)

The Prince has avoided the topic of his personal faith in the interviews he has given over the years. 'If I start talking about religion the press will say I'm barking,' he explained to Gyles Brandreth, adding, for good measure: '*You'll* say I'm barking.'[2] He has, however, pointed out he's a regular churchgoer usually alongside the Queen, and also admitted his interest in religion was late flowering. 'I was dragged into religious things', he said in 1991, 'by being invited to become involved in the reorganisation of St George's Windsor. Theological dialogue was really forced on me. I have never had any great difficulty about being an ordinary Christian.'[3]

In the 1960s he helped Robin Woods, Dean of Windsor, develop St George's House as a training college for clergy and a conference centre to discuss ecclesiastical issues. Religion was also one of the topics he discussed in three published volumes of letters with a later dean, Michael Mann, beginning with *A Windsor Correspondence.*

His own library included 634 books on religion. He has studied the Bible in depth and he has always been quick with a biblical quotation and reference. He has a reputation for taking preachers to task over the sermon they've just presented, and the late Queen Mother had in her collection a cartoon done by Hugh Casson which shows the Duke bearing down on some poor priest, reducing him to a quivering wreck.[4]

It's not just minor clerics that bear the brunt of the Duke's unique personality. At a service in Chichester Cathedral he startled a bishop in the congregation by winking at him as he processed through the nave.[5] Then at Prince Charles's confirmation at St George's Chapel, he surprised the officiating clergy by ostentatiously flicking through the Bible and ignoring the ceremony. Afterwards the Archbishop of Canterbury, Michael Ramsay, turned to the Dean of Windsor and was heard to utter the unecclesiastical comment: 'Bloody rude, that's what I call it.'[6]

The Prince's religious beliefs are also another aspect of his sensitive side, which for whatever reason he usually chooses to hide, and is therefore all the more surprising when it is revealed. In 2001 a retired courtier recalled a two-page document which Philip had sent round the palace not long before. In it he spelled out what Christ meant for us. 'There were 10 points – what the heart of Christianity is, why Christ died for us, and why we have responsibility for other people.' The former member of staff, who was not a great fan of the Prince, admitted: 'I'm not easily stirred, but I found it very moving.'[7]

67

ON THE POLICE DATABASE

In March 1960 Prince Philip visited New Scotland Yard and was asked if he'd agree to have his fingerprints taken for their souvenir file. HRH agreed, suggesting: 'Let's choose an interesting finger.'[1] The appropriate digit was then rolled on sensitised paper, the new invention which had replaced the messy inkpad method. When told that the Yard also had a set of Princess Margaret's prints – presumably in ink – Philip replied: 'Good for you!'

Later in the day he went to Leman Street police station in the East End to see a traditional 'cop shop' in action. During the visit there was a report of a smash and grab at Gardiner's Corner, Aldgate East. A patrol car hurried to the scene, with the Duke providing royal backup in the second car. The would-be thief had legged it by the time they arrived but Philip was able to experience a blue flashing light dash and see how the police used graphite powder to bring up a set of prints on the broken plate-glass window.[2]

68

A VERY MIXED MEDIA

The media were besotted with the Duke from the moment he was widely tipped to marry Princess Elizabeth. Partly it was because was he was the first glamorous figure to join the firm since his cousin, Princess Marina, in 1934, and secondly because he was marrying the hugely popular future queen.

Eileen Parker, wife of Philip's equerry, Michael Parker, recalled: 'One of Mike's special responsibilities was to act as a buffer between Prince Philip and the press, as reporters and cameramen apparently thought that the Prince was a more legitimate target for their thirst for news than the other members of the royal family.' Parker had to make sure the newshounds and snappers didn't get too close to Philip, especially when he was off duty.[1]

In the early days the Prince realised the benefit of working closely with Fleet Street and the newsreels as well as with the budding television industry. 'Yes, I made a conscious decision to talk to the media,' he later reflected, 'but not about me, only about what I'm doing, what I'm supporting.'[2] In 1951 he took part in a five-minute promotional film for one of his charities, the National Playing Fields Association, together with popular radio and TV star Wilfred Pickles. The short was shown in cinemas, with the audience encouraged to donate to the charity after each showing. He put in an assured onscreen performance though the director later admitted: 'You think he was calm? That's why we sat him at a desk. His left leg was jumping with nerves.'[3]

On 29 May 1961 the Duke appeared on the BBC's *Panorama*, making history as the first member of the royal family to give a television interview. The interviewer was the very deferential Richard Dimbleby and the subject was the uncontroversial topic of the Commonwealth Technical Training Week.

In the middle of the Swinging Sixties the Duke acknowledged members of the royal family could become 'museum pieces' if they weren't careful. The palace press officer, Richard Colville, felt his task was to keep the Queen and her family completely under wraps apart from their official appearances. Philip realised a new approach was long overdue and on Colville's retirement brought in William Heseltine, a young vibrant Australian, to shake up the monarchy's image. One of his first ventures was the 1969 landmark documentary *Royal Family* (see Chapter 76). By that time the Prince insisted on copyright and significant control by the court on such ventures, after an earlier attempt, *Royal Palaces*, had backfired. It was decided to produce *Royal Palaces* in 1965 after Jacqueline Kennedy's hugely successful television tour of the White House, and was fronted by the widely respected art historian and friend of the Queen Mother, Kenneth Clark. All went well until the screening for the Queen and Duke on 19 October 1966, when the royal couple, particularly the Queen, were appalled by Clark's jaunty tone and his occasional damning of her palaces with faint praise. 'All did *not* go well when I showed it to the monarch,' Clark reported to his wife. 'She was *furious* and would have liked to have stop it, but couldn't find a pretext for doing so.' He added, 'all she could say was that "it's so sarcastic," which means devoid of the slop and unction to which she is conditioned'. He went on to note she wouldn't speak 'to my poor producer', and swept out of the room, followed by her embarrassed courtiers.[4]

During the 1960s Philip's relationship with the newspaper industry entered choppy waters. Occasionally he could be obliging and charming to the media. Arriving at Dallas airport he was asked by one reporter: 'Are you still wearing your polka-dot underwear?' – a comment usually guaranteed to generate a ballistic response from the Duke, who that time joked: 'I'll wear almost anything providing it fits.'[5] He also managed to swerve an impromptu question during a TV interview about how he would feel if one of his children married a black person. An awkward answer could have had repercussions half a century later when Prince Harry met the mixed-race Meghan Markle.

In the 1960s the press first picked up on the Prince's outspokenness and early gaffes, such as his 1961 comment to British industry to 'get your finger out!' and his swipe at the country in general five years later: 'I'm fed up with making excuses for Britain.' British newspapers in particular started to build up files of Philip's comments, a task made much easier with digitalisation. As Jeremy Paxman said in relation to wrist slaps of the Duke by the press, 'every newsroom had a resident moralist ready to sermonise'.[6]

It didn't help that rather than rising above the media criticism, the Duke occasionally went for Fleet Street's jugular. In one year alone – 1962 – he described the *Daily Mirror* as 'not quite respectable', *The Times* as too stodgy and the *Daily Express* as 'a bloody awful newspaper'.[7] During a tour of a hospital in the Caribbean in the 1960s, the matron revealed one of the main problems was combating mosquitoes. Philip audibly sympathised in front of the press pack: 'I know what you mean. You have mosquitoes, we have the press.' The journalists took umbrage and gathered sulkily beneath a tree, making their displeasure known, until the Duke later apologised.

Press coverage of royal events was still largely deferential at this time, and it was the Continental media that was the problem. An analysis of press cuttings from 1960–72, largely concerned with the Queen and Philip, found sixty-three stories claiming that the Queen was on the verge of abdicating, another seventy-three that she was about to divorce the Duke, and ninety-three that she was pregnant – two of which they of course got right.

In 1973 the Prince poked fun at his reputation when he addressed the Newspaper Press Fund in Glasgow. A feature in *Time* magazine had recently declared the Prince no friend of the press. 'That's the trouble with reputations – they cling much more tenuously than the truth,' he told the assembled journalists, before joking: 'if anyone can offer me any advice about how I can improve this reputation or even offer any reason why I have it, I shall be more than grateful'.[8] Predictably, the following day's papers did both!

By the 1980s the rise of the paparazzi in Britain, the inevitable erosion of deference for the monarchy and all other institutions, and the tabloid circulation war – particularly between Rupert Murdoch's *Sun* and Robert Maxwell's *Mirror* – trivialised press coverage of the monarchy in the eyes of the Duke and the palace old guard. 'It is absolutely extraordinary what has happened in the last thirty years,' the Prince reflected in 2006. 'Before that we were accepted as normal. But now …'[9] As the Queen and Prince Philip entered late middle age, there was less interest in their private lives. Attention switched to the younger generation, particularly with the arrival on the scene of Lady Diana Spencer and, to a lesser extent, Sarah Ferguson a few years later. 'The media has turned us into a soap opera,' the Duke complained to biographer Gyles Brandreth.[10] He was still seething about it a few years later when he was interviewed by Jeremy Paxman: 'On the basis of the way the family have been treated by the media at the moment, I'm surprised people don't chuck it.' More than a decade later his prophecy came true when his grandson and his new wife did 'chuck it', having accused media outlets of running stories that are 'distorted, false or invasive beyond reason'.[11]

The Duke continued to make headlines over his occasional outbursts. The 'slitty-eyed' quip in China was a fine example that threatened to overshadow the Queen's landmark tour of that nation in 1986. Alan Hamilton, royal correspondent for *The Times*, asked students at a reception what the Duke had said to them. He and the rest of the press pack couldn't believe their luck when student Simon Kirby revealed Prince Philip had joked: 'If you stay here much longer you will all be slitty-eyed.' It was meant as banter, but the remark has haunted him ever since. 'The trouble with journalists', as he sees it, 'is that they have no sense of humour. Period.'[12]

Aged 85, he reflected on his press coverage: '*Now* I reckon I have done something right if I *don't* appear in the media, because I know that any appearance in it will be one of criticism.'

Irritation with media coverage of the royal family is one reason the Duke limits his perusal of the newspapers to an 'occasional glance' at the broadsheets. Of the rest he fumed, 'I can't cope with them. But the Queen reads every bloody paper she can lay her hands on,'[13] which of course is just the sort of Philip quip we all love.

69

DODGY PALACE LIFTS

Lift rides for the Queen and Duke are usually glitch-free, therefore it was a surprise when at the Palace of Westminster the royal couple ended up on a bit of a joy ride. They joined Black Rod on Level 1 of the House of Lords for the short descent to the ground, when a quick-fingered peer on the third floor managed to press his button first. His Lordship had the surprise of his life when the door opened and he found himself face to face with the monarch before the door shut and she whizzed back down.[1]

In May 1969 the Queen and Duke enjoyed an even more dramatic upsurge when they pressed a lift button, as the Princess Royal recently recalled: 'The Queen, Duke of Edinburgh, lady-in-waiting and me', during the state visit to Austria. 'I think we were all dressed up for a smart do somewhere. We went from the ground floor – we were only supposed to be going up two storeys – and it went up to the 19th floor, and this chap got in thinking he was going for a spa treatment. He was slightly surprised.'[2]

The Prince was less amused back in March 1960 when he found himself stuck in a Buckingham Palace lift with his cousin the Duchess of Kent and her daughter Princess Alexandra. The three, dressed in black tie and tiaras for the Royal Film Performance, were stuck between floors for ten minutes, delaying their arrival at the Odeon Leicester Square by twenty minutes.[3] They were there to see veteran Hollywood star Paul Muni in *The Last Angry Man* which, as one of the hosts from the Cinematograph Trade Benevolent Fund later said, was an ironic choice given the Prince's mood when he shook hands.

In 2007 the same lift stuck when Philip was due to escort President Kufuor of Ghana and his wife to a state banquet at the palace. The quick-thinking Prince used the luggage lift, to the amusement of the Queen who, gowned and tiara-ed, was watching the technical mayhem from a balustrade on the floor above and dashed to meet them, commenting, 'What a life one leads!'[4]

70

QUIPS, GAFFES AND BANTER: THE DUKE'S MEMORABLE CLANGERS 61-70

THOSE LESS FORTUNATE ...

61 During a 2012 visit to Bromley, Kent, he met 90-year-old Barbara Dubery sitting in a wheelchair outside, covered in a foil wrap to ward off the cold, *'Are they going to put you in the oven next?'*

62 Introduced to a blind girl, the Duke told her the joke about a blind man whirling his guide dog around his head, *'so he could have a look round'.*

63 To a blind woman with a guide dog outside Exeter Cathedral in 2002, *'Do you know they're now producing eating dogs for the anorexics?'*

64 To members of the British Deaf Association standing next to a steel band at the opening of the first Welsh Assembly in 1999, *'Deaf? If you're near there, no wonder you're deaf.'*

65 On stress counselling for servicemen in 1995, *'It was part of the fortunes of war. We didn't have counsellors rushing around every time somebody let off a gun, asking "Are you all right – are you suffering from a ghastly problem?" You just got on with it!'*

66 To another wheelchair-bound elderly lady at a care home in 2002, *'Do people trip over you?'*

67 Prince Philip told double amputee Trooper Cayle Royce that he should put wheels on his prosthetic limbs to move

around more quickly. Cayle, who had lost both legs in a bomb blast in Afghanistan, said Philip was 'my hero' and 'really comedy'.

68 At the Valentines Mansion in Redbridge in March 2012, on meeting disabled David Miller who drives a mobility scooter, *'How many people have you knocked over this morning on that thing?'*

69 At a reception at St James's Palace in 2014, the Duke was impressed with the wheelchair used by former rugby player Alastair Hignell, which could be raised or lowered as needed, *'That must be good for cocktail parties.'*

70 To Adam Hills, comedian and host of Channel 4's *The Last Leg,* who has a prosthetic limb, *'You could smuggle a bottle of gin out of the country in that artificial foot.'*

71

POESY PRINCE

Picture the Duke of Edinburgh enjoying peace of mind reading one of the 200-plus books of poetry he accumulated over the years, while a few hundred yards away, at Clarence House, the Queen Mother was doing exactly the same while lying in bed with a box of her favourite Elizabeth Shaw peppermint creams. (During the Second World War she was fortified by the chocolates and sent her sweet ration coupons directly to Elizabeth Shaw to secure her next box.)[1]

Queen Elizabeth's fondness for poetry is well documented. When, during the despair of early widowhood, the poet Edith Sitwell sent her a copy of new anthology *A Book of Flowers,* the Queen Mother was more than grateful. 'I started to read it, sitting by the river,' she wrote to Sitwell, 'and it was a day when one felt engulfed by great black clouds of unhappiness, and misery, and I felt a sort of peace stealing round my heart as I read such poems and heavenly words.'[2]

Queen Elizabeth apparently had no idea that her macho war hero of a son-in-law shared her passion for books of verse. When Philip's biographer Tim Heald raised the topic over lunch with her and Princess Margaret at Clarence House, the older lady 'gave me one of her famous beatific smiles, but made it plain … that she thought I was mad'. Turning to her younger daughter, she exclaimed: 'Did *you* know that Philip read poetry?' Margaret gave 'much the same disbelieving look' at Heald and admitted she had never heard of such a thing.[3]

Although Philip once claimed that his views on poetry are 'conventional' and 'conservative', he was familiar enough with twentieth-century verse to declare Dylan Thomas 'a brilliant poet' and to argue against inviting T.S. Eliot to speak at a conference as in his opinion the poet was 'deep, but narrow'.[4]

Several volumes of Eliot feature in Philip's collection, and he is more of a fan of the American-born poet than his wife or mother-in-law ever were. Queen Elizabeth once entertained friends with an account of a poetry evening at Windsor Castle during the Second World War at which Eliot recited *The Waste Land*. 'We had this rather lugubrious man in a suit, and he read a poem,' began the Queen Mother. 'I think it was called "The Desert". And first the girls [Elizabeth and Margaret] got the giggles, and then I did and then even the King.' Asked if the poem might have been *The Waste Land*, she replied: 'That's it. I'm afraid we all giggled. Such a gloomy man, looked as though he worked in a bank, and we didn't understand a word.'[5] (By delightful chance 'gloomy' Eliot was actually working for Lloyd's Bank in London when he wrote his most famous poem.)

72

... TALKING OF POETRY

When he was working as a full-time royal, the Duke received thousands of letters each year from a variety organisations and individuals. While the vast majority would be dealt with by his staff, Philip occasionally replied himself.

During their mammoth Silver Jubilee tour of the UK in 1977, the Queen and Duke happened to pass the eighteenth-century Windmill Bar in Hilltown, Dundee. The ever-curious Prince stopped, stared at the building and pointed at its windows. Regulars were intrigued by this and penned a poem to Philip, who was staying in the area overnight and it reached him via the Dundee City Chambers.

Clearly tickled by the gesture, Philip wrote a reply in verse which the pub later used in a publicity campaign to save it from demolition.

Entitled 'The Windmill Bar' and signed 'Philip', the poem is McGonagall-esque in style and contains lines such as …

From there 'cross the glen to the ramparts of Stirling,
Then into the station at Perth we were hauled,
But the sight the most glorious in store for us to see
Was the friendly old Windmill in Hilltown, Dundee.

He then went on to explain what had caught his eye as he passed by …

It wasn't the crowd coming out the door,
That caught my eye at quarter past four,

T'was the Ann Street windows that attracted my stare,
I wondered if anyone could be living up there,

Using a bit of artistic licence he even suggested the poem by the
regulars was a highlight of the Jubilee year …

There'll be many a kindness that'll long be remembered,
From the days of the Queen's Jubilee,
But none of the functions no matter how ordered,
Will quite match the verse from the Windmill, Dundee.[1]

Despite a public campaign to save the pub, which utilised the
Duke's poem time and again, the category 'B'-listed building was eventually knocked down and replaced by a housing
development.[2]

In a similarly light-hearted vein Philip replied to members of
the Oxford Union who once cheekily invited him to take part in
a debate on the monarchy. Despite being a real 'no-hoper' of a
request, which would almost certainly receive a thumbs-down
from the palace, the Duke once more took the time to reply …

One of the peculiarities of this home of democracy and
free speech is that there is a convention that members
of the royal family are expected to refrain from practising free speech on matters loosely termed political …
I presume this is in case any of us could be quite so pro-
foundly stupid as to say something with which members
might disagree.[3]

73

MAN BELONGING MRS QUEEN

One group of foreigners the Duke of Edinburgh has never upset is the Yaohnanen tribe of Tanna, a tiny island in Vanuatu, an archipelago country in the southern Pacific. The reason is simple: to the Yaohnanens, Philip is a divine being.

Royals are used to being venerated from time to time but should it happen like this in Blighty, the Prince would probably say something along the lines of 'get a grip'. As it is, he has always seemed to be chuffed by the relationship and has over the years sent the tribe three signed photos which are reverentially stored in a secret island location.

How it all started is a bit of mystery. It is thought to be linked to the tribe's ancient belief that the son of a mountain spirit travelled overseas to a far distant land where he married a powerful woman and would one day return to them. Before independence in 1980 Vanuatu was known as the New Hebrides, a joint Anglo-French colony. Formal photographs of the 'powerful woman' Queen and her husband adorned the walls of British government offices and would no doubt have caught the eye of any visiting locals. Fascination with the Duke grew following his solo visit in 1971 and a joint one with the Queen three years later.

At this time the Prince was unaware of his apotheosis and it took a letter from John Champion, the then British Resident High Commissioner, to break it to him that there was the 'Prince Philip Movement' in the South Pacific. Champion suggested a signed photo from the ducal god might be a nice gesture. This was duly sent and the delighted Yaohnanen mailed a pig-killing stick, called a *nal-nal*, to Buckingham Palace.

Another photo was taken of Philip, by now known as 'Man Belonging Mrs Queen', holding his *nal-nal* and that too became a much-treasured icon.

Neither the Duke nor Queen met the tribe during their time on Vanuatu, which is probably just as well. Travel writer Alexander Frater claimed the Yaohnanen are 'permanently spaced out on kava', an island brew more lethal than the strongest Scotch. Local lore says that, should the Queen see her husband drinking kava, she would be instantly executed by a single blow to the head using a giant root.[1]

Frater also alleges that former tribal elder Kalpapung once sent the Duke a *namba*, a penis gourd, which is a straw codpiece to hold the sexual organ in a permanently excitable state. The gift was for Philip to wear when he did eventually make it back to the island.

In the intervening years the tribe has remained content with its framed photographs of the deity. As Jack Naiva, chief of Yaohnanen village, explained to another writer, Matthew Bylis, Christians have 'been waiting 2,000 years for a sign from Jesus … our Philip sends us photographs! And one day he will come.'[2]

74

FEATURE FILM PHILIP

On screen, the Prince has been portrayed by two legends of the industry, a former Doctor Who, an animal rights activist and *Outlander*'s sadistic redcoat, Captain 'Black Jack' Randall.

A year after the wedding of the Prince and Princess of Wales in 1981, the American networks ABC and CBS managed to release two memorably forgettable biopics of Charles and Diana in the same week. Each had a stellar cast that failed to shine, thanks to truly awful dialogue and the stretching of truth way beyond its elastic limit.

In *Charles and Diana: A Royal Love Story*, Philip was played by Christopher Lee, who said he had moved to America in a bid to shake off his screen image as Dracula. He swapped his cape and fangs for the uniform of an Admiral of the Fleet and claimed 'there is nothing remotely distasteful about the idea' of recreating the marriage of the decade, despite it having more unintentional laughs than the worst Hammer horror film. Even his obituary stated: 'more surprising still was his acceptance of the role of Prince Philip in the ill-fated television film *Charles and Diana: A Royal Love Story*.'[1]

In *The Royal Romance of Charles and Diana*, the role of father-in-law of the bride went to Hollywood's former swash-buckling hero Stewart Granger, with Olivia de Havilland as the Queen Mother who helpfully teaches 'Diana' the correct way to walk downstairs. The *Washington Post*'s reviewer labelled it a piece of 'slack-jawed heraldic voyeurism incapable of, and apparently uninterested in, transforming remote news figures into believable mortals'.[2]

At least Granger was spared the fate of Dana Wynter, who, as the Queen, used the royal 'we' in nearly every utterance, the scriptwriters clearly thinking Elizabeth II spoke in the majestic plural from the moment she woke up. An example is the peculiar dialogue between her and Diana after a royal assassination attempt: 'Your Majesty, you can't! You can't go out to the balcony!' wails the Princess as her mother-in-law recklessly decides to make an appearance. 'Diana, we see your concern for our safety,' declares the monarch. 'But as the Royal Family we have no choice but to go forward and face our people. Because you see, my dear, we are the people.' Even

Queen Victoria, the most famous exponent of nosism, would have blanched at that one!

By chance, the two Dianas had slight royal connections. Diana in the Christopher Lee film was played by Caroline Bliss, whose grandfather, Sir Arthur Bliss, composed 'Processional' for the Queen's Coronation. Catherine Oxenberg, Diana in the Stewart Granger film, is the daughter of Princess Elizabeth of Yugoslavia, whose mother, Princess Olga of Greece and Denmark, was Philip's first cousin. Olga was also the sister of Princess Marina, wife of the Queen's uncle George, Duke of Kent, making Elizabeth a first cousin of the present Duke of Kent, Prince Michael and Princess Alexandra. There was another real royal connection when the actor Daniel Chatto, who played Prince Andrew in *The Royal Romance of Charles and Diana*, went on to marry Philip's niece, Lady Sarah Armstrong-Jones, the daughter of Princess Margaret.

There was no problem with the dialogue in the 2006 film *The Queen*, which explores the fallout from the death of the Princess of Wales in August 1997. Helen Mirren gave an Oscar-winning performance as the eponymous monarch and Peter Morgan was nominated for an Academy Award for Best Original Screenplay. This time the role of Philip went to American-born actor and animal rights activist James Cromwell, who said at the time that he didn't want to make the Duke as outrageous a figure as director Stephen Frears seemed to want: 'I had met Philip and have a lot of respect for him.' He admired the way the Prince coped with the restrictions of the role:

> He's been toeing the line for as long as she's been Queen. And he's learned all the protocol and he's had to eat it, by walking two steps behind her and having no say at all as a man in any decision. Winston Churchill told her, 'Never discuss anything having to do with this government with your husband.'[3]

Cromwell portrayed the Duke as curmudgeonly but supportive of the Queen, and his utterances were full of Philip-isms such as his reaction to the news that 'Elton John wishes to sing at the funeral. Should be a first for Westminster Abbey.' He grumbled that the funeral guest list would be 'a chorus line of soap stars and homosexuals', and felt that the public had overreacted to the passing of the Princess: 'sleeping in the streets and pulling out their hair for someone they never knew. And they think we're mad.'

Morgan and Frears spoke to every royal contact they could to research the background material and both have claimed Philip's cosy phrase 'Move over, Cabbage' as he climbs into bed with the Queen is based on reliable information,[4] and is from the French endearment '*mon petit chou*'.

The Prince will be familiar to fans of the Netflix series *The Crown*, in which he was played by former Doctor Who Matt Smith in series 1 and 2 and then by Tobias Menzies. Smith enjoyed playing the character and told *Variety* magazine:

> One of the interesting challenges for me was that I felt there was a sort of a misconception and a preconception about him, which reduced him a bit. And actually all the research I did found him to be brilliantly funny, very clever, very popular. In the royal house he's the most popular of all of them. If you've talked to any of the staff, Philip's the one they all love really.[5]

Matt Smith has dined out on the story of a friend of his who was at a dinner party attended by Philip. He couldn't resist asking the Prince if he'd watched *The Crown* and received a typical ducal retort: 'Don't be ridiculous.'[6]

Tobias Menzies, best known for his roles in *Outlander* as well as series 3 of *The Crown*, defends Philip against his portrayal in the series as an almost tyrannical father. 'I want to defend Philip in this regard,' he told *Harper's Bazaar*. 'There's a real contradiction in the end [because] there are also examples that Philip was a pretty hands-on dad, that he was pretty present, and parented with a lot of humour. You see Charles and Philip laughing. So, I can't really tell where the truth lies.'

Menzies has also argued that the Philip we know today and the one we thought we knew back then are two very different people. 'He was an outsider, coming into this very fusty, old-fashioned organisation. Over the years he's done a lot to bring it up to date and modernise it. He's been very influential on how that institution is run and how it organises itself – even though it may be hard to see now.'[7]

75

THE PRINCE AND THE PROFUMO SCANDAL

During the weekend of 27–28 July 1963 a well-dressed man walked into the Museum Street Gallery, Holborn, to view an exhibition of sketches by Stephen Ward, society osteopath and painter.

The man rapidly selected every portrait of the royal family on sale, paid for them with a bank draft for £5,000 and took them away immediately, declining to give a name.[1] It later emerged the discreet purchaser was Anthony Blunt, Surveyor of the Queen's Pictures and one of the Cambridge Five, who, nine months later, would confess to spying for the Soviet Union. His gallery mission was to protect senior members of the royal family, particularity Prince Philip, from association with Stephen Ward, then on trial at the Old Bailey for living off the immoral earnings of call girls Christine Keeler and Mandy Rice-Davies.

Showgirl Keeler lived with Ward in a non-sexual relationship at his apartment in London and his weekend cottage on the Cliveden estate of the 3rd Viscount Astor in Berkshire. It was at a pool party at Cliveden that Ward introduced Keeler to John Profumo, secretary of state for war, and his wife, the actress Valerie Hobson. Profumo was also introduced to the Soviet naval attaché Yevgeny Ivanov. Keeler began a short affair with Profumo which lasted for most of 1961. She also claimed to have slept with Ivanov. Rumours of the Keeler/Profumo affair eventually became widespread until the minister had to deny them in the House of Commons in March 1963.

Ward, facing police charges of immoral behaviour, split on Profumo and the press picked up on the story, forcing the minister to resign. Two days later Ward was arrested and formally charged. He decided to sell his portraits of royalty, society figures and film stars to raise money for his defence. On 30 July the judge, Sir Archie Marshall, gave a summing-up of the trial before the jury left to deliberate. It was so damning that Ward returned home and took an overdose of barbiturates, dying in hospital on 3 August, having been found guilty *in absentia*.

The downfall of Profumo and the murky reasons behind it rocked the Conservative government of Harold Macmillan. The prime minister privately feared that 'the tide of gossip might even lap around the royal family'.[2] One of the reasons it might was that Prince Philip had come into contact with Stephen Ward several times in London society and had also been sketched by him at Buckingham Palace for a magazine commission. They may have even met professionally, since Ward was an osteopath to the great and good, including Winston

Churchill, Paul Getty, Anthony Eden and Elizabeth Taylor. He treated several people known to Philip, among them actors Ava Gardner, Frank Sinatra and Danny Kaye, as well as King Peter of Yugoslavia, who was married to the Duke's first cousin Alexandra of Greece.

In her autobiography Christine Keeler claims Ward treated Philip.[3] Like the osteopath/artist, she wasn't always a reliable witness, since she goes on to write that Ward 'had no time for Philip and would always put him down in conversation for he hated the establishment'.[4] This conflicts with tales of the elaborate lengths he went to in mixing with the establishment and high society to further both his medical and artistic pursuits.

Ward and the Duke certainly went to the same parties from the late 1940s to the late 1950s. One was a lavish ball hosted by the actor Douglas Fairbanks Jnr on 18 June 1957 for the coming-out of his daughter Daphne, which was held at Cliveden. It was the evening of the first day of Royal Ascot and the Queen, resplendent in a white satin crinoline and wearing a pearl and diamond tiara, was accompanied by Philip and Princess Margaret.[5] Also, in his memoirs found after his suicide, Ward claims Philip had attended at least one his parties at Cavendish Square accompanied by 'a very attractive girl called Mitzi Taylor'.[6] It has to be remembered, of course, that at his trial Ward was branded a 'notoriously unreliable witness'. His biographers name a variety of eyewitnesses claiming to have seen the Prince at parties attended by Ward. Biographer Phillip Knightley goes into enormous detail about a Canadian model, this time called Maxie Taylor, arriving with the Prince as his plus one at the home of Fleet Street artist and cartoonist Arthur Ferrier on New Year's Eve 1946. The long anecdote ends with Jon Pertwee (later the third incarnation of Doctor Who) threatening to kick Philip's backside for interrupting his singing, at which point Ward intervenes, mentioning the forthcoming royal wedding. This was six months before the engagement of Philip and Elizabeth was announced. Equally risible is the claim that Philip was the 'Man in the Mask'[7] who had served dinner to Ward's guests wearing only a lace apron, a 1940s precursor to the Buff Butlers of today. Naturally this legend spread like wildfire through London's chattering classes, particularly during the trial period, and *Private Eye* labelled the Duke the 'Naked waiter'.

If Prince Philip did dine at Stephen Ward's apartment it wouldn't be the first or last time he unwittingly socialised with shady characters who later achieved notoriety. In January 1950, on a visit to Cairo, he was invited to a party at the home of Donald Maclean, another of the Cambridge Five. He joined fourteen other guests for a meal before ending the evening with a series of riotous games, including 'Murder'.[8]

As mentioned earlier (Chapter 44), Maclean's fellow Soviet spy, Kim Philby, attended one of the regular Thursday Club lunches. Mike Parker later recalled, 'he turned out to be the dullest man in the place'. Stephen Ward was also invited a few times (harmonica player Larry Adler claims the photographer Baron brought him). Parker thought there was something unsavoury about him and gave him a wide berth.[9]

One indisputable date on which the Prince and Ward met and spoke to each other was 9 June 1961 when Philip sat for the artist at Buckingham Palace. The osteopath had, by then, used his high-society client list as a springboard for his venture as a portrait artist. He went on to sketch famous names, including the prime minister, Harold Macmillan, and actress Sophia Loren, and an exhibition of his work was held in London in July 1963.

Ward was asked to produce sketches for the *Illustrated London News* and between March and July 1961 had the amazing opportunity, for a relatively unknown artist, to sketch eight members of the royal family. Quite how he achieved such a highly sought-after commission is unclear. The deal may have been brokered by the magazine's elderly managing editor, Sir Bruce Ingram, who had been a friend of the Queen's grandfather.[10]

Ward was delighted the Prince remembered him from the party at Cavendish Square before his marriage and recognised him: 'By Jove,' Philip said, 'You're the osteopath. I never connected you with this appointment.' They went on to talk about 'the old days, polo and the fact that he had a rare condition called "rider's bone" in the thigh'.[11] In the time allotted, Ward was able to produce a second, more informal, charcoal and pastel sketch which took him forty minutes, according to the inscription he added at the bottom. He gave the latter to a female friend. It was auctioned at Christie's in London in October 2011, realising £6,000.

Ward went on to sketch the Queen's cousin the Duke of Kent: 'he had a strange and difficult face'; her aunt Princess Marina: 'the most difficult to capture. The mouth is ever so slightly askew'; her sister Princess Margaret: 'the most difficult face he had ever done'; and her uncle, the Duke of Gloucester: 'an interesting Hanoverian face.' Having sketched eight royals in quick succession, Ward noticed by the time he got to the older Duke 'the strong family likeness I had encountered in things like the shape of the skull'.[12]

Stephen Ward's trial was set for the end of July 1963 and the osteopath/artist decided to sell 145 of his sketches, including his royal ones, in order to pay his legal costs. Prices ranged from 35 to 500 guineas with the royal portraits at the highest amount. Media interest was phenomenal and *The Times* reported 'chaotic scenes' at the press preview on the 22nd and 'when Miss Marilyn Rice-Davies [Mandy's birth name] looked in there was pandemonium'.[13]

It was four or five days later when the mysterious 'well-dressed man' came into the gallery and swept up the royal pictures. Frederick Read, who arranged the exhibition, claimed to have reason to believe that the money came from Canadian newspaper magnate Roy Thomson, who was elevated to the peerage 'for public works' in the following New Year's Honours List.[14] Most writers have identified the purchaser as Blunt. The Queen's biographer Sarah Bradford claims Blunt 'quietly bought them to save the royal family embarrassment'.[15] A few years earlier, investigative journalists Barrie Penrose and Simon Freeman write that in the 1980s Arthur Martin, head of DI, the elite section of MI5 with responsibility for Soviet counter-espionage, recalled that Anthony Blunt was asked by Michael Adeane, the Queen's private secretary, if he would perform a discreet favour and buy the royal works.[16]

There is one other mention of the Duke at the time of the trial. Artist Vasco Lazzolo was one of the few society figures who didn't desert Stephen Ward and agreed to stand as a witness for the defence. At the time he had been commissioned by the Fishmongers' Guild to paint Philip in his livery robes. Fearing the press might link his name with the Prince's, he briefed the Duke at the next sitting, offering to abandon the portrait if the sitter wanted to. 'Nonsense,' said Philip, 'we carry on.'[17] True to his word, Lazzolo supported Ward at his trial but at the party to celebrate the completion of the royal portrait a week after the osteopath's death he declared the latter's artistic merit as 'superficially competent ... his work has curiosity value but no aesthetic value.'[18] Lazzolo had known the Duke from his Thursday Club days and attended the unofficial stag party the club gave a week before the royal wedding.

London society gossipers apart, the first the public knew of the vague links between the Duke and scandal was a banner headline in the *Daily Mirror* on 24 June 1963. It trumpeted: 'Prince Philip and the Profumo Scandal' above the subheading – in much smaller font – 'Rumour is Utterly Unfounded'.

Journalists had picked up on a comment made by a Mr J.W. Salt, the Conservative agent for Walsall South, who told a party meeting: 'there is now a rumour floating around the country that a member of the Royal Family is involved with this lady' (i.e. Christine Keeler), although neither the *Mirror* nor Mr Salt revealed what 'the foulest rumour' was.[19]

In 1987 the rumours surfaced again when, during an interview on Radio Ulster, author Anthony Summers claimed that among photos found in Ward's flat after his death was one of two naked girls with three clothed men – Prince Philip, Baron and another man. The BBC apologised to Buckingham Palace, which declared the story 'old hat'.[20]

Then in January 2014, author Richard Davenport-Hines, whose book *An English Affair* had been published the previous year, said he believed the unfounded allegations about the Prince's involvement might account for why some of the Profumo/Ward documents are not set to be released until January 2064.[21]

Along with his so-called gaffes and rumours of his alleged affairs, Prince Philip's links to one of the greatest political scandals of the Queen's reign will, annoyingly for his reputation, keep rearing its head.

76

1969: THE YEAR THE QUEEN BANNED CHRISTMAS

In October 1969 Buckingham Palace announced that the Queen would not make her annual Christmas broadcast on either TV or radio and that a written message to the Commonwealth would be issued on Christmas Eve. It has so far been the only time since 1952 she has broken the tradition which was initiated by her grandfather George V in 1932.

There was a feeling among courtiers that the format was becoming stale and repetitive and needed a revamp. As Prince Philip explained during a press conference in November: 'Somehow or other we have got to find a better technique of doing it. And so we thought we'd take this year off and scratch our heads and see whether we can do something better.'[1]

The Duke also pointed out that 1969 had seen saturation coverage of the monarchy with the Investiture ceremony of the Prince of Wales at Carnarvon Castle and the broadcasting of the hugely successful documentary *Royal Family*. Ironically, it was the latter that was shown in the Queen's usual 3 p.m. Christmas Day slot.

Royal Family was the brainchild of two people: John Brabourne and William Heseltine. Brabourne was married to Philip's cousin Patricia Mountbatten and had masterminded a twelve-part ITV series on his father-in-law – *The Life and Times of Lord Mountbatten* – which was a critical and ratings success. The Queen attended a special preview of the series and dubbed its weekly TV slot 'Dickie time', using the war hero's family name. Heseltine was a young, vibrant Australian who had recently become the Queen's press secretary. The previous incumbent Major Richard Colville was dubbed 'the Abominable No-man' by the media for his general unwillingness to allow any media access to any private glimpse of the monarch and her family. Even senior members of the household found him difficult to get on with. 'We called him "Smiler" – ironically of course,' said one.[2]

Bill Heseltine recalled, 'there was nothing between the Court Circular and the gossip columns.'[3] He and Brabourne felt that 'the Royal Family was almost too dull, and one ought to lift the curtain of obscurity'.[4]

Brabourne suggested a royal documentary to Prince Philip when both were spending the weekend at the Norfolk home of Aubrey Buxton, an extra equerry to the Duke who also happened to be a director of Anglia Television. Philip was quickly on board with the idea, though the Queen was initially cautious, asking Brabourne: 'Will we have some say?'[5] She needn't have worried: the documentary was tightly controlled by a committee headed by the Duke, who came up with many ideas for the format, and Heseltine, who worked closely with the esteemed documentary-maker Richard Cawston, whom Brabourne and Philip had recruited for the joint BBC/ITV venture.[6]

Filming took place between 8 June 1968 and 18 May 1969, covering seventy-five days in the royal year in 172 locations. The forty-three hours of film were then distilled into a 110-minute film.

Curiously, the one member of the royal family who was not at ease with the filming was the Duke himself. Cawston and his team thought his role as overall commander-in-chief of the project would relax him. In the event, 'he had periods of pronounced sulkiness during the shooting'.[7] Much of it was caused by his overriding concern for his wife, who always found speaking before the cameras an ordeal. He once snapped at Cawston: 'Don't bring your bloody cameras so close to the Queen!'[8] Eventually he relaxed after 'he'd seen [she] had taken to it, and was going to do the part proud'.[9]

The Queen had initially been reluctant to take part. 'It's no good, I'm not a film star,' she told Heseltine, and she was concerned that people might think the resulting film too boring to watch. She also had problems getting used to the hand-held cameras and recording equipment which at times were too close for comfort. When she was talking to a group of Commonwealth ministers, she was startled when a microphone suddenly appeared beside her. Her elderly detective Albert Perkins – ironically dubbed 'the fastest gun in the west' by the crew – lunged and sent it flying with a karate chop.[10]

As filming progressed she began to relax, and occasionally invited Cawston to lunch to discuss her 'scenes' in advance. Before meeting ambassadors and the like in an audience, the Queen became adept at briefing them about the film and telling them what was wanted by the cameras. Sometimes this strategy backfired. Canadian Prime Minister Pierre Trudeau (father of the present prime minister, Justin Trudeau) was so overwhelmed he could only give monosyllabic answers to her questions. After he had bowed his way out of the room, the Queen turned to the crew and said: 'Well, he didn't have much to say for himself, did he?'[11] She had better luck with US President Richard Nixon. Realising that his visit would be a high point of the documentary, the Queen arranged for Prince Charles and Princess Anne to be there, telling Cawston: 'we must have something special for our film.'

The younger princes, Andrew and Edward, aged 8 and 4 when filming began, were very friendly with the team, and Edward was overheard asking: 'Mummy is it OK if I go and play with the film men?'

With the Queen relaxed, the film crew were also more at ease. An electrician on the team recalls the time they were filming the Queen looking through her priceless stamp albums. As he was reaching up to change a bulb, one of his colleagues goosed him from behind. He let out a yell and the Queen called over: '"Are you all right, Mr Gorringe?" I said: "I am now," and she asked, "Have you had a shock?" I replied, "Just a slight tickle, Ma'am," and we all collapsed laughing in front of her.'[12]

Another trick was played on a younger member of the crew while they were filming at Balmoral Castle, the Queen's private royal residence in Scotland. It became a bit of standing joke that

18-year-old Princess Anne had apparently developed a teenage crush on him. After he left for London, the others on the team sent a postcard of Balmoral from the local shop. The greeting was 'Sorry I didn't see you before you left, but I know how important your assignment was. See you in London.' They signed it 'A', addressed if to him at Lime Grove Studios, and by the time he was back in the office it had been passed around most of the BBC.[13]

The first family sequences were also shot on the Balmoral estate. When the crew arrived, one of them told Bill Heseltine that he'd just got back from filming at a nudist camp and recalled how a former beauty queen had stood on the top of a diving board, clutching something in her hand. This turned out to be her bathing cap, which she carefully arranged over her hair before diving in without another stitch on her.

The next morning Heseltine reported back: 'I told the Queen that story over dinner and she really liked it.' The electrician remembers: 'A few minutes later we were all lined up to meet Princess Anne and after she'd said, "how do you do?" Heseltine said: "Go on, tell Princess Anne that story about the nudist camp." Anne said: "Do tell me," so I had no choice. She thought it was hilarious.'[14]

The Princess wasn't always so charming. When the crew were waiting outside the Queen's apartments to set up a scene, Anne walked past them and they clearly heard her giving cheek to the monarch. As the teenager stormed out, one of the crew remonstrated: 'You shouldn't be talking to your mother like that!' A voice from inside the room called out, 'That's quite right!'[15] Princess Anne notoriously hated the documentary, later saying, 'I never liked the idea of *Royal Family*, I thought it was a rotten idea. The attention which had been brought upon one ever since one was a child, you just didn't need any more.'[16]

When they filmed the royal family enjoying a barbecue by the side of the River Dee, they realised they were on to a winner. The

Queen, dressed in a kilt and blouse, strolls over to Prince Philip and says: 'Well, that's the salad done.' The Duke, turning some sausages, replies: 'Well done. This, as you will observe, is not.' Today it all looks a bit awkward and contrived, but its impact in 1969 was staggering. It was the first time anyone had ever heard the Queen say anything that wasn't an official speech or broadcast, and she came across as very warm, relaxed and unstuffy.

Most of the scenes in the film took place as they would have done in the normal course of events. Some were complete setups, such as the one where the Queen pops into a shop near Balmoral with Edward to buy him an ice cream. Cameraman Peter Bartlett recalls: 'This was definitely contrived, as I had to pre-light the sweet shop. There was also a slight embarrassing moment because the Queen of course doesn't carry money, so I had to loan her half a crown.' (Millennials, that's pre-decimal coinage, not something she wore.) This explains why we see Her Majesty producing a single coin from an otherwise empty purse, saying: 'I'm afraid this is all I've got.'

The royals became adept at helping the team overcome technical problems. Electrician David Gorringe recalls a stuffy palace official ordering him to remove a lighting cable from under a priceless carpet:

> Princess Margaret came in, wearing her tiara, long white gloves and a ballgown. She looked fabulous with her beautiful dark blue eyes. Anyway she took one look at the cable [which was now on top of the carpet] and says to me: 'That looks terrible.' When I told her the story, she just said: 'Well let you and me get rid of it,' and with that she bent down and we both put it back.

In another sequence, Margaret was with the Queen at a gala at Covent Garden. Opera House officials said the team would not require an outside generator as their own system would cover it. They were wrong. Halfway through the National Anthem, the overloaded circuit blew up and everyone was left fumbling around in the dark. The Queen wasn't pleased when, later on, she sat down for dinner during the interval and the lights blew yet again. A row ensued between the chairman of the Board of Governors and Cawston's team, who were told 'this is all your fault', and it ended in a full-scale row. Eventually the Queen 'diffused' the situation herself by agreeing to arrive again during the second half while a bemused audience stood once more for the National Anthem.[17]

Prince Philip, initially so supportive of the idea, grew more and more miserable during every one of his own scenes. He found performing stunts such as pretending to answer an imitation phone call in order to appear hard at work a pointless exercise. He came across well in the final edit. Besides his usual position of three paces behind the Queen at key events, he appeared in a variety of other roles – piloting an aircraft, talking about conservation and carrying out his role as a charity patron. Reviewers were more impressed with his softer side. We saw him at his easel painting a landscape and, in one scene, taking Prince Edward for a boat ride on a loch. 'Get in,' yells the 4-year-old. 'Coming,' replies Philip, belying the occasional critical account of him in biographies as a remote authoritarian figure to his children.

Before the film was released, the royal family were given a special screening. It had been agreed all along that they had the right of veto, and Dick Cawston was worried that they might axe scene after scene. In the event it was passed in its entirety, though Prince Philip was concerned about the scene where a string on Prince Charles's cello snaps and stings Edward in the face, making him cry. In the end the Duke was persuaded it added to the naturalness of the whole programme.[18]

None of those present that day had any inkling the film would be such a success. During the first broadcast on BBC1, a two-minute interval was included halfway through. Later the Metropolitan Water Board reported that the sewerage system nearly reached saturation point as millions of loos were flushed in unison.

Dubbed 'Corgi and Beth', the film was initially given universal accolades for showing the royals as three-dimensional personalities. Any fears the Duke and his family had about how they would appears were allayed by the huge success of the programme. It would be seen by more people than any other documentary ever made in the UK: 30 million people watched it on BBC1 on 21 June 1969 and on ITV a week later, making it the third most watched TV programme in this country after the 1966 World Cup and the funeral of Diana, Princess of Wales.[19]

It would eventually be seen by 400 million people in almost 130 countries. It changed the public's perception of the Queen and her family and also changed how they appeared in future television programmes. The 1970 Christmas speech included footage of that year's tours of Canada, Australia and New Zealand. Future Christmas broadcasts would show unseen footage of royal weddings and christenings as well as images of overseas tours.

Subsequently it was criticised for being the first step on a slippery slope that ended with the royals appearing on *Wogan*, *Parkinson* and, most infamously, on Prince Edward's excruciating fundraising *It's a Royal Knockout*. It's been called 'Pandora's Box', 'a very good idea' by Philip's cousin Countess Mountbatten, 'a colossal mistake' by Sir David Attenborough – who thought the mystique of royalty would suffer – and 'the pivotal moment of the reign' by another TV legend, Sir Trevor MacDonald.

Whatever the views of the critics, the viewing figures showed that the public adored the film and in revealing the real personalities of the Queen and her family it probably saved them from becoming a complete irrelevance. For the future of the monarchy, embracing the television age was far better than trying to pretend it just wasn't happening.

77

CRASH, BANG, WALLOP: THE DUKE BEHIND THE WHEEL

After eighteen months of non-eventful retirement, in 17 January 2019 the Duke hit the headlines as well as three passengers in a Kia. The 97-year-old Prince was attempting to access the A149 from a lane in the royal Sandringham estate at around 3 p.m. when the two vehicles collided. The impact flipped his Land Rover onto its side and it ended up on the other side of the carriageway. He later told police he'd been 'dazzled by the sun', which would have been directly in his eyes at that time on a midwinter day.

The Duke was heard to yell, 'My legs, my legs!' and it was thought he might be trapped, until Roy Warne, a 75-year-old barrister and first on the scene, helped him free himself through the sun roof. The initial concern in the media for Philip's well-being was replaced by criticism when it was revealed that the 28-year-old driver of the Kia had a 9-month-old baby boy in the back seat. The child was unharmed, though a 45-year-old passenger suffered a broken wrist.

Press photos of a brand-new replacement Land Rover Freelander being delivered to Sandringham the following morning, swiftly followed by more photos of Philip driving it without a seatbelt, rapidly turned the situation into a PR disaster.

It was also the latest accident in an eventful eight-decade driving career.

Collisions with members of the public were nothing new. Even as a boy at Gordonstoun School in the late 1930s Philip was, according to his headmaster Kurt Hahn, prone to cycle 'regardless of safety rules'. On one occasion 'he avoided a crash with a baby in a perambulator by inches, thanks to his unusual agility; he appeased the mother by an apology that was irresistible'.[1]

To his credit, after his bumps, the Prince seems to have always checked to make sure the other party was uninjured.

It is unclear when the Prince passed his driving test but it is thought to have been after he left Gordonstoun School and started his naval career at Dartmouth College in 1939. His first documented crash occurred three years later, in March 1942, when he was 20. He was on shore leave, staying with the Mountbattens at their London home in Chester Street. After dinner with his party-loving older cousin David Milford Haven, the two borrowed the Earl's Vauxhall and set out on a tour of West End nightclubs. They headed back at 4.30 a.m. in the unlit streets, hit a traffic island, wrote off the car and tottered home covered in blood and cuts. 'So, after facing death many times at sea,' their forgiving uncle wrote to his daughter Patricia, 'they got their first wounds in the London blackout.'[2]

By the time of his next notable prang, on 21 October 1947, Philip was four weeks away from his wedding to the heir presumptive, and about to realise that even a minor road accident would guarantee blanket Fleet Street coverage. Returning to the training base at Corsham, Wiltshire, where he was instructing cadets, his black MG skidded at a corner, left the road and ended up in a hedge. Under the restrained headline 'Lieut. Mountbatten in Car Accident', *The Times* reported that Philip 'was slightly bruised and twisted his knee' but was able to carry out his teaching schedule. The two-seater car, unlike its owner, was 'fairly badly' damaged.[3] Other newspapers adopted a more jokey approach – 'Philip: Take it Easy' trumpeted the *Sunday Pictorial* – the sort of nannying style that would always irritate him the most.

John Dean, who was valet to the Duke for five and a half years from the time of the royal engagement (as well as a regular front-seat passenger) diplomatically recorded that 'although he has a passion for speed I always felt absolutely safe with him. His driving has the sure touch of the expert, fast yet without a trace of recklessness.' Ironically, Dean then offers a whole litany of reckless moments, from the Duke listening to the BBC's cricket coverage on the radio, commenting on the pretty girls they whizz past, clocking 100mph and refusing to stop for a snack, insisting, 'John I think it would be a good idea if you feed me with sandwiches as we drive along.'

His twin pet hates were apparently 'crawlers' holding up the traffic and those who pull up miles from the kerb, blocking the road. Regarding the latter, 'he would usually shout something, and in the cheerful camaraderie of the roads would ask the other driver to pull into the roadside'. It's not difficult to imagine what Edinburgh 'cheerful camaraderie' sounded like. Someone on the receiving end of it was the driver of an Austin Seven who blocked Philip's MG as he was about to overtake. When he did manage to draw level, 'the Duke leaned out of the window to make a testy crack about the "matchbox" that had been in its way'.

Royal speed demons of the late 1940s were helpfully kept on the road by the hopelessly deferential attitude of the police. Dean recalls the Duke being pulled over in his Austin Sheerline by two officers. Recognising the VIP occupant, 'they then drew themselves to attention and saluted. One officer said: "I beg your pardon, sir, I am sorry you have been troubled." The Duke said, "Quite right, quite right," and we drove on.'[4]

While most of the young Duke's bumps and scrapes were missed by the ever intrusive media, those involving his wife nearly always found their way into the papers. In February 1948, on their way to an engagement at the Admiralty, Philip was driving and Princess Elizabeth was in the passenger seat when they collided with a taxi, giving rise to public concern about the welfare of the newly-weds and the advisability of the Duke driving his young wife.

Royal vehicles hitting or being hit by commercial vehicles appears to have been a recurrent theme back in the day. In 1923 a car carrying the Queen's parents, the Duke and Duchess of York, to an engagement at the Guildhall hit the back of a dray cart being pulled by two horses. A pole from the dray cracked the wooden panelling of the nearside door of the royal car, which skidded on to the pavement.[5]

The Queen's grandmother, Queen Mary, was involved in a far more serious accident in May 1939, a few days before her seventy-second birthday. The royal car was returning from an engagement at Wisley Gardens when it collided with a lorry loaded with metal pipes at a busy junction in Wandsworth. The limousine was catapulted some distance before mounting the pavement and landing on its side. The widowed Queen was hurled across the feet of her equerry Lord Claud Hamilton and had to be rescued by a local painter who smashed a car window and placed his ladder in the vehicle for the royal party to use to climb out. Although bruised and shaken, Queen Mary managed to smile and wave at a crowd of onlookers who had gathered to watch proceedings. She was taken to the house of a nearby doctor and was heard to say, 'I shall be all right after I have rested for a few minutes. I am going to have a cup of tea and that is all I want.'[6]

The Regina v. lorry theme was reprised in 1956 when a car carrying Queen Elizabeth the Queen Mother and Princess Margaret had a bump with a 3-ton lorry on Brixton Hill, London. Mother and daughter were on the way to visit Lord Abergavenny, near Tunbridge Wells. *The Times* noted the delay was precisely four minutes.[7]

On 27 June 1957, five years in to her reign, the Queen was once again the front-seat passenger in a car accident. This time the Duke was at the wheel of his Lagonda when it crashed with another car in Gresham Road, Staines. The royal car lost a spotlight and the wing was damaged. By perfect coincidence, Philip was returning from the lunchtime AGM of the Automobile Association at the Savoy Hotel during which he had addressed members on road safety. Press coverage was more concerned about the passenger than the driver. The *Daily Express* headline 'Should Philip Drive the Queen?' was typical of Fleet Street's reaction.[8]

Seven years later, 7 June 1964, the Queen and Duke were in another Berkshire crash when the Duke's Rover collided with a Ford Popular driven by learner driver William Henry Cooper. The accident occurred outside the Rising Sun pub near Maidenhead and the royal couple had just been to the baptism of the Duke and Duchess of Kent's daughter Lady Helen Windsor. The Queen was said to 'be pale and shaken by the incident'. Mrs Cooper said later, 'I have driven twice with my husband and thought he was a good driver. My husband has

Philip and his Range Rover at the Royal Windsor Horse Show in 2005. (© Ian Lloyd)

failed his test about five times. He only grazed his knee in the impact although the rear of our car is badly damaged.'[9]

In January 1996 a Norfolk businessman received whiplash injuries and ended up in a neck-brace after a vehicle driven by the Duke hit his Mercedes 190 which had halted at a pedestrian crossing in the county. Mr Daynes said, 'The Prince's Range Rover came into the back of my Mercedes while I was waiting at a pedestrian crossing. It was entirely his fault … I noticed through my rear-view mirror that it was the Duke of Edinburgh who had been driving. It was quite a surprise.'

On 9 February 2019 the Duke's long and eventful life behind the wheel ended three weeks after his final car accident. Norfolk police said: 'We can confirm that the 97-year-old driver of the Land Rover involved in the collision at Sandringham on Thursday 17 January 2019 has today voluntarily surrendered his licence to officers. We will follow the standard procedure and return the licence to the DVLA.'

78

A FATHERLY BOND WITH JFK JNR

Fans of the Netflix series *The Crown* will no doubt recall an uncomfortable dinner hosted by the Queen and Prince Philip for US President John F. Kennedy and his wife Jacqueline. The hostess appeared jealous of the First Lady who in turn looked thoroughly miserable and injected herself with drugs to get through the evening. Needless to say the truth is far less dramatic, though it has to be said the encounter wasn't all plain sailing.

The main problem was that the Kennedys were staying with Jackie's once-divorced sister, Lee Radziwill, and her twice-divorced husband, Stanislaw. When the palace asked the Kennedys who they would like to invite to the dinner they naturally put Lee and Stas top of the list, while Jackie also asked for Princess Margaret, her rival in the glamour stakes, to be included and Jack requested Princess Marina of Kent, whom he had met when his father Joe was US ambassador in London in the late 1930s.

The royal household immediately replied that divorcees were not welcome dinner guests. Pressure from the office of Prime Minister Harold Macmillan forced the palace to back down and include the Radziwills for fear of upsetting the Special Relationship with the USA.

'Anyway the Queen had her revenge,' Jackie reported back to her close friend the writer Gore Vidal (who was also a vague relation since their two mothers were both wives of businessman Hugh D. Auchinloss), 'No Margaret, No Marina, no one except every Commonwealth minister of agriculture.' She also revealed: 'I think the Queen resented me. Philip was nice but nervous. One felt absolutely no relationship between them.'

Jackie, who was usually the embodiment of discretion, never referred to the meeting on record. If we believe Vidal's account, she found the monarch 'heavy going' and only human once when, in discussing their mutual need for stamina in such high-profile roles, the Queen said conspiratorially: 'one gets crafty after a while and learns how to save oneself'.

The evening ended with the Queen, mindful of Jackie's interest in all things equestrian, marching her through the Picture Gallery, halting at a van Dyck portrait and declaring, 'that's a good horse!'[1] Lee later recalled being escorted on the gallery tour by Philip, who joked: 'You're just like me – you have to walk three steps behind.'[2]

There can't have been any hard palace feelings about the divorcee debacle since in March 1962 Jackie and Lee enjoyed a private lunch with the Queen at Buckingham Palace. A year on, in November 1963, the Queen and Philip again met the Radziwills at a private dinner at the US ambassador's residence in London. Ten days later JFK was assassinated driving in an open-top car in Dallas. The royal couple immediately sent Jackie a private message of condolence. Later the Queen would recall, 'with all our hearts, my people shared his triumphs, grieved at his reverses and wept at his death.'[3]

At the time of the assassination the Queen was pregnant with Prince Edward so Philip represented her at the funeral in Washington. He flew from London with the prime minister, Alec Douglas-Home, and his wife, as well the leader of the opposition, Harold Wilson, and the Duke and Duchess of Devonshire (Andrew Devonshire's older brother had married JFK's sister Kathleen). Deborah Devonshire later recalled Philip inviting her to join him for dinner with Wilson during the flight, with the other guests on an adjoining table. The two men 'started talking about aeroplanes in such an incredible, technical way that it was quite impossible to listen to them and I found my mind wandering.'[4]

Given that Kennedy's funeral was only three days after his assassination it was, in the Duchess's words, 'not surprisingly, rather chaotic'. When Philip arrived at St Matthew's Cathedral he found he hadn't been allocated a seat and the Douglas-Homes had to move further back to make room for him. On the cathedral steps after the service, 'Debo' noted 'Prince Philip's stern blue look' as he contained his emotion. Others openly wept as the president's son John Jnr, 3 years old that day, saluted his father's coffin as it passed by to the presidential anthem 'Hail to the Chief'.

Inside the cathedral earlier, there had been more tears when 'John-John' called out, 'Where's my Daddy?' Things were no better for the Prince at the internment at Arlington Cemetery. He 'was jostled at the back again and behind a lot of soldiers, so he was not among the foreign visitors when they came away from the grave'.[5]

The Prince was accorded one special tribute by Jackie herself. At the White House later in the day she greeted the 220 representatives from 102 countries – thought to have been the largest collection of dignitaries at the passing of a head of state since the funeral of Britain's Edward VII in 1910. The majority were greeted by the widowed First Lady in the State Dining Room. However, she asked Philip – along with French President Charles de Gaulle, Ethiopia's Emperor Haile Selassie and Ireland's President Éamon de Valera – to join her for high tea in the Oval Office, where she inexplicably handed de Gaulle a fresh daisy.[6]

Leaving the reception, Philip was amused to see 'John-John' in full birthday party mode, running down the corridor hotly pursued by his flustered nanny. 'The kind-looking man watched me catch him,' Maud Shaw later recalled, '"I've got one like that," he grinned. "They're a handful aren't they?"'[7]

Eighteen months later Maud got to shake hands with the Duke after a tea party held at Windsor Castle hosted by the royal couple for Jackie and her family. It followed the inauguration of the John F. Kennedy Memorial at Runnymede by the Queen earlier in the day on an acre of land given to the American people in perpetuity. In a touching gesture Philip held the hand of John Jnr, by then aged 4, as they walked up the steep woodland path to the site honouring his father and namesake.

TAKE THE ****ING PICTURE: THE POTTY-MOUTHED PRINCE

During a visit to Brazil, Philip was to receive an aptly spherical gift from the national bowling club. Its president made a speech in fluent Portuguese for the assembled guests before turning to the Duke and in broken English declared, 'Balls, you know.' The Prince, smiling broadly, replied, 'And balls to you, sir.'

Visiting Magdalen College, Oxford, in 2008 to mark its 550th anniversary, the Queen and Duke joined 120 students and lecturers for a lunch of venison. Afterwards the royal couple were shown the college's famous Deer Park, prompting Philip to quip: 'How many of those buggers did you have to kill for lunch then?' On being told the ones they'd eaten had in fact come from Kent, he joked: 'Well, don't tell Charles. Because he likes to buy local.'

During the 1968 state visit to Brazil, it was reported Philip shouted out as one photographer ran alongside the royal motorcade, 'Shove off!' in 'the naval vernacular'. Later a journalist asked another passenger in the car to confirm the remark and was diplomatically told: 'I'd never heard the word before. I think it was French.'

An irate Prince Philip shouted to the present author – who thought he had considerably veered off the gravel Long Walk on to the verge to allow HRH and his four-in-hand to gallop past – 'Get off the ****ing grass!'

Unaware his protection officer had the car keys, Philip told him to 'b****r off', as he wanted to be alone. Climbing into the Range Rover, he noticed they were missing and yelled: 'Who's nicked the f***ing keys!', waking the Queen who opened the window to see what the commotion was all about.

In 1991 he was given the opportunity of taking control of a simulated space capsule at the HQ of NASA in Houston. His verdict: 'It was like a bloody great mechanical copulator.'

During the last phase of an overlong tour of HMS *Boxer*, the Duke made his feelings plain: 'Not another ****ing chamber!'

Faced again with yet another film crew and yet another boom microphone: 'Here comes that bloody machine again – why don't you stick it up your ****?'

Asked in the 1960s which of the countries he hadn't yet been to he would like to see, he replied: 'I would like to go to Russia very much – although the bastards murdered half my family.'

On being shown a piezo-meter water gauge (used to measure pressure of water) during a visit to Australia: 'A pissometer?'

During Cowes Week, Philip was sailing off the Isle of Wight when the owner of another boat shouted for his boat to move out of the way, cheekily calling him 'Stavros'. The Duke yelled back: 'It's not Stavros and it's my wife's ****ing water so I'll do what I ****ing please!'

The Duke's most famous four-letter rant came in 2015 during a visit to the RAF Club to mark the seventy-fifth anniversary of the Battle of Britain. Philip grew visibly impatient with a photographer setting up a group shot of him and surviving members of 'The Few', and snapped, 'Just take the f***ing picture!'

80

QUIPS, GAFFES AND BANTER: THE DUKE'S MEMORABLE CLANGERS 71–80

OFFICIALDOM

71 **Mayors:** While being escorted on a tour of Liverpool Docks by Lord Derby, Philip was asked by his lordship if he wouldn't mind stopping for a minute at the dock gates to meet the mayors of Bootle and Crosby. *'I haven't come here to see your bloody mayors. I came to meet the dockers,'* snapped the Prince. After grudgingly shaking hands he was told by Lord Derby: *'I must tell you that one of your bloody mayors was a docker, and the other works on the railways. The people here would have been very upset if you hadn't met them.'*

72 **Politicians:** To Conservative MP Jeremy Hunt, *'Who are you?'* Hunt replied that he was health secretary but had been culture secretary at the time of the London Olympics, *'Well they do move you people on a lot.'*

73 **Politicians:** Greeting MP Joan Walley at a palace reception, *'And who do you represent?'* 'Stoke on Trent,' she replied. *'Ghastly place, isn't it?'*

74 **Chairmen:** *'Occasionally I get fed up, going to visit a factory, when I am being shown around by the chairman, who clearly hasn't got a clue and I try to get hold of the factory manager but I can't because the chairman wants to make sure he's the one in all the photographs.'*

75 **MPs**: In Ghana he was told their parliament only had 200 members. The Duke replied, *'That's about the right number. We have 650 and most of them are a complete bloody waste of time.'*

76 **Mayors again:** On a visit to a town where the mayor proudly showed off a model of a new housing development, zoned according to price, the Duke took it upon himself to correct his description of 'the lower income area', calling it *'the ghetto'*.

77 **More mayors:** On the approach of the robed mayor and other civic dignitaries during a visit to Nottingham, *'Here comes the chain gang.'*

78 **Chairmen again:** On meeting Sir Michael Bishop, chairman of Channel 4 TV in 1996, *'So you're responsible for the kind of crap that Channel Four produces.'*

79 **Civil servants:** While meeting one in 1970: *'You're just a silly little Whitehall twit: you don't trust me and I don't trust you.'*

80 **Even more mayors:** When he was introduced to David MacIsaac, the newly appointed Mayor of Slough, Berkshire, in 2008, Philip quipped, *'Are you going to put on weight with all the meals you attend as mayor?'* Meeting him a few months later he gave him a quick once-over and said, *'I told you you would get fat!'*

81

ROYAL WINKER

It began in October 1957 with a cheeky piece in the *Spectator* under the headline 'Does Prince Philip Cheat at Tiddlywinks?'

The recently formed Cambridge Tiddlywinkers (club tie: light blue spots on a dark background with descendent gold winks), having had no luck finding opponents in over two years, saw it as an opportunity to boost their flagging cause. They wrote to the Duke suggesting he appoint a team of royal champions to try to scotch the magazine's damaging slur.

Philip used his media contacts and persuaded *The Goon Show* cast – Harry Secombe, Peter Sellers and Spike Milligan – to represent him. The showdown took place at Cambridge University's Guildhall in front of a tightly packed crowd of 600, including the senior proctor, students and townspeople. Prince Philip was unable to be there but telegraphed a morale-boosting message:

AT ONE TIME I HAD HOPED TO JOIN MY CHAMPIONS BUT, UNFORTUNATELY, WHILE PRACTISING SECRETLY, I PULLED AN IMPORTANT MUSCLE IN THE SECOND OR TIDDLY JOINT OF MY WINKING FINGER.

He ended with: *WINK UP, FIDDLE THE GAME AND MAY THE GOONS' SIDE WIN.*[1]

Sadly, without the benefit of the Duke's 'cheating', his champions were trounced by the Varsity team, 120½ to 55½. The real winner of the night was tiddlywinks itself, which had been in the doldrums since its Victorian parlour game heyday. In 1960 the Duke commissioned a 'Prince Philip Silver Wink' trophy. According to an exclusive in *Winking World* 'H.R.H. the Duke of Edinburgh has presented a very fine trophy, a mounted silver wink, to be competed for between all the winking Universities in Britain.' By the 1960s some thirty-seven British universities were winking for it.[2]

In 2008, to commemorate the half-century of the University v. Goon match, a second royal match was held at Cambridge.

This time the Duke's champions were made up of members of the Savage Club, a London club set up for gentlemen in literature and the fine arts whose honorary members have included Edward VII, George V, George VI and Prince Philip.[3] Alas they lost 24 to 18 so Philip never did restore his tiddlywink reputation.

82

TURNING THE QUEEN DECIMAL

Among the Duke's multifarious duties was the presidency of the Royal Mint Advisory Committee, a position he held from 1952 to 1999. This meant in effect that for forty-seven years he was in charge of how his wife appeared on all the coins and medals issued by the Royal Mint during this period.

It was kick-started shortly after the death of George VI when Mary Gillick, a 71-year-old recently widowed sculptor, was asked to produce the first image of Elizabeth II to be used on coinage. Philip was so involved with the design that he visited Gillick's studio to see how work was progressing. Thanks to his involvement, Gillick was able to secure a one-hour sitting with the new Queen and settled on an uncrowned Renaissance-style profile. Elizabeth, hearing that the sculptor wanted to depict her with hair bound in a thin laurel wreath similar to the coinage of Queen Anne, apparently asked not to look too much like Julius Caesar.

Philip's committee approved the new design, the Queen approved it even more at a Privy Council meeting in November 1952, and from then on it became the image of Elizabeth II her subjects spent until decimalisation. In actual fact, he had reservations about these earlier likenesses. He didn't think they were very lifelike, and after all he was the most qualified person to judge.[1]

Philip or not, Gillick's work must have found favour with the Mint since she went on to sculpt a joint image of the royal couple in 1953 for medals used to commemorate royal visits to certain countries. Two years later she produced a sculpture of Philip for a solo medal of him.

The Duke also had a hand in producing the heptagonal 50p coin and apparently had concerns about the sexlessness of Britannia, wanting a fuller figured 'body in the right proportions that fills the robes'. For the obverse he didn't have to worry about the shape of his wife's body, just the position of her head. 'Putting "70" in front of "Elizabeth" looks ridiculous,' he argued, 'all those initials are better behind the Queen's head, and it also keeps the lettering that much further away from the face.'[2]

Fittingly, the last Royal Mint coin approved by the Duke was some eighteen years after he relinquished his role as committee president. To mark his official retirement from public life in 2017 a special £5 coin was produced and was struck by the Prince of Wales at the Royal Mint on 11 July 2017. The Latin inscription reads 'NON SIBI SED PATRIAE' which translates as 'Not for himself but for his country'.

83

A SENSITIVE TOUCH

Behind the defensive outer shell and the irascible nature there is another Prince Philip that relatively few people get to see. In the words of a former courtier: 'He is actually remarkably kind-hearted, but goes to enormous lengths to hide it.'[1]

His cousin Countess Mountbatten believed the clue lay in his early years. 'My feeling about him is that he has a much more sensitive centre than people have ever understood because he's had to build a hard shell around himself to survive the circumstances in which his life has been lived.'[2] Former Dean of Windsor, Michael Mann, opted for a more dramatic analogy: 'What he did was build a picket line around himself with machine-guns on it. You are not admitted through that line unless you are totally trusted.'[3]

While he'll be best remembered for firing a few rounds from his picket line at journalists, photographers and anybody inadequately prepared, over-familiar or totally indecisive, he has, in the words of Marcus O'Lone, land agent at Sandringham, 'an inclination to always support the underdog'.[4]

There are examples of fair play stretching back to his early years. According to his childhood friend Hélène Cordet, when he was aged 4 he gave 'his own battered' toy as well as 'his new one' to her sister Ria who had been left out of the gift distribution by a tactless visitor.[5] John Wynne, a classmate at Cheam School, recalled a similar selfless act: 'When we were both eleven and a half or twelve we dead-heated in the high jump and, at the prize-giving, I pushed him forward to go and collect the cup. When he came back he gave it to me. "That's yours," he said.'[6]

As an employer he inspired loyalty. John Dean, his valet in the late 1940s and early 1950s, remembered him as 'pleasant and courteous to servants' though he could be demanding and bark orders 'in naval fashion'. When the Prince called Dean 'a stupid clot' the two men didn't speak to each other for a few days.[7]

Others fared better. Returning from his naval duties in the Mediterranean for the baptism of Princess Anne in October 1950, the Prince brought his Maltese steward, Vincent, home with him. The latter was not only allowed to attend the service but was introduced to George VI by Philip. 'The gesture endeared Philip to all Malta and is still remembered,' wrote his cousin Alexandra of Yugoslavia with cousinly overstatement a decade later.[8] Even temporary staff could be bowled over by him. Lady Pamela Hicks recalls that on the 1953–54 Coronation tour, 'when we left New Zealand the local typists who were helping out, said "the best investment ever made was to have Prince Philip in the royal family," they were so impressed. They thought he was wonderful, very kind and sensitive.'[9]

Some members of the royal household couldn't stand his abrasive, confrontational manner. There is the story of Sir Michael Adeane, the Queen's private secretary from 1953 to 1972, standing in front of his mirror on the first day of his retirement. He suddenly started to roar with laughter as he was in the middle of shaving. 'What on earth are you laughing at?' asked his wife. 'Oh', he replied, 'I just thought, I'll never have to work with that man again!'[10]

Mike Parker, private secretary to Philip at the beginning of the reign, had a different experience and sounded euphoric reflecting on it half a century later:

My God! Amongst his own people like us, or people who worked for him, he was a delight to work for: he was funny, direct … absolutely fabulous. If at any time he got steamed up about something, he would apologise like anything. He would say: 'Well I'm sorry about that. I was wrong; you were right.' He was marvellous at that. We all loved him dearly. And we still do.[11]

Another member of Philip's household during the early years, Squadron Leader Peter Horsley, the equerry-in-waiting, recalled muddling up the seating plan before an official luncheon

Philip has a kind side that he often chooses to keep hidden. Here he smiles for the camera while judging at the Royal Windsor Horse Show in 2010. (© Ian Lloyd)

in Ottawa. Philip, unfazed, called out: 'Just sit anywhere.' Everyone did and the meal was a great social success.[12]

Brian McGrath, a later private secretary to the Duke, interviewed for a 2008 documentary, said: 'You know the thing about Prince Philip is that no one ever leaves him.'[13] McGrath was himself proof of that since he retired from the key post in 1992 after ten years but remained an extra equerry and was allowed to keep his palace office right up until his death aged 90 in 2016 with the agreement from the Duke that he was allowed to bring in his labrador to work.

Surprisingly for such a stubborn man, he is willing to apologise if he thinks he is in the wrong, as Mike Parker pointed out. Philip memorably let rip at Major Sir Rennie Maudsley, Keeper of the Privy Purse in 1970, calling him 'a silly little Whitehall twit' (see Chapter 80), but soon afterwards the startled courtier received a two-page letter from the Prince saying that he didn't know what had got in to him.[14]

Unlike the Queen and other members of the family who find it difficult to pour out their emotions on paper, Philip has always been able to express himself touchingly and from the heart in his letters. An example is the handwritten letter he penned to a yachting friend who was suffering from terminal cancer and had only weeks to live. Philip had met him through his links with the Royal Yachting Association and wrote to him in hospital. He also sent him the insignia of a Commander of the Royal Victorian Order – an award instituted for those providing personal service to the royal family – for his voluntary work in the sailing world.[15]

In the aftermath of the murder of his uncle Lord Mountbatten in August 1979, Philip wrote a 'long and lyrical' letter to his cousin Patricia Brabourne, who was recovering in hospital from her horrific injuries. She had also lost one of her twin sons, Nicholas, in the atrocity and was too ill to attend his funeral. The Duke, who was at the funeral, wrote 'a graphic description of the occasion and how everyone present had felt – exactly what a grieving mother needed to hear about the funeral of her fourteen-year old son'.[16] Patricia later commented: 'it was an incredibly kind and thoughtful gesture and it helped and consoled immeasurably.'[17]

Even Simon Kirby, the embarrassed student who revealed the Duke's 'slitty-eyed' gaffe to the press in China (see Chapter 68), received a handwritten letter from Philip after he sent a letter of apology to Buckingham Palace and the Foreign Office. While the Foreign Office sent a friendly but formal letter of acknowledgement to Kirby, the Prince wrote: 'I certainly do not blame you for all the fuss and humbug your comments may have generated in the British media.' He went on to blame the media and pointed out that on his subsequent visit to China it was clear that 'very few people were aware of the incident anyway'. He ended by wishing the student an interesting and enjoyable time during the remainder of his stay in China.[18]

84

DIANA: A COMPLICATED DAUGHTER-IN-LAW

In theory, Diana was the ideal choice to marry the heir to the throne. Born at Park House on the Sandringham estate in July 1961, she had grown up on the periphery of royal life. Her father Johnny Spencer was an aristocrat – Viscount Althorp, later Earl Spencer – a former equerry to the Queen who accompanied Elizabeth and Philip on their mammoth 1953–54

Coronation tour of the Commonwealth. Diana's grandmothers were both ladies-in-waiting and close friends of the Queen Mother. Crucially, she was probably the last woman in 1980s Britain who was required to be a virgin on her wedding day. As Charles's great-uncle Lord Mountbatten coyly phrased it, the Prince 'should choose a suitable, attractive, sweet-charactered girl before she has met anyone else she might fall for'.[1]

Prince Charles's authorised biography suggests that Philip more or less commandeered his eldest son into proposing to Diana. 'An intervention from the Duke of Edinburgh had a powerful if not decisive impact on the Prince of Wales,' writes Jonathan Dimbleby. The Duke's letter to his son went on to warn that any further delay in making his feelings clear would cause lasting damage to Diana's reputation. Prince Charles 'interpreted his father's attitude as an ultimatum'.[2]

The tone of this father/son letter, labelled 'bullying' by later biographers, was disputed by one of Philip's relatives in a 2001 profile of the Duke. 'I've seen that letter,' the relative revealed, 'and it was the most charming letter you can imagine from a loving father giving very sensible advice.'[3]

Had he been so 'bullied' by his father, it is unlikely that Charles, during his engagement, would have arranged a meeting with the Duke, during which he voiced his concerns about marrying Diana. A cleric who was close to the pair and privy to the discussion later recalled: 'What I understand happened on that occasion is that Charles told Prince Philip he wasn't sure he'd done the right thing. His father, thinking it was for pre-marriage nerves, told him that he had to make up his mind, that he must either go for it or let the girl off the hook.'[4] Philip himself seems to have been delighted with the match. Three weeks before the engagement was announced he told friends: 'Isn't it wonderful that they are going to get married? We're delighted.'[5]

Once Diana Spencer joined the royal family, Philip was one member of the firm who made a concerted effort to help her adjust to life as a princess, mindful of his own uncomfortable welcome from courtiers and family friends, both before and after marrying Princess Elizabeth. At one full family gathering he helped her overcome her insecurity by playfully waltzing her into dinner when she appeared nervous.[6]

In the early years he maintained a good relationship with his first daughter-in-law, though he was said to be enraged when Diana occasionally stole the limelight from the Queen. One such occasion was the 1984 State Opening of Parliament, when the Princess opted for a radically new hairstyle, and the ensuing press coverage totally eclipsed anything the Queen said or did during one of the major set-piece events of the royal year.[7]

As the Wales' marriage disintegrated during the second half of the 1980s and early 1990s the Queen and Duke were passive observers, reluctant to get involved until things came to a head midway through the 'annus horribilis' of 1992. On Sunday 7 June, the first serialisation of Andrew Morton's explosive biography of Diana was serialised in the *Sunday Times*. The fairy-tale romance that the nation had fallen for hook, line and sinker, only a decade before, was exposed as a sham, and an incredulous public lapped up details of Diana's bulimia, her suicide attempt and Charles's adultery with a previously unheard-of Camilla Parker Bowles.

The serialisation coincided nicely with the peak of the social season, which may have been great for newspaper sales but was awkward for the royal family since Diana was a key attendee at a series of events, including Trooping the Colour, the Order of the Garter Service at Windsor and Royal Ascot. It was during the racing week that the Queen and Duke convened a meeting at Windsor Castle with Charles and Diana to discuss the fallout from the Morton book. Diana found the meeting very frank and, given the circumstances, even friendly. She very much wanted a trial separation while her parents-in-law, listening sympathetically, urged the warring couple to try to make a go of it for the sake of each other, their sons and the monarchy. Diana agreed to another meeting the following day but then changed her mind and headed back to Kensington Palace.[8]

The Queen and Philip tried again to discuss the matter with the Waleses a few months later during the annual summer break at Balmoral Castle. 'It was just impossible,' the Duke claimed later. 'She didn't appear for breakfast. At lunch, she sat with her headphones on, listening to music. And then she would disappear for a walk or a run. Believe me, we tried.'[9]

Philip tried another approach and wrote a series of letters to his daughter-in-law over the summer months of 1992. Like the Charles letter, they have often been interpreted as critical of the recipient, usually by journalists who hadn't read them or been made aware of the contents. Newspaper reports even suggested Philip used the words 'harlot' and 'trollop' in them, and Diana's private secretary, Patrick Jephson, remembers her telling him bitterly, 'he thinks I'm just in it for the publicity.'[10] Diana showed them to two of her friends, Rosa Monckton and Lucia Flecha de Lima. The former later recalled the letters 'caused excitement and alarm at the same time', with a sensitive and overwrought Princess either laughing or crying at the contents. Rosa added, 'Actually he [Philip] was pretty wonderful. All he was trying to do was help. And Diana knew that.' Lucia also praised Philip: 'They were good letters. He is a good man.'[11]

The letters resurfaced ten years later during the inquest into the deaths of Diana and her companion Dodi Fayed. Under sworn testimony, Philip's private secretary, Brigadier Miles Hunt-Davis, told the court there was 'not a single derogatory term within the correspondence'. The jury were shown extracts in which Diana called the Duke 'Dearest Pa', and signed off with

'Fondest love'. In one of them Philip said he was eager to 'do my utmost to help you and Charles to the best of my ability', adding, 'I have no talents as a marriage counsellor!!!' To which she responded, 'You are very modest about your marriage guidance skills and I disagree with you! This last letter of yours showed great understanding and tact.'[12]

In 1993 the Princess acknowledged the help she had been given by her parents-in-law when she memorably announced her resignation from public duties in her 'Time and Space' speech at a Headway Charity lunch at London's Hilton Hotel. She told the rapt audience: 'I would also like to add that this decision has been reached with the full understanding of the Queen and the Duke of Edinburgh, who have always shown me kindness and support.'

That 'kindness and support' evaporated two years later when Diana made her extraordinary *Panorama* interview. Besides her comments that 'there were three of us in this marriage, so it was a bit crowded,' and 'I'd like to be a queen of people's hearts', she dropped in the real bombshell statement that in her opinion Charles wasn't cut out for the 'suffocating' role of king.

Philip found it frustrating that the behaviour of Charles, who had admitted adultery in his own, jaw-dropping interview the previous year, and now Diana were undermining the respect he and the Queen had generated for the monarchy over the previous four decades. The Duke told his wife there was no alternative to divorce for the Prince and Princess of Wales and the Queen wrote firm letters to both of them instructing them to end their acrimonious marriage.[13]

Charles and Diana divorced on 28 August 1996. The final meeting between Philip and Diana came the following spring when on 9 March they both attended Prince William's confirmation at Windsor when three generations of the royal family put on a united front for the sake of 14-year-old William as well as for the monarchy.

85

FROZEN-OUT FERGIE

It all started so well. When Sarah Ferguson began dating Prince Andrew the world warmed to her over-enthusiastic zest for life, the mischievous glint in her eye and clear adoration of the good-looking Prince, still basking in his post-Falklands hero status.

For the royal family it seemed to be a match made in heaven. Sarah's father, Ronald 'Major Ron' Ferguson, was a first-rate polo-playing chum of Philip's, who appointed him to run Guards Club, the royal polo venue at Smith's Lawn in Windsor Great Park. It was here that the young Sarah and Andrew, born four months apart, got to know each other watching their fathers play in countless matches.

Like Diana and Camilla Parker Bowles, 'Fergie' (as she was inevitably dubbed by the tabloids) has royal Stuart blood flowing through her veins. All three are descended from that friskiest of monarchs, Charles II, albeit via the wrong side of the sheets. The Merry Monarch's liaison with his French-born mistress Louise de Kérouaille produced his seventh and youngest illegitimate son Charles Lennox, 1st Duke of Richmond, the ancestor of all three royal women.

Following her marriage in July 1986, the new Duchess of York forged a strong bond with her father-in-law, who found her far more straightforward to deal with than the emotionally complicated Princess of Wales. At her wedding reception she sat between Philip and ex-King Constantine of Greece. It's been suggested the two shared a bawdy sense of humour and the older Duke was over the moon when Sarah learned how to fly light aircraft and helicopters.

The honeymoon period with the press lasted not much longer than the Yorks' actual honeymoon cruise around the Azorean Islands on the royal yacht *Britannia*. By the late 1980s the tabloids moved into overdrive and started to lambaste her for everything, from weight gain, fashion misses (who can forget the orange wrap likened to a duvet that she wore to the film premiere of *White Mischief*), her many holidays and that sheer exuberance everyone had adored back in 1986 but which now seemed graceless. When she waved and called out the first name of a butler before a Windsor Castle dinner, Philip 'looked at me askance and said: "Surely you have outgrown flirting with the staff?"'[1]

A significant problem for the young Duchess was the separation from her husband, whose naval duties included a six-month tour in the Far East and another lengthy deployment to the North Atlantic. For her father-in-law, such duties were second nature and he was far from sympathetic, telling Sarah, 'Well the Mountbattens managed, and so can you.'[2] In a 2001 interview for an American magazine she said Philip gave them an ultimatum a week after their wedding that she couldn't live with Andrew in the ports near to where he was stationed. She went on to say if she was in the same predicament then – i.e, 2001 – she would have defied her father-in-law, even though 'he's very frightening – the Duke of Edinburgh.'[3]

It was the official separation for the Yorks, announced on 19 March 1992, that was the beginning of the end for the Philip/Fergie relationship. At first he was sympathetic to her plight and, in the words of one senior courtier to biographer Graham Turner, Philip 'wrote a series of very helpful letters to the Duchess of York when she was in difficulty. I've seen them and I thought they were loving and supportive. He got fed up with her only when she consistently ignored his advice.'[4] In the same newspaper profile, 'a long-standing female friend' of the

Duke's recalled, 'I know for a fact that he tried to help Sarah York. He saw her a great deal because she asked to see him, but she did exactly the opposite of what he advised time after time, and, in the end it nearly drove him mad.' Apparently Philip said to the same friend, 'The time she wasted asking for my advice.'[5]

The straw that broke the camel's back was the infamous toe-sucking scoop by the *Daily Mirror* showing a topless Fergie with her 'financial advisor', John Bryan, examining more than her stocks and shares during a poolside consultation. Unfortunately Sarah was staying with the Queen and Duke and their children at Balmoral Castle at the time. Philip began what would be a two-decade avoidance tactic with his soon-to-be-former daughter-in-law. 'As soon as I came in through one door he'd be falling over the corgis to get out of the other.'[6] In future Fergie's occasional meetings with the Queen at Sandringham or Balmoral were choreographed so as not to coincide with Philip's own visits to the estates. As always, his overriding priority was for the effect on the monarchy and particularily on the Queen, coming as it did halfway through her 'annus horribilis' of 1992. One senior courtier who was part of the Balmoral house party recalled, 'The Queen was grey and ashen and completely flat. She looked so awful, I felt like crying.'[7]

Asked nearly a decade later by Gyles Brandreth why he no longer saw Sarah, the Duke's reply was a straightforward: 'I don't see her because I don't see much point.'[8] On another occasion he told the same author, 'Her behaviour was a bit odd.'[9]

With the new Millenium there was a thawing of relations. When the Duke was eighty in June 2001, Sarah sent him a twelve-piece dinner service, for which she received a friendly note of thanks signed off with an affectionate 'With love, Pa.' It's not generally known that she has occasionally dined with the Queen and Duke at Windsor Castle. Then in October 2018 in a public show of unity the two were positioned inches from each other on the official wedding photos of the Yorks' youngest daughter Princess Eugenie and husband Jack Brooksbank.

86

BIBLIO-PHIL

Prince Philip's library is part of a suite of rooms in the north wing of Buckingham Palace overlooking Green Park. Shielded by trees and from the noise and stares of a packed Constitution Hill, for almost seventy years it's offered him the ideal sanctuary to study, learn and research.

As with most members of the royal family his reading matter is supplied by Hatchards of Piccadilly, which has held royal warrants since the time of George III. The Duke has also given his royal warrant to Bibliophile, a postal book bargain retailer of new and out-of-print titles.

Those that have glimpsed the 10,000 or so works agree that it is packed with worthy tomes rather than pot-boilers. 'I think that you would be right to say that I read more for information and instruction than indulgence,' he once admitted.[1]

A palace-approved book from 1947 says his collection then included works by the historian G.M. Trevelyan and *England in the Seven Years War* by Sir Julian Corbett, which apparently made an impression on him. When at sea he read the Lord Peter Wimsey novels of Dorothy L. Sayers – *Murder Must Advertise, Unnatural Death, The Nine Tailors* and so on. Unexpectedly, the younger Philip was also a fan of Lewis Carroll's *Alice* books.[2]

Philip's library is unsurprisingly arranged and catalogued in shipshape fashion. Two other approved biographers have been given a detailed breakdown of the modern collection.

Tim Heald, writing in 1991, was given the result of a stock-take by the Prince's staff done on 22 November 1990. It lists:

560	books on birds
486	religion
373	horses, especially equestrianism
203	poetry
170	fiction – mostly classics including Arthur Conan Doyle, R.M. Ballantine, Saki, Somerville and Ross and H.G. Wells, as well as the heroic naval sagas of C.S. Forester and Captain Marryat.

Surprises on the Heald list include Françoise Sagan's *Bonjour Tristesse* (an account of a girl's summer romance which scandalised French society when it was published in 1954). Also, given that the only things the Duke is known for cooking are steaks on a barbecue, there is a collection of cookery books, from classic Elizabeth David through to the Roux brothers and Antonio Carluccio's book on mushrooms.[3]

Gyles Brandreth, writing in 2004, lists 'some 11,000 books' including:

1,000+	on wildlife, and conservation
600	equestrianism
494	sport
990	art
781	birds[4]

87

NORTH OF WATFORD GAP

Prince Philip's favourite local is the Waterside Inn at Bray, Alain Roux's three-Michelin-starred restaurant, where his grand-children took him to celebrate his ninetieth birthday. He's also done his fair share of queuing at burger vans at carriage-driving events and in his younger days it was said, 'He knows what it is to eat steak and chips in sleazy seaport cafés.'[1]

Prince Philip once surprised breakfast-munching holiday-makers and lorry-drivers when he popped into a Little Chef on the A1 at Doncaster. The Duke was on his way north to a carriage-driving event in Cumbria in August 2014. While his security team and staff queued for drinks and snacks, the 93-year-old Philip was happy to pace up and down in the dining area. Asked by a member of staff if he wanted a seat he replied, 'Oh no. I'm just stretching my legs,' before carrying on his wander around.

In its previous life as a Happy Eater, the same café famously served Prime Minister John Major a fry-up on his way to the Young Conservatives' Conference in Scarborough.

The Duke is not the only royal to visit the chain. In the 1990s his youngest son Edward and girlfriend Sophie Rhys-Jones popped in to the Little Chef at Selby for a bite to eat. Prince and Princess Michael stopped off at Membury Services on the M4 dressed in full mourning following the funeral of their brother-in-law, Sir Angus Ogilvy, in January 2005. The Princess has even agreed to open a Happy Eater off the A3 near Guildford, memorably quipping, 'We'll go anywhere for a free meal!'

88

PRINCE PHILIP: THE GODFATHER

The Duke is godfather to more than twenty people. He was 23 when he was asked by his childhood friend Hélène Cordet to be godfather to her son and 97 when he became godfather to Inigo Hooper, the great-grandchild of his first cousin, the late Patricia, Countess Mountbatten of Burma.

1 **Professor Max Boisot (1943–2011):** Rumours persisted for years that Max Boisot was Prince Philip's illegitimate son, mainly because Philip was a close friend of his mother, cabaret star Hélène Cordet, and had been best man at her wedding, and because Max was born out of wedlock. The father was in fact a French airman called Marcel Boisot who remained a discreet secret after he deserted Hélène. Philip was not only godfather to the baby but contributed to his school fees at his own alma mater, Gordonstoun.

2 **Louise Cordet (b. 1945):** Another godchild (and supposed love child) of the Prince's is the sister of Max Boisot. Again fathered by Marcel Boisot, Louise took her mother's surname when she began a pop career in the 1960s. She was dubbed the 'Queen of the Twist' and was a one-hit wonder with 'I'm Just a Baby'. When Hélène sought Prince Philip's advice about the media rumours about his alleged fathering of her children he told her, 'Look, if you like you can sue them, but I don't think it's worth it. On the contrary, it will just stir up more trouble.'

3 **Mark, 9th Lord Henniker (b. 1947):** His mother, Osla Henniker-Major (née Benning), was Prince Philip's first girlfriend. Mark married Lesley Foskett in 1973 and runs the 2,000-acre Thornham estate in Suffolk. Their 21-year-old son Freddy committed suicide in 2005. His mother said, 'he frequently lost his way and found real difficulty in understanding the purpose of life'.

4 **Nicky Phillips (1947–91):** Prince Philip's childhood friend Gina Wernher married Harold 'Bunnie' Phillips (a former lover of Philip's aunt Edwina Mountbatten) in 1944. Gina was godmother to Prince Andrew and Philip was godfather to her only son Nicholas. The latter inherited the family estate, Luton Hoo in Bedfordshire, in 1977, and attempted to develop it into a profitable concern. It was used as the setting for films such as *Four Weddings and a Funeral* and *Eyes Wide Shut*, as well as TV adaptations of *Bleak House* and *Rebecca*. Unfortunately Nicky's business ventures failed and he committed suicide in 1991 aged 43, leaving debts of £23 million, forcing the family to sell the estate to Elite Hotels eight years later.[1]

5 **The 3rd Earl Mountbatten of Burma (b. 1947):** The eldest son of Philip's cousin Patricia, the Earl was born Norton Knatchbull. The following year Patricia was godmother to Prince Charles and in 1982 Norton was godfather to Prince William. He married Penelope Eastwood in October 1979 two months after the murder of his grandfather Earl Mountbatten by the IRA. He has suffered from ill health for several years and Penelope runs the family estate Broadlands in Hampshire. His heir is 38-year-old Nicky Knatchbull, who knew Prince William at Eton and is a former drug addict. He uses the name Five Dimensional Nick for his work as a musician and film-maker. In January 2019 it was announced he was engaged

to Ambre Saint-Clare, who is a 'mer-lesque artiste' or performing mermaid.[2]

6 **Paul Brandram (1948–2020):** A paternal relation, Paul was the son of Philip's first cousin Princess Katherine of Greece who, like the Duke, was a grandchild of George I of Greece, the brother of Britain's Queen Alexandra. At the time of her death in 2007 she was the last surviving great-granddaughter of Queen Victoria. In 1947 she married Captain Richard Brandram who won the Military Cross during the Italian Campaign but who was dismissed from the Royal Artillery following a court martial in 1950. Paul worked in the City and married twice.

7 **Colin Neville (b. 1948):** Colin was the son of General Sir Robert Neville, a former Governor of the Bahamas and an ADC to George VI who captained Philip's polo team at Cowdrey Park

8 **Julie Parker (b. 1948):** Julie was the daughter of Philip's old navy friend (and later private secretary) Mike Parker and his wife Eileen. In 1972 she married Timothy Buxton, though they were divorced in 1986. Their granddaughter Francesca Mitchell, born in 2012, has the middle name 'Lilibet', which is the name the Queen is called by close members of her family.

9 **Princess Margareta of Romania (b. 1949):** The Princess's father, King Michael of Romania, was, like Prince Philip, a descendant of George I of Greece. Since Michael's death in 2017 Margaret has been styled Custodian of the Crown of Romania since the country is a republic. In her twenties she had a five-year relationship with the future British prime minister, Gordon Brown, while studying at Edinburgh University. In a 2007 interview with the *Daily Telegraph* she revealed: 'It was a very solid and romantic story; I never stopped loving him, but one day it didn't

seem right any more, it was politics, politics, politics, and I needed nurturing.'

10　**Peter, 5th Lord Mottistone (1949–2013):** Philip served with Peter's father, David Seeley, later 4th Lord Mottistone, in the British Pacific Fleet in 1945. The two naval officers were afterwards stationed in Malta and when Peter was born on the island in 1949 Philip and Princess Elizabeth attended the baby's christening ceremony on board HMS *Chequers*.

11　**Philip Howard-Johnston (b. 1950):** His father, Rear-Admiral 'Johnny' Howard-Johnston was involved in the Battle of the Atlantic in the Second World War and his mother was the daughter of the First World War hero Douglas Haig. In 1969 he established 'Howard-Johnston Cars', a used-car firm in Edinburgh.

12　**Philip Lawson Johnston (b. 1950):** Another Philip named after the Duke. He is the son of the 2nd Lord Luke and is a specialist glass engraver. He was awarded a royal warrant for supplying engraved glass to the Queen.

13　**Annabel Cope (b. 1952):** The daughter of the Queen's cousin and confidante, the late Hon. Margaret Rhodes, Annabel, along with Princess Anne, was a bridesmaid at the 1960 wedding of Princess Margaret to Antony Armstrong-Jones.

14　**Princess Maria Tatiana 'Tania' of Yugoslavia (b. 1957):** The Princess is the granddaughter of Philip's youngest sister Sophie. Her father, Prince Andrew (the son of King Alexander I of Yugoslavia), committed suicide in America in 1990 aged 60. Now called Tania Thune-Larson, a graduate of the London College of Printing, she is a successful photographer and landscape artist.

15　**Lady Camilla Hipwood (b. 1957):** Camilla is the daughter of the 15th Earl of Westmorland and dated Prince Charles before marrying the polo player Howard Hipwood.

16 **David Gerard Leigh (b. 1958):** David's father, William Gerard Leigh, was one of Philip's polo-playing chums and travelled with the Duke to play in some of the South American clubs in the early 1960s. His niece Laura dated Prince Harry in 2003.

17 **The Hon. Philip Astor (b. 1959):** The son of the 2nd Viscount Astor of Hever, Philip once owned the Tillypronie estate, dubbed 'the most expensive estate' in Scotland, that was built by Sir John Clark, the son of Queen Victoria's physician. He memorably had a 300ft rabbit – the symbol of Hugh Heffner's playboy empire – carved into the landscape. His wife Justine Picardie is editor-in-chief of *Harper's Bazaar UK.* His cousin once removed, William Astor, is married to David Cameron's mother-in-law, Annabel.

18 **Prince Christopher of Yugoslavia (1960–94):** Unusually, the Duke was also godfather to Maria Tatiana's brother Christopher. Christopher led a private life as a science teacher on the island of Islay using the name Christopher George. He was killed in May 1994 at the age of 34 when he was cycling home in the early hours of a Saturday morning and collided with a car. He died before an ambulance could arrive. Prince Philip had to break the news to Christopher's grandmother, Princess Sophie, who was staying at Windsor Castle for the annual Royal Windsor Horse Show.

19 **George, Earl of St Andrews (b. 1962):** The eldest son of the Duke and Duchess of Kent, he was named after his grandfather George, Duke of Kent, the Queen's uncle. His grandmother, Princess Marina, was Philip's cousin. He is probably best known these days as the father of model Lady Amelia Windsor, who is also a contributing fashion editor at Tatler.com.

20 **Ashley Hicks (b. 1963):** Ashley is only son of Philip's cousin Lady Pamela Hicks (youngest daughter of Earl Mountbatten

of Burma) and her husband David. He has followed in his father's footsteps and become an interior designer. He had two daughters with his first wife Allegra Tondato and two sons with his second Katalina.

21 **Lady Henrietta Purbrick (b. 1964):** Henrietta is the daughter of Philip's friend and former treasurer and private secretary, Lord Rupert Nevill, and granddaughter of the 4th Marquess of Abergavenny. She is married to Colonel Tim Purbrick, whose uncle Reggie is married to showjumper Lizzie Purbrick, who was found guilty in 2018 of criminal damage for swilling pig's blood all over her ex-lover Lord Prior's flat.

22 **Prince Philippos of Greece (b. 1986):** The youngest son of former King Constantine II of Greece, he shares his godfather's birth name – Prince Philippos of Greece and Denmark. Educated at Washington DC's Georgetown University, since 2014 he has been a financial analyst with the New York company Ortelios Capital.

23 **Inigo Hooper (b. 2018):** Seventy-five years after becoming a godfather for the first time, 97-year-old Prince Philip stood as godfather to his first cousin three times removed. Inigo Norton Sebastian Mountbatten Hooper is the grandson of Norton, the 3rd Earl of Mountbatten, one of the Duke's first godsons. The ceremony took place at Romsey Abbey, near to the Mountbatten family home of Broadlands, and Philip took a private helicopter from Sandringham to the event, which coincided with President Trump's tea party with the Queen at Windsor in July 2018.

89

PHILIP THE GOOD FATHER

Throughout the 1970s and 1980s, every year without fail, Philip invited his four children to join him for a break at Craigowan Lodge on the Balmoral estate. Here they would enjoy a private get-together away from the press and public. It was strictly a closed shop with no partners – not even the Queen – invited. None of them missed a year and none of them has ever said what was discussed or what events took place.[1]

90

QUIPS, GAFFES AND BANTER: THE DUKE'S MEMORABLE CLANGERS 81-90

OPENINGS AND UNVEILINGS

81 At the opening of the National Cyber Security Centre, the Prince was being briefed about hacking and asked the member of staff if he spoke Russian or Chinese. When the hapless employee said no, Philip replied, *'Let's hope they don't attack when you're on duty.'*

82 In 2015 the Queen unveiled two statues of herself and Philip at Canterbury Cathedral to mark the Diamond Jubilee. The Duke mused that the Queen looked more like Barbara Windsor and he resembled Boris Karloff, and was heard to mutter: *'I'm sure the pigeons will like it.'*

83 Opening a new Mathematics Centre at Cambridge University in the Millennium year of 2000, *'This is a lot less expensive than the Dome – and I think it will be a lot more useful!'*

84 Opening the new de Havilland Campus at Hertfordshire University in 2003: *'During the Blitz, a lot of shops had their windows blown in and put up notices saying, "More open than usual". I now declare this place more open than usual.'*

85 At the opening of the Theatr Clwyd in Flintshire in 1976 an official told the Queen, *'We seem to have lost His Royal Highness!'* Unfazed, she replied, *'Don't worry, he's probably gone through a door he's not supposed to.'* He had, and emerged on the opposite side of the theatre.

86 During a 2005 visit to an engineering school, which was closed so he could officially open it: *'It doesn't look like much work goes on at this university.'*

87 To a Filipino nurse at the opening of a new cardiac centre at Luton and Dunstable University Hospital: *'The Philippines must be half empty, you're all here running the NHS.'*

88 When the Queen asked him the date so she could write it in a Visitors' Book, he quipped: *'March the 8th, as it says on the plaque you've just unveiled!'*

89 A line he used at many an opening over his last few working years, *'Ladies and gentlemen, you're about to see the world's most experienced plaque-unveiler.'*

90 At the opening of the Animal Health Trust Farm in Essex in 1957, someone had forgotten a vital component of the ceremony. The Duke declared, *'It gives me the greatest pleasure to declare this laboratory open … and if someone will lend me a key I will unlock it.'*

91

CHARITY CASE

The Duke of Edinburgh is president, patron or member of more than 780 organisations. Although he ceased to be actively involved in them when he retired from public duties in 2017, his name remains linked with them. At the time of the Golden Jubilee in 2002 Buckingham Palace estimated he had chaired almost 1,454 meetings to do with his organisations.

Just a week after his wedding in November 1947, it was announced that the Duke had accepted the role of patron of the London Federation of Boys' Clubs. The following year he began another lifelong association with a youth charity when he became President of the National Playing Fields Association (NPFA), which was set up to promote parks and green spaces for play and sports for young people. His approach to his first presidency would be typical of his commitment to the organisations he involved himself with over the next seventy years. 'I want to assure you that I have no intention of being a sitting tenant in the post,' he told the NPFA. True to his word, in the early years he worked every morning at their office in Buckingham Gate and launched a £500,000 appeal. He organised charity cricket matches featuring legends of the sport such as Denis Compton and received £7,000 from a Butlins holidaymakers' reunion.[1]

For ten years (1951–61) he was president of the Automobile Association (although he wasn't the first member of the family to be involved: Princess Anne was made its millionth member when she was born the previous year). Again he was hands-on, suggesting everything from motorway landscaping to, ironically – given his own career behind the wheel – accident prevention. Ahead of the Queen's Coronation on 2 June 1953 he was in the useful position of being able to ask the organisation to manage the road signing, parking and traffic control. Half a century before most of us cottoned on to the idea, he suggested cutting down the amount of diesel exhaust fumes that he pointed out were polluting the air.[2]

Nor was his fundraising confined to the UK. He seized opportunities on his overseas travels to partake in everything from charity dinners to money-raising polo matches. Once he accepted the offer to dive into the swimming pool of Miami man who promised $100,000 for one of his charities if he would do so.[3]

So hands-on is Philip that he has frequently ended up designing, presenting and paying for the trophies linked to his organisations. When the Grand Order of Water Rats – the showbusiness fundraising charity – proposed a Prince Philip Greyhound Trophy, he said, 'What about a silver lamppost?' In the end he came up with the design on a silver dog collar. He even founded a bag-piping trophy for the Pakistan Army, having been impressed by a display of their massed bands during the Queen's state visit of 1961.

Similarly, when the Argentine Polo Association needed a trophy for its annual thirty-goal tournament, he sketched one featuring a silver polo stick which would be decorated with the winners' names added one by one with silver labels. In his sketch he added names: 1) James Snitch, 2) Augustus Bull, 3) William Clot etc. Then, mindful of how over-seriously many people take a royal commission, he added the instruction: 'These names NOT to be engraved.'[4]

The Duke has always been involved with many large charities and institutions, from the British Dental Association to the World Wide Fund for Nature. Over the years he has also lent his support to an eclectic group of patronages and organisations, some of which reflect his hobbies and interests as well as his occasional desire to support the offbeat. These include:

Accrington Camera Club – Life Member. A Lancashire club supporting photography. The Duke has always been a keen 'snapper'.

All England Lawn Tennis and Croquet Club – Honorary Life Member. His interest in the Wimbledon Championship is minimal – preferring to leave royal support to the Duke of Kent (President) and Duchess of Cambridge (Patron). He and the Queen memorably attended the 1977 Women's Singles Final and presented the trophy to Britain's Virginia Wade.

Alvis Owner Club – Honorary Member. He was a fan of the sports saloon and is also a member of the Reliant Owners' Club.

Band of Brothers – Honorary Life Member. Amateur Kent cricket club. Philip played cricket in his youth and supports several organisations associated with it.

Boy Scouts Association of Argentina – Honorary Member. One of his many overseas commitments. Presumably he kept quiet about it during the Falklands War.

British Model Flying Association – Patron. He's flown nearly every type of fully grown aircraft so it's natural he'd support the plastic and balsa wood ones.

British Railway Modellers of North America – Honorary Member. Who'd have thought?

Caravan and Motorhome Club – Patron. No need for a static caravan when you have a stately home here and there, but the Caravan Club did present the young Charles and Anne with a Royal Caravan in 1955 made of ash-clad aluminium. Philip added a tow-bar to his Hillman Husky and towed the small caravan around the grounds of Buckingham Palace, more evidence that he was not the cold and remote father figure some biographers have suggested.

Chilean Air Force – Honorary Pilot. He didn't put many hours of flying time in with them.

Concrete Society – Honorary Member. Promotes concrete technology and use. He qualifies for a free copy of *Concrete* magazine.

Eccentrics Club – Honorary Life Member. A London club that attracted aristocrats, literary and political figures.

Federation of All Japan Karatedo Organisations – Honorary Ninth Dan. Don't mess with him on a dark night, he's a top-belt karate royal.

Friends of Mount Athos – Honorary Member. Society that promotes the history and heritage of the twenty Orthodox Monasteries on this peninsula in north-east Greece. It is one of the few official links he maintains with the land of his birth. Prince Charles is also a patron.

Friends of the Sea Otter – Honorary Member. An endangered species – a cause close to his heart.

Hastings Winkle Club – Member. Fundraises for local charities.

Honourable Order of Kentucky Colonels – Honorary Colonel. Another fundraising group – sits nicely with his Honorary Sheriffdom of Harris County, Texas.

Hull Kung Fu Club – Honorary Member. Another martial arts belt for his valet to iron.

Lepra – Donor. Thirty years before Diana, Princess of Wales, made headlines by her involvement with AIDS charities, the Queen and Philip were equally ground-breaking when they visited a leper colony in Nigeria to allay the irrational fears that surrounded the disease at that time.

Merioneth Brass Band Association – Patron. Philip was created 1st Earl of Merioneth and Baron Greenwich when he received the Dukedom of Edinburgh on the eve of his wedding.

Press Club – Honorary Member. Despite his aversion to the Fourth Estate, the Duke supports two other media organisations – the Edinburgh Press Club and the Los Angeles Press Club.

St Edmund Hall Teddy Bears Cricket Club – Honorary Member. Students of 'Teddy' Hall in Oxford asked him to support this and he was tickled by the idea.

92

THE DEATH OF DIANA

Shortly after 1 a.m. on Sunday 31 August 1997, the Queen's assistant private secretary, Robin Janvrin, was awoken by the insistent ringing of the telephone. On the other end of the line was British Embassy in Paris with the devastating news that Diana, Princess of Wales, and her companion Dodi Fayed had been involved in a horrific car crash in the French capital. Fayed had been killed outright along with the driver of the Mercedes, Henri Paul. Diana's injuries were serious but the exact extent of them was still unclear.

Janvrin was based at Craigowan Lodge, the large detached villa on the Balmoral estate often used by the Queen on short visits to her Deeside retreat. He contacted the castle and then dashed the few hundred yards to where the Queen, Prince Philip and Prince Charles, all dressed in their nightwear, were anxiously waiting to hear further news.[1]

Shortly after 4 a.m. the embassy confirmed to Janvrin that Diana had died from massive internal injuries. The Queen and Philip's first thoughts were for their grandsons William and

Harry, who were also staying at the castle. Their grandparents counselled Charles to let them sleep on and to take the radios out of their room and the TV out of what was still known as the nursery. It was decided that Charles would fly to Paris with Diana's two sisters in an aircraft of the Queen's Flight to bring the Princess's body home, leaving William and Harry in the care of their grandparents.

How the Queen behaved and reacted in this situation can be gauged by an account of an earlier, almost parallel, situation. In August 1979 Earl Mountbatten was murdered when the IRA detonated a bomb that was on board his small fishing boat. Also killed that day was a local boy who assisted the family and Nicholas Knatchbull, Mountbatten's grandson. Nicholas's twin, aged 15 that year, the same age as Prince William, was himself injured and was hospitalised with his critically wounded parents. On his release he was invited to stay with the Queen at Balmoral. In his memoirs Timothy recalled the monarch acting 'like a mother duck gathering in lost young'. She kissed him, fed him sandwiches and helped him to unpack. 'She was in almost unstoppable mothering mode,' he recalled.[2]

In the following days she got her doctor to care for Tim's wounds, monitored when he should go to bed and decided when he was fit to go out with her own sons on the grouse moors. 'She was caring and sensitive and intuitive,' he remembered. He was also grateful that she sat next to him at meals and listened to him pour out his grief about the horrific explosion and the loss of his twin. 'She didn't probe. She has a brilliant way of using her ears as magnets and getting people to talk. I spoke to her in a way I hadn't spoken, articulating things other people hadn't drawn out of me.'[3]

On the day of Diana's death, the Queen and Duke carried out the normal activities of the day, hoping their grandsons would find some comfort in the familiar routines of life on the estate while suffering the reeling shock of what had happened to them. 'The boys were very calm,' recalled one who was present. 'They simply busied themselves helping Prince Philip get the food for the usual barbecue picnic. They ate a very good supper.'[4]

Had the British public been made aware of this and Tim Knatchbull's account of his own visit, they might have been less critical of the Queen's decision to remain with her grandsons at Balmoral in the aftermath of their mother's death. Those close to the Queen have (and had) no doubt her decision to stay with William and Harry rather than to hot-foot it to London to console sobbing members of the public – who, for the most part, had never known the Princess – was definitely the right one.

For Margaret Rhodes, the Queen's cousin and close confidante, it was an obvious choice:

> The Queen's priority was for her two grandsons. Of course she wanted to be close to them and to make sure they were all right. I mean what else was she to do? I think all the criticism hurt her terribly. Balmoral was the ideal place for them all to be as a family. It's private and secluded and peaceful, and I know William and Harry adore the Queen and Prince Philip, and would have wanted to have been with them.[5]

Criticism grew during the week, fanned by negative newspaper headlines. 'The media were circling, looking to blame someone other than themselves,' recalled one of the Queen's advisors.[6]

The Queen and Duke were particularly infuriated over the growing anger from the papers that Buckingham Palace was not flying a flag at half-mast. 'The editors know perfectly well why the flag is not flying,' a guest at Balmoral heard her say over tea on the Tuesday. 'The flagpole would still be bare even if I had died. It *never* flies at half-mast. The trouble is I have been around too long.'[7] For the whole of her life the only flag that had flown at the palace was the Royal Standard when the monarch was in residence. Counselled by Prince Philip, who was as unyielding as she was on the issue, the Queen was not about to change a century-long tradition on the insistence of the Fourth Estate.

By Thursday the negative press coverage reached a crescendo with headlines screaming: 'SHOW US YOU CARE', 'WHERE IS OUR QUEEN?', 'SPEAK TO US MA'AM'. Plans for the Queen and Duke to travel to London on the royal train on Saturday morning were abandoned. Urgent damage limitation meant they needed to fly down on Friday afternoon and to be seen to be reacting to the distraught crowds in the capital. Being forced to yield to pressure was, in Philip's mind, the Queen's greatest public humiliation.[8]

On the eve of their departure, Philip also suggested the family should once again attend a church service at nearby Crathie Kirk, where the minister Bob Sloan led prayers for Diana. On the way back to the castle the Queen and Duke, together with Charles, William and Harry, paused to read messages left with hundreds of floral tributes outside the entrance to the estate.

Returning to London, Philip was by the Queen's side during the tense walkabout outside Buckingham Palace, where there was an almost tangible sigh of relief from courtiers when the brooding crowd treated the couple with respect rather than abuse. Neither the Queen nor the Duke like to parade their emotions in public and there was a moment of exasperation from the Prince when a woman in the crowd urged the monarch 'to take care of the boys, Ma'am!' 'That's what we've been doing,' Philip interjected, repeating, 'That's what we've been doing!'[9]

Inside the palace, press officer Mary Francis noted the Queen and Philip 'spent a long time talking about what the mood was, and what was on people's minds, wanting to understand but not quite being able to be just out there and mingle and hear as private individuals'.[10]

By coincidence, the present author interviewed the Queen's cousin Margaret Rhodes at her home in Windsor Great Park, a few days after Diana's funeral to talk about the Queen and Philip's forthcoming Golden Wedding Anniversary. Before discussing the latter, and hearing I'd been in London covering Diana's funeral, Mrs Rhodes unexpectedly went off-piste with: 'Look what on earth's happening? Whatever is going on in London? I've never seen anything like it in my life. Why are people behaving like this?' She had been due to drive up to Balmoral to join the Queen and Duke and it was clear just how baffled those close to the couple were about the near-hysterical mood of the country and how much they wanted to try to offer some shred of comfort to Elizabeth and Philip.

Also on the Friday after Diana's death, Philip made a decision which, with the benefit of hindsight, may not have been wise for his grandsons. At the age of 76 there were no plans for him to walk behind Diana's coffin and both William and Harry were themselves reluctant to do so. He made the suggestion: 'If you don't walk, you may regret it later. I think you should do it. If I walk, will you walk with me?' The young princes readily agreed, although Harry in particular later regretted having to walk in front of thousands of sobbing members of the public and the lenses of hundreds of photographers and TV cameras.

Perhaps Philip's motivation was the thought of a rainy November day sixty years earlier when, as a 16-year-old, and after another tragic accident, he had chosen to walk in the funeral procession of his favourite sister Cécile, his brother-in-law and his two small nephews.

93

IS THERE ANYONE THERE? PART 1

One evening in the Coronation year of 1953, a medium called Lilian Bailey was led blindfolded into the drawing room of a Kensington mansion to give a reading to a group of clients. As usual she channelled her spirit guide, one William Hedley Wooton, whom she claimed had been a captain in the Grenadier Guards who had been killed at the Battle of Ypres.

After the reading was finished the blindfold was removed and Mrs Bailey was startled to see in front of her nearly every senior royal, led by the Queen, the Queen Mother, Prince Philip, his cousin Princess Marina, Duchess of Kent, with her son Edward, Duke of Kent, and his sister Princess Alexandra.[1]

The meeting came a year after the death of King George VI and it was said that the Queen Mother was apparently anxious to make some kind of contact with him. Similarly the Duchess of Kent had also been widowed when her husband, Prince George, was killed in an air crash in 1942, leaving her bereft and with three young children aged 6 and younger to look after.

It is believed that Lilian was recommended to the royals by Lionel Logue, the speech therapist credited with helping King George to overcome a chronic stammer, a story immortalised in the film *The King's Speech*. She was also known to Gillian Benson, a niece of the 3rd Earl of Dudley.

The Queen Mother was no stranger to the world of spiritualism since, according to family legend, her younger brother David Bowes Lyon was thought to have the power of second sight. When their brother Michael was reported missing, feared dead, during the First World War, David remained optimistic, claiming to have 'seen' him in a house surrounded by fir trees and with his head bandaged. David was proved right since Michael was eventually located as a prisoner of war.[2]

Biographer Christopher Wilson has found no proof that Bailey's spirit guide, William Wooton, ever existed on this side of the Great Divide and says that Bailey's claim to having been awarded an OBE can also be disproved.[3] Nevertheless, Queen Elizabeth went on to have other consultations with the medium and even gave her a brooch as a thank-you.[4]

The Queen Mother, Queen and Prince Philip are not the only members of the royal family to have had a brush with spiritualism. After the death of Prince Albert, Queen Victoria turned to a book called *New Philosophy: All About the Future*, which claimed that the spiritual journey continued after death. She also believed her beloved servant John Brown had second sight. Her daughter-in-law Queen Alexandra is said to have tried to contact her late husband, Edward VII, via a medium called John Sloan. Edward himself was a client of Count Louis Hamon, who used the name Cheiro, Europe's most celebrated medium and palmist. A favourite royal medium was Bertha Harris whose clients included Queen Mary, George VI and Edward VIII's lover, Wallis Simpson (presumably not at the same time!).

Nothing has ever emerged about what was revealed during any of the consultations, including the Kensington one attended by the Queen and Duke. Also, one can only guess at what Prince Philip said after listening to the dubious utterings of Lilian Bailey via her very questionable guide from the other world.

94

IS THERE ANYONE THERE? PART 2

It's not generally known that Prince Philip has had an interest in the paranormal, in particular UFOs, as far back as the beginning of the Queen's reign. The unusual hobby was first brought to light in a 2011 biography of the Prince. Author Philip Eade discovered that the Duke had been regular subscriber to *Flying Saucer Review.*[1]

In the late 1940s and early 1950s there was a spate of apparent UFO sightings, mainly in the USA, that were widely reported in the press. The Air Ministry had a 'UFO Desk' to record reports of interplanetary craft. Even the prime minister, Winston Churchill, was moved to write an excited memo to the secretary of state for air, Lord Cherwell: 'What does all this stuff about flying saucers amount to? What can it mean? What is the truth? Let me have a report at your convenience. WSC 28 July 1952.'[2]

Churchill wasn't the only member of the establishment concerned with it. Philip's uncle, Earl Mountbatten, wrote to his eldest daughter Patricia that he was convinced UFO's 'come from another planet' and that they 'were not "aeroplanes" with silly little almost human pilots but are themselves the actual inhabitants: Martians, Venusians, Jupiterians or what have you.' He even wrote a detailed report of a sighting over his own Broadlands estate witnessed by a retired British Army sergeant, one Frederick Briggs, who was working as a bricklayer on the estate and who 'says he saw a large craft that looked like a child's top hovering over a field. He says a column came down from the centre of the craft, and there appeared to be a humanoid figure descending with the pillar.' Mountbatten adds Briggs 'did not give the impression of being the sort of man who would be subject to hallucinations, or would in any way invent such a story'.[3]

The other influence on Philip's extraterrestrial beliefs was a member of his own household, Sir Peter Horsley, the Duke's equerry from 1949 to 1956. Horsley had been a deputy commander-in-chief of Strike Command during the war, someone whose honesty and integrity should have been in no doubt. Having said that, he was a man who was subject to the odd paranormal encounter. After his Mosquito was shot down during a mission, the recovering Horsley believed he had received messages from several of his fellow officers who were, in fact, all dead.[4]

The equerry clearly won Philip over to his point of view. The Duke asked him to follow up any credible reports of sightings and invited witnesses to Buckingham Palace to give their accounts personally. According to Eade, he even wrote to Timothy Good, a renowned Ufologist, pointing out 'there are many reasons to believe that they exist'.[5] It is unclear just how convinced the Prince was about UFOs or whether it was another example of his ever-inquiring mind keeping its options open.

Certainly Sir Peter Horsley drew the line at telling his boss about his meeting with a real-life alien at a flat in London. The extraterrestrial chap called himself 'Mr Janus' and said he could read minds. Horsley recalled in his memoirs, 'He didn't say he was a visitor from another planet – but I had that impression. I believe he was here to observe us. I never saw him again.'

During their meeting Mr Janus said he wanted to meet Prince Philip – whom he described as 'a man of great vision, a person of world renown, and a leader in the realm of wildlife and the environment. He is a man who believes strongly in the proper relationship between man and nature which will prove of great importance in future galactic harmony.'[6] (Even the most cynical reader would have to admit that if aliens do exist, they are pretty well clued up about the British royal family.)

Not all the establishment was as willing to consider Horsley's point of view as Prince Philip was. When Horsley's memoirs were published in 1997, a senior official at the Ministry of Defence commented, 'How unfortunate that the public will learn that the man who had his finger on the button of Strike Command was seeing little green men.'[7]

95

CARTOON CHARACTER

The Duke takes humour seriously. An inventory of his Buckingham Palace library at the time of his seventieth birthday showed he had collected 174 books of humour. Among them were several annuals by Carl Giles, the *Daily Express* cartoonist. There was also a copy of Osbert Lancaster's *Parkinson's Law*, for which Philip wrote the foreword ('You can get away with the most unpalatable truth if you can make it appear funny.').[1] Latterly he admired Matt, of the *Daily Telegraph*. In February 2018, Philip led tributes marking Matthew 'Matt' Pritchett's thirty years with the *Telegraph*. 'Successful cartoonists', wrote Philip, 'do not only need to be able to draw, they have to think of subjects to illustrate. Matt has shown that he has a genius for both, as well as the ability to think of wonderfully appropriate swipes at the idiocies of contemporary life.'[2] When Philip retired in August 2017, Matt drew a sketch of curtains and a cord opened to reveal a disc on the wall carrying the message 'Unveil Your Own Damn Plaque'.

The seventieth birthday inventory tells us that Philip, who for many years was patron of London's Cartoon Museum, himself owned 197 original cartoons, many of which bravely take the mickey out of him. Most of them are displayed in private royal lavatories throughout the various estates, thereby allowing the Duke the last laugh.

96

CRY FREEDOM

One of the benefits of being the long-lived consort of a popular monarch is the gradual accumulation of freedoms or citizenships of towns and cities. Prince Philip has around twenty of them scattered across the globe.

In June 1948 he received the Freedom of the City of London. It was of course only three years since the end of the war and in a poignant speech he looked back on his war service and said:

> In every kind of human activity there are those who lead and those who follow … I would like to accept the Freedom of this City, not only for myself, but for all those millions who followed during the Second World War. Our only distinction is that we did what we were told to do, to the very best of our ability, and kept on doing it.

By the time he received the Freedom of the City of Glasgow in 1955 he had honed his bantering style of public speaking and joked: 'The ceremony is full of charm and dignity unlike the ownership of Glasgow which I understand can be obtained with a couple of drinks any Saturday night.' A remark greeted with thunderous civic applause rather than a Glasgow kiss.

In the UK the Duke has received the freedom of London (1948), Greenwich (1948), Edinburgh (1949), Belfast (1949), Cardiff (1954), Glasgow (1955), Windsor and Maidenhead (1995). His Commonwealth 'freedoms' are Melbourne (1956), Calgary (1959), Dar es Salaam (1961), Nairobi (1963), Bridgetown (1964) and Perth (2012). He has three non-Commonwealth 'freedoms': Guadalajara (1964), Acapulco (1964) and Los Angeles (1966). In addition he has the citizenship of Montevideo (1962) and of Chicago (1966).

He seems to have done rather well with US territories since he is also a deputy sheriff of Harris County, Texas, and an honorary deputy sheriff of Los Angeles County.

Perhaps his most impressive, and least expected, title is that of Grand Commander of the Order of Maritime Merit of the San Francisco Port Authority (1968).

97

FUN PHIL FACTS

- The Duke carried out 22,219 solo engagements between the Queen's accession in 1952 and his retirement in 2017.
- He gave 5,496 speeches over the same sixty-five years.
- He carried out 637 overseas visits on his own as well as attending all the Queen's overseas state visits and Commonwealth visits.
- On a visit to the Francis Crick Institute, a major biomedical research centre developing ways of preventing and treating

serious infections, Philip revealed he hadn't had flu for the past forty years.
- He has sat for some 220 portraits.
- He gained his RAF wings in 1953, his helicopter wings in 1956 and his private pilot's licence in 1959.
- He flew fifty-nine types of aircraft in forty-four years.
- He gave up flying in 1997 aged 76, having completed 5,986 hours of flying time.
- His mother's childhood name for him was 'Bubbikins'. She even addressed a letter to 'Dear Bubby-kins' in 1965 when she was 80 and he was 44.
- In his eightieth year he carried out 559 engagements.
- After Edmund Hilary and Tenzing Norgay succeeded in climbing Mount Everest on 29 May 1953 the expedition leader Sir John Hunt brought out the expedition rum and first of all toasted the patron of the expedition, the Duke of Edinburgh.[1]
- The only area of land he owns in his own right are a few acres near Wood Farm in Norfolk.[2]
- The Duke designed the stained-glass windows in the new private chapel at Windsor Castle during the restoration of the state apartments following the 1992 fire.
- Former royal footman Charles Oliver revealed the Duke always takes his electric glass-lidded frying pan with him so that he can make his own fried breakfast.
- He also sometimes rustled up a mean late-night scrambled eggs and smoked haddock for the Queen after the kitchen staff have left, and he has been known to pluck and clean the snipe he'd shot that day.[3]
- A keen amateur painter himself, Philip always gives the artists he sits for the third degree. Royal portrait painter Richard Stone, who has painted Philip three times, recalls, 'the Duke is the only sitter who will rummage through my paintbox talking about oil colour and asking questions about colour mixes.'

Richard Stone's 2001 oil portrait of the Duke of Edinburgh.
(© Richard Stone)

- The Prince also told Richard Stone that when he was engaged to Princess Elizabeth and staying with the royal family at Windsor Castle he would get up in the night and wander around the state apartments with a torch admiring the pictures. Says Stone, 'I like to think of him creeping around the castle in the dark to see all the Gainsboroughs and van Dycks.'[4]

- The Duke took up playing polo while he was stationed in Malta from 1949 to 1951. Arthritis in his hands forced him to retire at fifty in 1971. At the time his handicap was 5.
- He then took up competition carriage driving. He won one World Team Gold as a member of the British team. His best individual place in a championship was sixth.
- The Duke is entitled to a forty-one-gun salute from the King's Troop Royal Horse Artillery on his birthday, 10 June.
- According to art historian Roy Strong, when Margaret Thatcher became prime minister, her husband Denis asked the Duchess of Kent to arrange a meeting for him with Philip to talk about their three-steps-behind role of consort.[5]
- The Duke's Standard reflects his multinational background. Consisting of four quarters, it features the three lions and hearts from the Danish royal coat of arms, the white cross on a blue background from the Greek national flag and white stripes from the Battenberg coat of arms. The fourth quarter depicts Edinburgh Castle.
- Philip became the longest-serving consort of a British sovereign on 17 April 2009 when he outlived Charlotte of Mecklenburg-Strelitz, who was the consort of George III for fifty-seven years and fifty days.
- He is the oldest surviving great-great-grandchild of Queen Victoria and Prince Albert.
- Prince Philip is the longest-living British royal male in history. He is the third longest-lived British royal personage after his mother-in-law, the Queen Mother, who lived until she was 101 years and 238 days. The record for oldest British royal ever is held by the Queen's aunt, Princess Alice, Dowager Duchess of Gloucester, who lived until she was 102 years and 309 days.

98

MY HUSBAND AND I

It was an unlikely match. He was an outspoken, fast-driving jack the lad with a girl in every port who relished his freedom. She was the methodical, organised, dutiful princess who never rocked the boat and whose only contact with the opposite sex was during an eightsome reel at Balmoral.

He came from a broken home after his parents separated when he was 9. Hers was an ultra-tight unit, labelled 'us four' by her devoted papa.

Their love was a slow-burning one that had developed through letter-writing over six years of wartime separation, and then more frequent meetings as the conflict subsided and Philip returned from sea. What he lacked was a home and the stability of family life. What she needed was stimulation, a link with the outside world, someone to broaden her horizons and to give her a glimpse of life outside the rarefied atmosphere of court life.

When their relationship finally blossomed during the summer of 1946, the couple gave few clues away, even to those close to them. Peter Ashmore, the King's equerry, recalled Philip's three-week stay at Balmoral, when the couple came to what Philip called 'an understanding'. Ashmore noted: 'They certainly did not drool over each over. They scarcely held hands.'[1] That was hardly a surprise, since Philip had never been shown much affection from Prince and Princess Andrew. Growing up at a time when hugs and embraces between parents and children were hardly ever the norm, his own situation was exacerbated by his mother's long absence in sanatoria and her later self-isolation during her recovery and his father's removal

The look of love: The Queen and Duke share a private moment before setting off for Royal Ascot in their carriage procession. (© Ian Lloyd)

from the scene when he moved to Monte Carlo with his mistress. Elizabeth, the ever-dutiful daughter, had had public emotion trained out of her at an early age, particularly by her emotionally constrained grandmother Queen Mary.

Mike Parker recalled trying to encourage Philip to show some kind of public affection to his wife: 'He doesn't wear his heart on his sleeve,' Parker commented in a 1992 interview:

> I always wanted to see him put his arms around the Queen, and show her how much he adored her. What you'd do for any wife. But he always sort of stood to attention. I mentioned it to him a couple of times. But he just gave me a hell of a look.[2]

Both of them were, and would remain, overshadowed by the two greatest showmen the royal family had nurtured: the

Queen Mother, who adored her every public appearance, and Dickie Mountbatten, Philip's vainglorious and ambitious uncle.

Love and marriage did help both of them to evolve. Elizabeth was emotionally controlled and the fact he wasn't all over her was something she quite liked. What Philip gave her was excitement and a huge contrast with a deferential royal household and chinless aristocrats who had followed the traditional Eton College, Guards Officer path to adulthood. Philip's childhood traumas had given him almost impenetrable defence barriers. He was unable to cope with intimacy and warmth but, as Lady Mountbatten reflected: 'Philip had a capacity for love which was waiting to be unlocked and Elizabeth unlocked it.'[3] His passion was clear in a letter to his new mother-in-law written shortly after the wedding. 'Cherish Lilibet? I wonder if that word is enough to express what is in me?' He felt Elizabeth was 'the only "thing" in this world which is absolutely real to me'. He ends the letter, 'very humbly, I thank God for Lilibet and for us'.[4] Elizabeth was similarly enamoured, writing to her parents from Scotland that she and her new husband 'behave as though we had belonged to each other for years! Philip is an angel.'[5]

Their two happiest years were spent on the island of Malta where Philip was stationed from 1949 to 1951 and where Elizabeth spent several lengthy visits, taking on the life of an officer's wife and basing herself at Villa Guardamangia, owned by the Mountbattens.

During their Malta years Philip's career advanced. He was promoted to lieutenant commander and was given command of HMS *Magpie*. Meanwhile, back in the UK, the couple had moved into the refurbished Clarence House where Philip was very much the *pater familias,* in charge of the decision-making and head of their small family.

All this changed with the death of the King on 6 February 1952. As we have seen, within twelve months Philip had to cope with leaving the navy, being ostracised by courtiers and politicians who would only deal with the young Queen and the almighty snub of not being able to pass on his Mountbatten surname to his children.

As Lady Mountbatten's husband John Brabourne noticed, since his marriage Philip's 'life changed completely. He gave up everything.'[6] His strategy henceforth was to carve a niche for himself. He became obsessed, in his own words, with making 'a sensible contribution'. In the decades ahead he would take on almost 800 patronages and very much ran the private estates of Balmoral and Sandringham as well as being Ranger of Windsor Great Park. Elizabeth also ensured that while she was head of the country, he was head of the family, making key decisions about the children's futures. The Queen grew resigned to his determination to excel in his own areas, joking in their late forties: 'I gave up trying to stop him years ago.'[7]

Philip's frustration with his subordinate role and his annoyance that, in the early days of her reign, his dutiful wife slavishly followed the wishes of the palace old guard and Winston Churchill, led him to occasional bursts of temper. These were witnessed by courtiers, friends and relations. 'He could be brutal,' recalled a former member of staff who heard him berate the Queen. 'Don't talk such rubbish' or 'You're completely wrong' were typical slights.[8]

The Queen's cousin Margaret Rhodes recalled Philip's disconcerting habit of jumping down people's throats. 'He was like that with the Queen. He'd say "why the bloody hell?" "what the bloody hell?" I think she did find it disconcerting.'[9] Philip's uncle, Earl Mountbatten, who liked to think of himself as Elizabeth's knight in shining armour, also witnessed a Philip outburst against his wife. He was a backseat passenger when Philip was driving the three of them around Cowdrey Park at breakneck speed. As he approached each bend at full throttle the Queen kept giving a sharp intake of breath. Philip shouted: 'If you do that once more, I'll put you out of the car!' When they were safely on *terra firma* Mountbatten asked Elizabeth why she let his nephew talk to her like that. 'But you heard what he said,' explained the Queen, 'and he meant it.' Lady Pamela Hicks later commented, laughingly, 'My father couldn't believe what he'd heard.'[10]

Deep down, the Prince was aware he could occasionally make hurtful comments. To a family friend he once made the revealing comment: 'I don't seem able to say nice things to people, though I'd like to. Why is that?'[11]

In the early days the Queen, aware of the huge sacrifice Philip had made, tolerated his outbursts. After all, he had not only given up a promising naval career but also turned his back on a life lived without press intrusion and the restrictions of court life. 'She would clam up and wouldn't fight back,' recalled a close friend. 'It was very much like that in the first ten or fifteen years of their married life.'[12]

What he did give the Queen, right from the beginning, was his total support. Mike Parker recalled: 'He told me the first day he offered me a job, that his job, first, second and last, was never to let her down.'[13]

The Duke always knew the Queen is not a natural performer in public as her mother was, and on hundreds of walkabouts while Elizabeth made polite chit chat with the crowds it is Philip who always bantered with them. When he spotted a small child clutching flowers for the monarch, he'd often lift the youngster over the crush barriers himself and direct them to the Queen. He has been known to shout 'back off' (and other four-letter instructions) to photographers getting too close to her and to ease tension with the odd joke or too. When the Queen was about to be waylaid by one of her most persistent male fans loaded down with gifts for the monarch outside a Norfolk church, Philip could be heard muttering: 'There he goes again, blather, blather, blather.'

In private he is notably deferential to the Queen. Guests at Balmoral Castle have noted how he pours a drink for the Queen, handing it to her with a 'here you are darling' aside. Once he was unavoidably detained and arrived for dinner after her. An equerry was astonished to see him formally bow and apologise: 'I'm very sorry I'm late.'[14]

The arrival of Elizabeth and Philip's 'second family' – Andrew in 1960 and Edward in 1964 – heralded a new phase in the marriage. The Queen was now a decade into her role as head of state. She was more confident in her approach to dealing with ministers and private secretaries and the authoritarian Alan Lascelles and Winston Churchill had long since left office. On 8 February 1960, eleven days before the birth of Prince Andrew, the Queen issued an Order-in-Council stating that that she and her family would be known as the House of Windsor but that her descendants would take the name Mountbatten-Windsor. It corrected what Philip had felt to be the huge personal snub from eight years before when she confirmed she and her descendants would be known as the House of Windsor, thereby stopping Philip from giving his surname to his own children and eventual grandchildren. The prime minister, Harold Macmillan, noted: 'The Queen only wishes (properly enough) to do something to please her husband – with whom she is desperately in love.' Deeply suspicious of Philip and his uncle, the prime minister added, 'what upsets me ... is the Prince's almost brutal attitude to the Queen over all this.' He added cryptically: 'I shall never forget what she said to me that Sunday night at Sandringham.'[15] Macmillan wasn't the only insider to witness Elizabeth's clear adoration of her husband. A senior courtier during these same years recalled: 'She was quite definitely in love with Philip.'[16]

Philip himself inadvertently gave a clue to their intimacy when he fact-checked a manuscript by biographer Tim Heald. The author wrote: 'It was generally known that at the Palace the royal couple had separate bedrooms.' In the margin the Prince scrawled: 'wrongly.'[17] Another glimpse of their physical intimacy in the 1960s came from Chief Petty Officer William Evans, head of Mountbatten's personal staff at Broadlands, the Earl's Hampshire mansion where Elizabeth and Philip had honeymooned some fifteen years earlier. Evans recalled the Queen, then in her mid-thirties, screaming with laughter and shouting 'Stop it! Philip, stop it, stop it stop it!' as Philip ran after her, pinching her bottom repeatedly and growling: 'Get up there, girl, get up there.'[18]

The Prince's cheeky approach to his wife (every pun intended) was reminiscent of an earlier anecdote from the time his cousin Patricia Knatchbull said she'd only just realised what a lovely complexion Elizabeth had. At which point Philip piped up, 'Yes and she's like that all over!'[19]

By then the Queen was beginning to answer her husband back more. Former private secretary Martin Charteris later commented, 'Prince Philip is the only man in the world who treats the Queen simply as another human being. And of course it's not unknown for the Queen to tell Prince Philip to shut up. Because she's the Queen that's not something she can easily say to anybody else.'[20]

As with many couples they agreed on the big things but squabbled on the minor ones. One former courtier told biographer Graham Turner, 'he and the Queen have phenomenal rows', but that they soon blow over: 'There's a terrific mutual tongue-lashing and then they end up the best of friends.'[21]

In the tight-knit palace environment some of these rows inevitably happened in front of members of the household. Martin Charteris recalled one on the royal yacht *Britannia* when the

Queen declared: 'I'm not going to come out of my cabin until he's in a better temper. I'm going to sit here on my bed until he's better.'[22] On other occasions her technique is to throw up a smokescreen when he is in a mood. By changing the subject or talking in riddles she confuses him, throws him off guard, as he prefers straightforward arguing to such a cryptic approach.[23]

Among those they trust, the Queen has often been able to poke fun at her husband, whether he's there or not. Susan Crosland, wife of the then foreign secretary, Anthony Crosland, later wrote about accompanying the Queen and Duke on the royal yacht during their 1976 state visit to the USA. *Britannia* was caught in a storm off the American coast and the Queen joked: 'I have *never* seen so many grey and grim faces round a dinner table. Philip was not at all well.' She paused before adding, 'I'm glad to say', and started giggling. Susan Crosland realised: 'I'd forgotten her consort is an Admiral of the Fleet.'[24]

In November 2017 the royal couple marked their Platinum Wedding Anniversary. The same year the Duke retired from public duties and based himself at Wood Farm on the Sandringham estate while the Queen carried on her usual round of engagements. Philip once said the secret of a happy married life was for each partner to pursue their own interests. They remained a rock-solid team and, as Lady Pamela Hicks commented: 'What is so lovely is that they are still so much in love with each other.' The Queen lights up when he's around, when he walks into a room or when he pays her a compliment. Once her dress designer, the late Ian Thomas, was making some adjustments to the hemline of her dress, when Philip happened to walk past the open door and he said: 'Hmh, nice dress.' Thomas said the Queen 'flushed scarlet' at the compliment.[25] They haven't completely softened with old age. 'They are not a sweet "Darby and Joan"', says Lady Pamela. 'They're both *very* strong characters.'[26]

The Queen, resplendent in a golden silk dress, arrives with Philip for a celebratory concert at the Royal Festival Hall on the eve of their Golden Wedding Anniversary, 19 November 1997. (© Ian Lloyd)

In the two decades since the deaths of her mother and sister in the spring of 2002, Elizabeth has relied on him even more as the touchstone for the values she grew up with: duty, self-sacrifice, service to Queen and country. They speak every day on the telephone from wherever they happened to be. During the lockdown in spring 2020 Philip left Wood Farm and joined the Queen at Windsor and, over the summer, at Balmoral. It was the longest the two have been together apart from their early tours and their time in Malta as a young naval couple.

Neither of them likes to share their private thoughts about their marriage with the outside world. There was one notable exception. At the time of the Golden Wedding in November 1997, three months after the death of Diana had rocked the monarchy to its core, they paid a tribute to each other in their speeches. On the eve of the anniversary Prince Philip said:

> The main lesson that we have learned is that tolerance is the one essential ingredient of any happy marriage … It may not be quite so important when things are going well, but it is absolutely vital when the going gets difficult. You can take it from me that the Queen has the quality of tolerance in abundance.

The Queen paid a more tangible tribute to her husband to mark his ninetieth birthday. She gave him the title of Lord High Admiral, a position only ever held by the sovereign. For the man who had given up his own promising career to help support her for the rest of his life it was a touching gesture and one that apparently moved him close to tears.

99

QUIPS, GAFFES AND BANTER: THE DUKE'S MEMORABLE CLANGERS 91-100

.... JUST GENERALLY RUDE

91 When Chief Anyaoku, then Secretary-General of the Commonwealth, arrived for a reception at Buckingham Palace wearing full traditional Nigerian robes, Philip laughed and said, '*You look like you're ready for bed.*'

92 Introduced to Stephen Judge, a guest at a palace garden party who had a small, well-sculpted beard. '*What do you do?*' asked Philip. '*I'm a designer, sir,*' replied Mr Judge. '*Well, you're obviously not a hirsute designer,*' the Prince said, adding for good measure: '*Well, you didn't design your beard too well, did you? If you are going to grow a beard, grow a beard. You really must try harder.*'

93 To the author's great-uncle who, asked by the Duke how he got to work each day, said, '*I cross the Manchester Ship Canal in a ferry,*' to which the Duke responded: '*What's the matter, can't you swim?*'

94 A pre-Meghan Markle quip in 2000, '*People think there's a rigid class system here, but dukes have even been known to marry chorus girls. Some have even married Americans.*'

95 Talking about fire alarms in 1998 to a woman who had lost two children in a fire, '*They're a damn nuisance – I've got one in my bathroom and every time I run a bath the steam sets it off.*'

96 Double standards: To a hunt saboteur who admitted to eating meat, *'It's like saying adultery is alright as long as you don't enjoy it!'*

97 Children: To 13-year-old Andrew Adams who very much hoped to go into space one day, *'You could do with losing a bit of weight.'*

98 Blood sports: The Duke was not impressed with claims that those who slaughter meat have a greater moral authority than those who take part in blood sports, *'I don't think a prostitute is more moral than a wife, but they are doing the same thing.'*

99 The younger generation: At a ceremony for the Duke of Edinburgh Awards honouring some of the country's finest young achievers, *'Young people are the same as they always were. They are just as ignorant.'*

100 Malta: During the 2007 royal visit to an engaged couple in their thirties: *'How long have you two been at it?'*

100

I DID IT MY WAY

Trying to get Prince Philip to comment meaningfully on his legacy has defeated all his biographers and interviewers.

Half a century ago, writer Basil Boothroyd asked him: 'What are your proudest achievements?' Fifty-year-old Philip retorted: 'I doubt whether I've achieved anything likely to be remembered.' At 70 he told Tim Heald, 'I am not really interested in what goes on my tombstone.'

Aged 80 he was deeply depressed about the state of the monarchy. According to one friend, he felt 'that everything he has tried

Philip with the Queen, Charles and William at the 2001 Braemar Games. The Duke's influence on Elizabeth II and two future monarchs will be very much at the heart of his legacy. (© Ian Lloyd)

to put into it is disintegrating before his eyes. What has happened over the past ten years [i.e. the 1990s – with the 'annus horribilis' of 1992, the 'war of the Waleses' and the death of Diana] has caused him more grief and anxiety than anything else.'[1]

Ten years later and even TV newsreader Fiona Bruce, at her most unctuous, failed to elicit anything positive from the Duke, whose first answer was an unequivocal: 'I didn't want to do this interview.' He managed to dismiss his ninety years on the planet in a series of staccato negatives – traumatic childhood: 'I don't try to psychoanalyse myself'; lack of a teenage family home: 'It was no great deal. I just lived my life', and his best chance of immortality, the DofE Award: 'I've no reason to be proud.'

One thing he has agreed on is his lack of fondness for the ageing process, something he flippantly refers to as 'anno domini'. At 50 he vowed he didn't want to live to be 80. At 80, watching the seemingly eternal Queen Mother, still appearing in public in her centenary year, he declared: 'God, I don't want to live to be 100. I can't imagine anything worse.' Quite how he felt as his own ten-decade milestone loomed is anyone's guess.

Queen Elizabeth and the late King were of course a hard act to follow for both the Queen and Duke, and for Philip there was that irritatingly over-productive forebear, Prince Albert, who left a daunting array of achievements from concocting the Great Exhibition to designing Balmoral Castle.

The Duke's own contribution to the family firm is more than he could ever have imagined. As the Queen herself said on the day of their Golden Wedding in 1997: 'I, and his whole family, and this and many other countries, owe him a debt greater than he would ever claim, or we shall ever know.' On his role in the monarchy he did once grudgingly admit: 'All I'll say is that I've tried to help keep it going while I've been here.'

As we've seen, he's helped more than 800 organisations as a more than hands-on patron, president, colonel etc., including his eponymous award scheme.

He has been the Queen's 'strength and stay', as she put it, in what has been the most public marriage in the world, and unlike some of his more libidinous and morally bankrupt overseas royal contemporaries, he has failed to mire the House of Windsor with scandal or corruption. Of course critics will highlight the trail of destruction caused by his 'dontopedalogy' – which he defined as 'the science of opening your mouth and putting your foot in it'. A percentage of his so-called gaffes are jaw-droppingly rude, but most have been taken well by the recipients, or blown out of proportion by thrilled journalists and by an increasingly politically correct and ready-to-be-outraged world.

His role as a father has also had mixed results. His tough-love approach alienated the sensitive young Charles, who sought solace with his grandmother Queen Elizabeth, though he proved a fine role model for the more resilient Anne. His indulgence of Andrew and Edward, neither of whom were to be high achievers like their father or models of diligence like their mother, has had its repercussions over the years. Edward's involvement with *It's a Royal Knockout* was a low point for the monarchy but a tiny blip compared with Andrew's baffling, ill-advised, friendship with Jeffrey Epstein.

We've seen how he tried to help his daughters-in-law Diana and Sarah until both went too far – Diana with her *Panorama* interview and Fergie with her topless, toe-sucking debacle. He is hugely popular with all eight of his grandchildren and it's a shame he wasn't playing an active role in the royal family's future at the time of Harry and Meghan's decision to move abroad. The Duke left Sandringham moments before Harry arrived for the summit with the Queen, Charles and William that would decide his future relationship with the family firm. His unwillingness to meet the grandson he had, not so long before, admired for his war record and his charity work including the Invictus Games, was a definite snub to the younger Prince. After all Philip, had spent the best part of seven decades sublimating his own desires and ambitions to those of his wife and the monarchy. Harry's decision to throw in the towel in search of personal goals, was, according to one family friend, 'for his grandpa hugely disappointing and a dereliction of duty.'[2]

Like the Sussexes, Prince Philip has grown to detest the media. In their case it was for personal attacks or encroaching photographers; for the Duke it was the resulting trivialisation of the monarchy that has upset him the most. While Harry and Meghan are fixated by themselves, the Duke resolutely refuses to reflect publicly on his life: 'I am not going to write an autobiography,' he once said. 'I don't spend a lot of time looking back.'[3]

Inevitably the media will spend a lot of time looking back over the next few years. There will be page after page about his outspokenness and his private life, but the newspapers know their readership well, and also know that, at grassroots level, the Duke of Edinburgh has many fans and admirers. They know that he has embodied the old-fashioned virtues of duty, self-sacrifice and service, quite literally, to Queen and country. His Second World War contemporaries would regard it all as second nature, along with the joshing sense of humour, so loved by Philip, that boosted morale. Like them, and the Queen, he is the last of a truly remarkable generation.

NOTES

1. Born with Two Birthdays
1 Judd, Denis, *Prince Philip: A Biography* (Michael Joseph, 1980) p50

2. 'My Place of Rest'
1 Yugoslavia, HM Queen Alexandra of, *Prince Philip: A Family Portrait* (Hodder & Stoughton, 1960) p31
2 Ibid.pp31–2
3 Brandreth, Gyles, *Philip and Elizabeth: Portrait of a Marriage* (Century, 2004) p57
4 Boothroyd, Basil, *Prince Philip: An Informal Biography* (McCall, 1971) p143
5 Sinclair, Marianne (ed.), *The Wit & Wisdom of the Royal Family* (Plexus, 1990) p35

4. A Slice of Battenburg
1 *The Life and Times of Lord Mountbatten*, Associated-Rediffusion Television, 1968, Episode 1
2 Ziegler, Philip, *Mountbatten: The Official Biography* (Collins, 1985) p24
3 *Life and Times of Lord Mountbatten*, Episode 1
4 Vickers, Hugo, *Alice: Princess Andrew of Greece* (Hamish Hamilton, 2000) p7
5 Warwick, Christopher, *Ella: Princess Saint and Martyr* (Wiley, 2006) p312
6 Lady Pamela Hicks, telephone interview, 15 November 2019
7 Ziegler, *Mountbatten*, p24
8 Lady Pamela Hicks, telephone interview, 15 November 2019
9 Smith, Charles, *Lord Mountbatten: His Butler's Story* (Stein and Day, 1980) p35ff
10 Eade, Philip, *Young Prince Philip* (Harper Press, 2011) p30

5. Phil the Greek
1 *Daily Telegraph* 18 July 2018
2 Rocco, Fiammetta, 'A Strange Life: Profile of Prince Philip', *Independent* 13 December 1992

3 Ibid

6. Paris and a Bohemian Aunt
1 Bertin, Celia, *Marie Bonaparte: A Life* (Harcourt Brace Jovanovich, 1982) p18
2 Ibid.pp85–6
3 Ibid.p94
4 Vickers, Hugo, *Alice: Princess Andrew of Greece* (Hamish Hamilton, 2000) p358
5 Bertin, *Marie Bonaparte* p36
6 Ibid.p92
7 Ibid.p97
8 Ibid.p235

7. Baby Steps in Britain
1 Hough, Richard, *Louis and Victoria: The Family History of the Mountbattens*, 2nd edn (Weidenfeld & Nicolson, 1984) p171
2 Court Circular, *The Times* 19 December 1922

8. Family Tragedy No. 1
1 *The Queen's Mother-in-Law*, Channel 4, 2012
2 Ibid

9. First Meeting
1 *Aberdeen Press and Journal* 3 December 1934
2 Eade, Philip, *Young Prince Philip: His Turbulent Early Life* (Harper Press, 2012) p101

11. No Fixed Abode
1 *Daily Telegraph* 21 May 2001
2 Brandreth, Gyles, *Philip and Elizabeth: Portrait of a Marriage* (Century, 2004) p68
3 Eade, Philip, *Young Prince Philip: His Turbulent Early Life* (Harper Press, 2012) p103
4 *Daily Telegraph* 21 May 2001
5 Ibid
6 Yugoslavia, HM Queen Alexandra of, *Prince Philip: A Family Portrait* (Hodder & Stoughton, 1960) p60

7 Brandreth, *Philip and Elizabeth* p176
8 *Daily Telegraph* 21 May 2001
9 Ibid
10 Yugoslavia, HM Queen Alexandra of, *Prince Philip* p102

12. Not a Hard Act to Follow
1 *Evening Telegraph and Post* 17 December 1935
2 *Aberdeen Press and Journal* 2 August 1935
3 Brandreth, Gyles, *Philip and Elizabeth: Portrait of a Marriage* (Century, 2004) p330

13. Family Tragedy No. 2
1 Eade, Philip, *Young Prince Philip: His Turbulent Early Life* (Harper Press, 2011) pxvii
2 Ibid.pxix
3 Brandreth, Gyles, *Philip and Elizabeth: Portrait of a Marriage* (Century 2004) p71

14. The Nazi Link
1 Brandreth, Gyles, *Philip and Elizabeth: Portrait of a Marriage* (Century, 2004) p72
2 Parker, John, *Prince Philip: His Secret Life* (St Martin's Press, 1990) p53
3 Petropoulos, Jonathan, *Royals and the Reich: The Princes von Hessen in Nazi Germany* (Oxford University Press, 2006) p114
4 Heald, Tim, *The Duke: A Portrait of Prince Philip* (Hodder & Stoughton, 1991) pp42–3
5 *Prince Philip: The Plot to Make a King*, Channel 4, 2015
6 Petropoulos, *Royals and the Reich* p248
7 Ibid.p4
8 Ibid.p102
9 Ibid.pp278–9
10 Parker, *Prince Philip* pp104–5

15. Girls, Girls, Girls
1 Yugoslavia, HM Queen Alexandra of, *Prince Philip: A Family Portrait* (Hodder & Stoughton, 1960) p62
2 Ibid.p77
3 Heald, Tim, *The Duke: A Portrait of*

Prince Philip (Hodder & Stoughton, 1991) p69
4 Brandreth, Gyles, *Philip and Elizabeth: Portrait of a Marriage* (Century, 2004) p164
5 Ibid.
6 Yugoslavia, HM Queen Alexandra of, *Prince Philip* p63
7 Eade, Philip, *Young Prince Philip: His Turbulent Early Life* (Harper Press, 2012) p121
8 *Daily Telegraph* 31 October 2011

16. First Love
1 Baring, Sarah, *The Road to Station X* (Wilton 65, 2004) p35
2 McKay, Sinclair, *The Secret Life of Bletchley Park* (Aurum Press, 2010) p172
3 Eade, Philip, *Young Prince Philip: His Turbulent Early Life* (Harper Press, 2012) p144
4 *Daily Telegraph* 28 March 2011
5 Eade, *Young Prince Philip* p144
6 Ibid.p145
7 Ibid.p146
8 De Courcy, Anne, *Debs at War: How Wartime Changed Their Lives* (Weidenfeld & Nicolson, 2005) p105
9 *Daily Telegraph* 15 February 2013
10 Eade, *Young Prince Philip* p159
11 Ibid.p147

17. A Practical Joker
1 Eade, Philip, *Young Prince Philip: His Turbulent Early Life* (Harper Press, 2012) p49
2 Brandreth, Gyles, *Philip and Elizabeth: Portrait of a Marriage* (Century, 2004) p17
3 Yugoslavia, HM Queen Alexandra of, *Prince Philip: A Family Portrait* (Hodder & Stoughton, 1960) p39
4 Ibid.p56
5 *Daily Telegraph* 21 May 2001
6 Pimlott, Ben, *The Queen* (HarperCollins, 2001) p171
7 Paxman, Jeremy, *On Royalty* (Penguin, 2007) p235
8 *Daily Telegraph* 22 May 2001

18. Breaking and Entering
1 Dean, John, *HRH Prince Philip, Duke of Edinburgh* (Robert Hale, 1954) pp45–6
2 Wharfe, Inspector Ken, *Diana: Closely Guarded Secret* (Michael O'Mara, 2002) p102
3 Parker, Eileen, *Step Aside For Royalty* (Bachman & Turner, 1982) p48
4 Ibid.p81

19. It's Not for Me, It's for a Friend
1 Boothroyd, Basil, *Prince Philip: An Informal Biography* (McCall, 1971) p50
2 Ibid.
3 Email from Tracey Trussell, M BIG (Dip), 29 April 2020
4 Lady Pamela Hicks, telephone interview, January 2020
5 Sacks, David, *The Alphabet: Unraveling the Mystery of the Alphabet from A to Z* (Arrow Books, 2004) p165
6 Leslie, Ann, *Killing My Own Snakes: A Memoir* (Pan Books, 2009) pp369–70
7 *Daily Telegraph* 21 May 2001

21. Two Degrees of Separation
1 Aston, Sir George, *His Royal Highness the Duke of Connaught and Strathearn* (George G. Harrap, 1929) p31
2 *Dundee Evening Telegraph* 23 January 1942

22. For Queen and Country
1 Brandreth, Gyles, *Philip and Elizabeth: Portrait of a Marriage* (Century, 2004)

23. Naval Hero
1 Eade, Philip, *Young Prince Philip: His Turbulent Early Life* (Harper Press, 2012) p136
2 Boothroyd, Basil, *Prince Philip: An Informal Biography* (McCall, 1971) p128ff
3 'Prince Philip Reveals His Role In Royal Navy's WWII Battle of Cape Matapan for First Time', *Huffington Post* 17 April 2012 www.huffingtonpost.co.uk/2012/04/17/prince-philip-royal-navy-battle-cape-matapan-world-war-two_n_1430568.html

4 Boothroyd, *Prince Philip* p129
5 Eade, *Young Prince Philip* p137
6 Heald, Tim, *The Duke: A Portrait of Prince Philip* (Hodder & Stoughton, 1991) p64
7 Yugoslavia, HM Queen Alexandra of, *Prince Philip: A Family Portrait* (Hodder & Stoughton, 1960) p70
8 Eade, *Young Prince Philip* p200

24. 1945: The Final Surrender
1 *A Right Royal Rescue*, BBC Radio 4, 27 January 2006
2 Lee, Arthur S. Gould, *The Royal House of Greece* (Ward Lock & Co., 1948) p279
3 Ibid.
4 *Prince Philip: The War Years*, BBC1, 19 August 1995

25. The Moment They Clicked
1 Crawford, Marion, *The Little Princesses* (Duckworth, 1993) pp85–6
2 Ibid.p85
3 Yugoslavia, HM Queen Alexandra of, *Prince Philip: A Family Portrait* (Hodder & Stoughton, 1960) p75
4 Ibid.
5 Shawcross, William, *Queen Elizabeth the Queen Mother: The Official Biography* (Macmillan, 2009) p578
6 Eade, Philip, *Young Prince Philip: His Turbulent Early Life* (Harper Press, 2012) p154
7 Shawcross, *Queen Elizabeth* p578

26. Pathway to Love
1 Pearson, John, *The Ultimate Family: The Making of the Royal House of Windsor* (Michael Joseph, 1986) pp81–2
2 James, Robert Rhodes, *Chips: The Diaries of Sir Henry Channon* (Penguin, 1970) pp350–1
3 Boothroyd, Basil, *Prince Philip: An Informal Biography* (McCall, 1971) p17
4 Yugoslavia, HM Queen Alexandra of, *Prince Philip: A Family Portrait* (Hodder & Stoughton, 1960) p72
5 Rhodes, Margaret, *The Final Curtsey* (Umbria Press, 2001) p69

6 Ellis, Jennifer (ed.), *Thatched with Gold: The Memoir of Mabell, Countess of Airlie* (Hutchinson, 1962) p227
7 Bradford, Sarah, *George VI* (Weidenfeld & Nicolson, 1989) p420
8 Ibid.p421
9 Ziegler, Philip (ed.), *Personal Diary of Admiral the Lord Louis Mountbatten, 1943–1946* (Collins, 1988) p125
10 James, *Chips* p483
11 Pimlott, Ben, *The Queen* (HarperCollins, 2001) p97
12 Ibid.p98
13 Yugoslavia, HM Queen Alexandra of, *Prince Philip: A Family Portrait* (Hodder & Stoughton, 1960) p84
14 *Daily Telegraph* 2 April 1946
15 Pimlott, *The Queen* p100
16 Dean, John, *HRH Prince Philip, Duke of Edinburgh* (Robert Hale, 1954) p36
17 Shawcross, William, *Queen Elizabeth the Queen Mother: The Official Biography* (Macmillan, 2009) p624
18 Countess Mountbatten, telephone interview, January 1945
19 Morgan, Janet, *Edwina Mountbatten: A Life of Her Own* (Fontana, 1992) p401

27. The Mystery of Their Engagement
1 Boothroyd, Basil, *Prince Philip: An Informal Biography* (McCall, 1971) pp32–3
2 Yugoslavia, HM Queen Alexandra of, *Prince Philip: A Family Portrait* (Hodder & Stoughton, 1960) p86
3 Ibid.

28. Philip Flunks and Exam
1 Parker, Eileen, *Step Aside for Royalty* (Bachman & Turner, 1982) p95
2 *Daily Telegraph* 21 May 2001
3 Parker, *Step Aside* p94
4 Ibid

29. An Unwelcome Welcome
1 Brandreth, Gyles, *Philip and Elizabeth: Portrait of a Marriage* (Century, 2004) p193
2 Sir Edward Ford, interview with the author, September 1997

3 Shawcross, William, *Queen Elizabeth the Queen Mother: The Official Biography* (Macmillan, 2009) p626
4 Turner, Graham, *Elizabeth: The Woman and the Queen* (Macmillan, 2002) p32
5 Strong, Roy, *The Roy Strong Diaries 1967–1987* (Weidenfeld & Nicolson, 1997) p221
6 Ellis, Jennifer (ed.), *Thatched with Gold: The Memoir of Mabell, Countess of Airlie* (Hutchinson, 1962) p225
7 Eade, Philip, *Young Prince Philip: His Turbulent Early Life* (Harper Press, 2012) p180
8 Turner, *Elizabeth* p30
9 Ibid.
10 Brandreth, *Philip and Elizabeth* p183
11 Sir Edward Ford, interview with the author, September 1997
12 Turner, *Elizabeth* p30
13 Pimlott, Ben, *The Queen* (HarperCollins, 2001) p104
14 Eade, *Young Prince Philip* p181
15 Crawford, Marion, *The Little Princesses* (Duckworth, 1993) p100
16 Eade, *Young Prince Philip* p179
17 Brandreth, *Philip and Elizabeth* p182
18 Heald, Tim, *The Duke: A Portrait of Prince Philip* (Hodder & Stoughton, 1991) p53
19 Judd, Denis, *Prince Philip: A Biography* (Michael Joseph, 1980) p125
20 Bradford, Sarah, *George VI* (Weidenfeld & Nicolson, 1989) p420
21 Turner, *Elizabeth* p32

31. Philip the Jewellery Designer
1 Vickers, Hugo, *Alice: Princess Andrew of Greece* (Hamish Hamilton, 2000) p326
2 Ibid
3 Field, Leslie, *The Queen's Jewels* (Weidenfeld & Nicolson, 1987) p85
4 Vickers, *Alice* p326
5 Menkes, Suzy, *The Royal Jewels* (Grafton Books, 1985) p14
6 Field, *The Queen's Jewels* p144

32. An End to His Vices
1 Heald, Tim, *Princess Margaret: A Life Unravelled* (Weidenfeld & Nicolson, 2007) pp32-33
2 Eade, Philip, *Young Prince Philip: His Turbulent Early Life* (Harper Press, 2012) p175
3 Lady Pamela Hicks, telephone interview, January 2020
4 Yugoslavia, HM Queen Alexandra of, *Prince Philip: A Family Portrait* (Hodder & Stoughton, 1960) p108
5 Ibid. pp61–2

34. Pre-Wedding Jitters?
1 Yugoslavia, HM Queen Alexandra of, *Prince Philip: A Family Portrait* (Hodder & Stoughton, 1960) p97
2 Bocca, Geoffrey, *Elizabeth and Philip* (Henry Holt & Co., 1953) p76
3 Yugoslavia, HM Queen Alexandra of, *Prince Philip* p98
4 Brandreth, Gyles, *Philip and Elizabeth: Portrait of a Marriage* (Century, 2004) p195
5 Bocca, *Elizabeth and Philip* p76
6 Parker, Eileen, *Step Aside for Royalty* (Bachman & Turner, 1982) p37
7 Dean, John, *HRH Prince Philip, Duke of Edinburgh* (Robert Hale, 1954) p55
8 Ibid. p56
9 Countess Mountbatten, telephone interview, January 2015
10 Brandreth, *Elizabeth and Philip* p197

35. Philip's Austerity Wedding
1 James, Robert Rhodes, *Chips: The Diaries of Sir Henry Channon* (Penguin, 1970) p509
2 Ellis, Jennifer (ed.), *Thatched with Gold: The Memoir of Mabell, Countess of Airlie* (Hutchinson, 1962)
3 Interview with Lady Pamela Hicks, October 2017
4 James, *Chips* p510
5 Interview with Lady Pamela Hicks, October 2017

37. Honeymoon Hysteria
1 Dean, John, *HRH Prince Philip, Duke of Edinburgh* (Robert Hale, 1954) p61

2 *Daily Mirror* 21 November 1947
3 Smith, Charles, *Lord Mountbatten: His Butler's Story* (Stein and Day, 1980) p86
4 *Daily Herald* 24 November 1947
5 Pimlott, Ben, *The Queen* (HarperCollins, 2001) p144

38. Philip and a Royal Mistress
1 Brandreth, Gyles, *Philip and Elizabeth: Portrait of a Marriage* (Century, 2004) p177
2 Heald, Tim, *The Duke: A Portrait of Prince Philip* (Hodder & Stoughton, 1991) p76
3 Vickers, Hugo, *Alice: Princess Andrew of Greece* (Hamish Hamilton, 2000) p315
4 Ibid. pp308–9
5 'Andrée Lafayette' at www.imdb.com
6 *Indianapolis Star* 28 January 1923
7 *Lit de parade de Valtesse de la Bigne*, Musée des arts décoratifs, Paris

39. A Working Royal
1 Yugoslavia, HM Queen Alexandra of, *Prince Philip: A Family Portrait* (Hodder & Stoughton, 1960) p105

41. Philip and Charles: Good Cop or Bad Cop?
1 *The Prince of Wales Talks of His Feelings about Next Tuesday's Investiture*, BBC1, 26 June 1969
2 Dimbleby, Jonathan, *The Prince of Wales: A Biography* (Little, Brown and Co., 1994) p21
3 Brandreth, Gyles, *Charles and Camilla: Portrait of a Love Affair* (Century, 2005) p119
4 'Royal Row: How Prince Philip dubbed Prince Charles BLOODY STUPID after naive error', *Daily Express* 23 January 2019, www.express.co.uk/news/royal/1076732/royal-news-prince-philip-prince-charles-queen-elizabeth-ii-bloody-stupid-spt
5 Dimbleby, *Prince of Wales* p62
6 Ibid. p65
7 Brandreth, Gyles, 'I've Just Got to Live With It', *Sunday Telegraph* 16 May 1999

8 *Daily Telegraph* 22 May 2001
9 *Daily Telegraph* 27 May 2001
10 *The Times* 4 February 1971
11 *Daily Telegraph* 10 November 2003
12 Heald, Tim, *The Duke: A Portrait of Prince Philip* (Hodder & Stoughton, 1991) p233
13 Brandreth, Gyles, *Philip and Elizabeth: Portrait of a Marriage* (Century, 2004) p333
14 Dimbleby, *Prince of Wales* p257

42. Ol' Blue Eyes
1 Dean, John, *HRH Prince Philip, Duke of Edinburgh: A Portrait by his Valet* (Robert Hale, 1954) p116
2 Ibid.
3 *The Times* 11 December 1951
4 'Royal News Princess Margaret's Sinatra Letter for Sale', *Female First* 20 April 2006 www.femalefirst.co.uk/royal_family/Princess+Margaret-16684.html
5 Warwick, Christopher, *Princess Margaret: A Life of Contrasts* (André Deutsch, 2000) p142
6 *Daily Mirror*, 16 March 1966

43. Two Dukes and the King of Jazz
1 Shew, Betty Spencer, *Royal Wedding* (MacDonald & Co., 1947) p20
2 Lawrence, A.H., *Duke Ellington and his World* (Routledge, 2001) p347
3 George, Don, *Sweet Man: The Real Duke Ellington* (G.P. Putnam's Sons, 1981) p131
4 *Reading Evening Post* 27 November 1973
5 Smith, Kent, *Duke Ellington* (Melrose Square Publishing, 1992) p81
6 Tucker, Mark (ed.), *The Duke Ellington Reader* (Oxford University Press, 1993) p244
7 *Daily Telegraph* 21 April 2016
8 *The Times* 19 August 1919
9 *Daily Telegraph* 21 April 2016

44. The Thursday Club
1 Pimlott, Ben, *The Queen* (HarperCollins, 2001) p271
2 Parker, Eileen, *Step Aside for Royalty* (Bachman & Turner, 1982) p80

3 Ibid.
4 Parker, John, *Prince Philip: His Secret Life* (St Martin's Press, 1990) p119
5 Brandreth, Gyles, *Philip and Elizabeth: Portrait of a Marriage* (Century, 2004) p302
6 Ibid
7 Parker, *Step Aside*, p80

45. First Home
1 *The Times* 15 August 1947
2 *The Times* 30 July 1947
3 *The Times* 1 September 1947
4 Bradford, Sarah, *Elizabeth: A Biography of HM the Queen* (William Heinemann, 1996) pp148–59

46. Princess Anne: The Son He Never Had
1 *Independent* 13 December 1992
2 Boothroyd, Basil, *Prince Philip: An Informal Biography* (McCall, 1971) p202
3 Heald, Tim, *The Duke: A Portrait of Prince Philip* (Hodder & Stoughton, 1991) p240
4 Ibid. p232
5 *Independent* 13 December 1992
6 Brandreth, Gyles, *Philip and Elizabeth: Portrait of a Marriage* (Century, 2004) p335
7 Hoey, Brian, *Anne, The Princess Royal* (Grafton, 1989) p51
8 Longford, Elizabeth (ed.), *The Oxford Book of Royal Anecdotes* (Oxford University Press, 1990) p511
9 Hoey, *Anne* p155
10 Heald, *The Duke* p232
11 Brandreth, *Philip and Elizabeth* p343
12 Ibid. p336

47. 'The Whole World Had Dropped on His Shoulders'
1 *Daily Telegraph* 22 May 2001
2 Boothroyd, Basil, *Prince Philip: An Informal Biography* (McCall, 1971) p65
3 Parker, Eileen, *Step Aside for Royalty* (Bachman & Turner, 1982) p103
4 Boothroyd, *Prince Philip* p65
5 *Daily Telegraph* 22 May 2001
6 Brandreth, Gyles, *Philip and Elizabeth:*

Portrait of a Marriage (Century, 2004) p258

7   Boothroyd, *Prince Philip* p65

8   Brandreth, *Philip and Elizabeth* p257

9   *Prince Philip: The Plot to Make a King*, Blakeway Productions, Channel 4, 2015

10 Ibid

11 Catterall, Peter (ed.), *The Macmillan Diaries: The Cabinet Years 1950–1957* (Macmillan, 2003) p151

12 Ibid.p 150

13 Boothroyd, *Prince Philip* p64

14 Vickers, Hugo, *Cecil Beaton: The Authorized Biography* (Weidenfeld & Nicolson, 1985) p359

15 Yugoslavia, HM Queen Alexandra of, *Prince Philip: A Family Portrait* (Hodder & Stoughton, 1960) p142

16 Brandreth, *Philip and Elizabeth* pp258–59

17 Ibid.p259

18 Hibbert, Christopher, *The Court of St James's* (Weidenfeld & Nicolson, 1979) p231

19 Countess Mountbatten, telephone interview, January 2015

48. 'That Damn Fool Edinburgh'

1   Pimlott, Ben, *The Queen: A Biography of Elizabeth II* (HarperCollins, 1996) p185

2   Longford, Elizabeth, *Elizabeth II* (Weidenfeld & Nicholson, 1993) p155

3   Eade, Philip, *Young Prince Philip: His Turbulent Early Life* (Harper Press, 2012) p160

4   Interview with Countess Mountbatten, January 2015

5   *Prince Philip: The Plot to Make a King*, Blakeway Productions, Channel 4, 2015

6   Paxman, Jeremy, *On Royalty* (Penguin, 2007) p291

49. And to Crown It All …

1   Pimlott, Ben, *The Queen* (HarperCollins, 2001) p204

2   *Daily Express* 18 November 2019

3   *Daily Telegraph* 17 May 1999

4   Pimlott, *The Queen* p209

5   *The Queen's Coronation: Behind Palace Doors*, Channel 4, 2008

6   Eade, Philip, *Young Prince Philip: His Turbulent Early Life* (Harper Press, 2012) p277

7   Yugoslavia, HM Queen Alexandra of, *Prince Philip: A Family Portrait* (Hodder & Stoughton, 1960) p144

51. Don't Call Me Albert!

1   Brandreth, Gyles, *Philip and Elizabeth: Portrait of a Marriage* (Century, 2004) p249

2   Strober, Deborah and Gerald, *The Monarchy: An Oral History of Elizabeth II* (Hutchinson, 2002) p105

52. Mother-in-Law Trouble

1   Turner, Graham, *Elizabeth: The Woman and the Queen* (Macmillan, 2002) p23

2   Shawcross, William, *Queen Elizabeth the Queen Mother: The Official Biography* (Macmillan, 2009) p625

3   Ibid

4   Ibid.p626

5   Turner, *Elizabeth* p86

6   Ibid.p85

7   Boothroyd, Basil, *Prince Philip: An Informal Biography* (McCall, 1971) p101

8   *Daily Telegraph* 22 May 2001

9   Ibid

10 Heald, Tim, *Princess Margaret: A Life Unravelled* (Weidenfeld & Nicolson, 2007) p235

11 Curtis, Sarah (ed.), *The Journals of Woodrow Wyatt: Volume Two* (Macmillan, 1999) pxiv

12 Ibid.p311

53. What Have You Come As?

1   Wheeler-Bennett, John W., *George VI: His Life and Reign* (St Martin's Press, 1958) p626

2   James, Robert Rhodes, *Chips: The Diaries of Sir Henry Channon* (Penguin, 1970) p518

3   *Dundee Evening Telegraph* 13 July 1949

4   *Birmingham Daily Gazette* 16 July 1949

5   *Dundee Evening Telegraph* 13 July 1949
54. Edinburgh Green
1   Moran, Joe, *On Roads: A Hidden History* (Profile Books, 2010) p28-29
2   Pigott, Peter, *Royal Transport: An Inside Look at the History of Royal Travel* (Dundurn, 2005) p130
3   *The Times* 25 August 1951
55. The Rumours
1   *Daily Telegraph* 22 May 2001
2   Pimlott, Ben, *The Queen* (HarperCollins, 2001) p721
3   *Confessions of a Prince,* BBC World Service, 14 May 2020
4   *Daily Mail* 13 July 2017
5   Judd, Denis, *Prince Philip: A Biography* (Michael Joseph, 1980) p167
6   Forster, Margaret, *Daphne du Maurier: The Secret Life of the Renowned Storyteller* (Doubleday, 1993) p279
7   Heald, Tim, *The Duke: A Portrait of Prince Philip* (Hodder & Stoughton, 1991) p249
8   Ibid.p248
9   Parker, John, *Prince Philip: His Secret Life* (St Martin's Press, 1990) p139
10 Kelly, Kitty, *The Royals* (Warner Books Inc., 1997) pp193–5
11 Higham, Charles and Moseley, Roy, *Princess Merle: The Romantic Life of Merle Oberon* (Coward-McCann, 1983) p273
12 Ibid.p296
13 Brandreth, Gyles, *Philip and Elizabeth: Portrait of a Marriage* (Century, 2004) p304
14 Ibid.p318
15 Ibid.p311
16 Bradford, Sarah, *Elizabeth* (William Heinemann, 1996) p401
17 *The Times* 18 April 2009
18 *Daily Mirror* 15 January 1996
19 Turner, Graham, *Elizabeth: The Woman and the Queen* (Macmillan, 2002) p37
20 *Daily Mail* 11 November 1997
21 Smith, Sally Beddell, *Elizabeth the Queen* (Random House, 2012) p415

22 Brandreth, *Philip and Elizabeth* p299
23 Ibid.
24 Interview with the Hon. Mrs Rhodes, March 2006
25 Brandreth, *Philip and Elizabeth* p290
26 Ibid.p299
27 *Daily Mirror* 14 January 1996
28 Brandreth, *Philip and Elizabeth* pp290–1
29 Paxman, Jeremy, *On Royalty* (Penguin, 2007) p237
30 Smith, *Elizabeth the Queen* p416
31 Turner, *Elizabeth* p111
32 Brandreth, *Philip and Elizabeth* p318
33 Turner, *Elizabeth* p110
34 Lees-Milne, James, *A Mingled Measure* (John Murray, 1994) p183
35 *Daily Telegraph* 22 May 2001
56. Tours de Force
1   Smith, Sally Beddell, *Elizabeth the Queen,* (Random House, 2012) p99
2   Yugoslavia, HM Queen Alexandra of, *Prince Philip: A Family Portrait,* (Hodder & Stoughton, 1960) p153
3   Brandreth, Gyles, *Philip and Elizabeth: Portrait of a Marriage* (Century, 2004) p181
4   Pimlott, Ben, *The Queen* (HarperCollins, 2001) p270
5   Ibid. pp270-1
6   Brandreth, *Philip and Elizabeth,* p287
7   Pimlott, *The Queen,* p271
8   Ibid. p272
9   *The Times,* 30 January 1959
10 *The Guardian,* 28 May 2010
57. The Day the Queen Sported a Beard
1   *Daily Mirror* 18 February 1957
58. When is a Prince Not a Prince?
1   The National Archives, LCO 6/3677, HRH Philip Duke of Edinburgh 1954–1957
2   Ibid
3   *London Gazette,* 21 November 1947
61. The Dukebox
1   Crawford, Marion, *The Little Princesses* (Duckworth, 1993) p30
2   Shew, Betty Spencer, *Royal Wedding* (MacDonald & Co., 1947) p18

3   Ibid
4   *The Times* 29 July 1947 p4
62. The Queen Raises Philip's Six-Bar Limit
1   Thorpe, D.R. (ed.), *Who Loses Who Wins: The Journals of Kenneth Rose, Volume Two* (Weidenfeld & Nicolson, 2019)
64. Sartorial Star
1   Dean, John, *HRH Prince Philip, Duke of Edinburgh* (Robert Hale, 1954) p47
2   Ibid.p36
3   Turner, Graham, *Elizabeth: The Woman and the Queen* (Macmillan, 2002) p30
4   *Daily Telegraph* 21 May 2001
5   Turner, *Elizabeth* p30
6   Ellis, Jennifer (ed.), *Thatched with Gold: The Memoir of Mabell, Countess of Airlie* (Hutchinson, 1962) pp228–9
7   Dean, *HRH Prince Philip* p50
8   Ibid.p49
9   *Daily Telegraph* 22 May 2001
10 Brown, Craig, *The Book of Royal Lists* (Routledge and Kegan Paul, 1982) pp118–19
11 *Daily Telegraph* 22 May 2001
65. Royal Variety: Not Always the Spice of Life
1   Brandreth, Gyles, *Philip and Elizabeth: Portrait of a Marriage* (Century, 2004)
2   Private information
3   Delfont, Lord, *Curtain Up: The Story of the Royal Variety Performance* (Robson Books Ltd, 1998) p116
4   Private information
66. Man of Faith
1   Judd, Denis, *Prince Philip: A Biography* (Michael Joseph, 1980) p18
2   Brandreth, Gyles, *Philip and Elizabeth: Portrait of a Marriage* (Century, 2004) p51
3   Heald, Tim, *The Duke: A Portrait of Prince Philip* (Hodder & Stoughton, 1991) p235
4   Ibid.p235
5   *Daily Telegraph* 21 May 2001
6   Judd, *Prince Philip* p124

7   *Daily Telegraph* 21 May 2001
67. On the Police Database
1   Butler, Peter, *The Wit of Prince Philip* (Leslie Frewin Ltd, 1965) p123
2   *The Times* 31 March 1960
68. A Very Mixed Media
1   Parker, Eileen, *Step Aside for Royalty* (Bachman & Turner, 1982) p79
2   Brandreth, Gyles, *Philip and Elizabeth: Portrait of a Marriage* (Century, 2004) p224
3   Judd, Denis, *Prince Philip: A Biography* (Michael Joseph, 1980) p143
4   Stourton, James, *Kenneth Clark: Life, Art & Civilisation* (William Collins, 2016) pp288–9
5   Duncan, Andrew, *The Reality of Monarchy* (Heinemann, 1970) p115
6   Paxman, Jeremy, *On Royalty* (Penguin, 2007) p236
7   Parker, John, *Prince Philip: His Secret Life* (St Martin's Press, 1990) p226
8   Ibid
9   Paxman, *On Royalty* p236
10 Brandreth, *Philip and Elizabeth* p2
11 *Guardian* 20 April 2020
12 Paxman, *On Royalty* p236
13 Ibid.p237
69. Dodgy Palace Lifts
1   *Metro* 21 March 2012
2   *Anne the Princess Royal at 70,* ITV, 29 July 2020
3   *Illustrated London News* 9 April 1960
4   Lloyd, Ian, 'Party Palace Secrets', *Daily Mail* 18 July 2015
71. Poesy Prince
1   www.elizabethshaw.co.uk
2   Shawcross, William, *Queen Elizabeth the Queen Mother: The Official Biography* (Macmillan, 2009) p672
3   Heald, Tim, *The Duke: A Portrait of Prince Philip* (Hodder & Stoughton, 1991) p198
4   Ibid.p197
5   A.N. Wilson in *Spectator* 30 June 1990
72. … Talking of Poetry
1   *Herald* 24 February 1999
2   *Courier* 19 February 2019

3 Duncan, Andrew, *The Reality of Monarchy* (Heinemann, 1970) p110

73. Man Belonging Mrs Queen

1 Heald, Tim, *The Duke: A Portrait of Prince Philip* (Hodder & Stoughton, 1991) p144
2 Baylis, Matthew, *Man Belonging Mrs Queen: Adventures with the Philip Worshippers* (Old Street Publishing, 2013)

74. Feature Film Philip

1 *Daily Telegraph* 7 June 2016
2 *Washington Post* 20 September 1982
3 'Interview: Helen Mirren and James Cromwell', *IGN* 17 May 2012 www.ign.com/articles/2006/10/05/interview-helen-mirren-and-james-cromwell
4 *Sydney Morning Herald* 16 December 2006
5 '"The Crown" Star Matt Smith on Naughty Prince Philip, the First Female Doctor and Pay Parity', *Variety* 21 August 2018 variety.com/2018/tv/news/the-crown-star-matt-smith-onnaughty-prince-philip-the-first-female-doctor-pay-parity-1202910694/
6 Ibid
7 *Harper's Bazaar* 18 November 2019

75. The Prince and the Profumo Scandal

1 Knightley, Phillip and Kennedy, Caroline, *An Affair of State: The Profumo Case and the Framing of Stephen Ward* (Atheneum, 1987) p248
2 Pimlott, Ben, *The Queen* (HarperCollins, 2001) p320
3 Keeler, Christine, *Secrets and Lies: The Trials of Christine Keeler* (John Blake, 2014) p30
4 Ibid.p38
5 *Tatler* 3 July 1957
6 Eade, Philip, *Young Prince Philip: His Turbulent Early Life* (Harper Press, 2012) p217
7 Ibid.pp217–18
8 Sutherland, Douglas, *The Great Betrayal: The Definitive Story of Blunt, Philby, Burgess and Maclean* (Times Books, 1980) p80

9 Heald, Tim, *The Duke: A Portrait of Prince Philip* (Hodder & Stoughton, 1991) pp105–6
10 Summers, Anthony and Dorril, Stephen, *Honey Trap: The Secret Worlds of Stephen Ward* (Weidenfeld & Nicolson, 1987) p205
11 Knightley and Kennedy, *Affair of State* p65
12 Ibid
13 *The Times* 23 July 1963
14 *London Gazette* 31 December 1963
15 Bradford, Sarah, *Elizabeth* (William Heinemann, 1996) p307
16 Penrose, Barrie and Freeman, Simon, *Conspiracy of Silence: The Secret Life of Anthony Blunt* (Vintage Books, 1988) p407
17 Knightley and Kennedy, *Affair of State* p210
18 *Daily Herald* 10 August 1963
19 *Daily Mirror* 24 June 1963
20 Eade, *Young Prince Philip* p218
21 *Independent* 5 January 2014

76. 1969: The Year the Queen Banned Christmas

1 *The Times* 10 November 1969
2 Author interview with Sir Edward Ford, September 1997
3 Pimlott, Ben, *The Queen* (HarperCollins, 2001) p379
4 Ibid. Interview with former private secretary Lord Charteris
5 Lacey, Robert, *Royal: Her Majesty Queen Elizabeth II* (Little, Brown and Co., 2002) p222
6 Ibid
7 Boothroyd, Basil, *Prince Philip: An Informal Biography* (McCall, 1971), p68
8 Lacey, *Majesty* p282
9 Boothroyd, *Prince Philip* p68
10 Ibid.
11 Ibid
12 Author interview with David Gorringe, May 2009
13 Author interview with Peter Bartlett, May 2009

14 Private information

15 Private information

16 *Queen and Country* documentary, 2002

17 Author interview with David Gorringe, May 2009

18 Author interview with Peter Bartlett, May 2009

19 'Features: Britain's Most Watched TV – the 1960s', British Film Institute (BFI), available at web.archive.org/web/20051122221448/http:/www.bfi.org.uk/features/mostwatched/1960s.html (accessed 28 September 2020)

77. Crash, Bang, Wallop: The Duke Behind the Wheel

1 Eade, Philip, *Young Prince Philip: His Turbulent Early Life* (Harper Press, 2012) p98

2 Ziegler, Philip, *Mountbatten: The Official Biography* (Collins, 1985) p307

3 *The Times* 23 October 1947.

4 Dean, John, *HRH Prince Philip, Duke of Edinburgh* (Robert Hale, 1954)

5 *The Times* 13 October 1923

6 *People's Journal* 27 May 1939

7 *The Times* 11 February 1956

8 *The Times* 28 June 1957

9 *The Times* 8 June 1964

78. A Fatherly Bond with JFK Jnr

1 Vidal, Gore, *Palimpsest: A Memoir* (Random House, 1995) p123

2 Radziwill, Lee, *Lee* (Assouline, 2015)

3 Smith, Sally Beddell, *Elizabeth the Queen* (Random House, 2012) p166

4 Devonshire, Deborah, *Wait for Me! Memoirs* (Farrar, Straus & Giroux, 2010) p321

5 Ibid.

6 Leigh, Wendy, *Prince Charming: The John F Kennedy Jr. Story*, rev. edn (Signet, 1999) p88

7 Shaw, Maud, *White House Nannie: My Years With Caroline and John Kennedy Jr.* (Signet, 1966) p123

81. Royal Winker

1 'Wink Up and Fiddle', *Sports Illustrated* 7 April 1958

2 North American Tiddlywinks Association, Facebook page

3 'Royal Match of Tiddlywinks', University of Cambridge News website 3 March 2008 www.cam.ac.uk/news/royal-match-of-tiddlywinks

82. Turning the Queen Decimal

1 Boothroyd, Basil, *Prince Philip: An Informal Biography* (McCall, 1971) p275

2 Ibid.

83. A Sensitive Touch

1 Interview with Sir Edward Ford, 1997

2 Turner, Graham, *Elizabeth: The Woman and the Queen* (Macmillan, 2002) p25

3 Ibid.p26

4 *The Duke: A Portrait of Prince Philip*, ITV documentary, 2008

5 Judd, Denis, *Prince Philip: A Biography* (Michael Joseph, 1980) p61

6 Turner, *Elizabeth* pp26–7

7 Brandreth, Gyles, *Philip and Elizabeth: Portrait of a Marriage* (Century, 2004) p227

8 Yugoslavia, HM Queen Alexandra of, *Prince Philip: A Family Portrait* (Hodder & Stoughton, 1960) p121

9 Lady Pamela Hicks, telephone interview, 8 October 2019

10 *Daily Telegraph* 21 May 2001

11 Strober, Deborah and Gerald, *The Monarchy: An Oral History of Elizabeth II* (Hutchinson, 2002) p238

12 Eade, Philip, *Young Prince Philip: His Turbulent Early Life* (Harper Press, 2012) p269

13 *The Duke: A Portrait of Prince Philip*, ITV documentary, 2008

14 Turner, *Elizabeth* pp26–27, 106

15 Heald, Tim, *The Duke: A Portrait of Prince Philip* (Hodder & Stoughton, 1991) p227

16 Lacey, Robert, *Royal: Her Majesty Queen Elizabeth II* (Little, Brown and Co., 2002) pp260–1

17 Countess Mountbatten, telephone interview, January 2015

18 Heald, *The Duke* p246

84. Diana: A Complicated Daughter-in-Law

1 *Daily Telegraph* 28 March 2011
2 Dimbleby, Jonathan, *The Prince of Wales: A Biography* (Little, Brown and Co., 1994) p282ff
3 *Daily Telegraph* 22 May 2001
4 Turner, Graham, *Elizabeth: The Woman and the Queen* (Macmillan, 2002) p134
5 Bradford, Sarah, *Diana* (Viking, 2006) p87
6 Ibid.p97
7 Ibid.p134ff
8 Brandreth, Gyles, *Philip and Elizabeth: Portrait of a Marriage* (Century, 2004) p349
9 Paxman, Jeremy, *On Royalty* (Penguin, 2007) p274
10 Jephson, Patrick, *Shadows of a Princess* (HarperCollins, 2000) p253
11 Brandreth, *Philip and Elizabeth* p351
12 Smith, Sally Beddell, *Elizabeth the Queen* (Random House, 2012) p366
13 Turner, *Elizabeth* p155

85. Frozen-Out Fergie

1 York, Sarah Duchess of, *My Story* (Simon & Schuster, 1996) p188
2 Ibid.pp162–3
3 *Daily Mirror* 17 July 2001
4 *Daily Telegraph* 22 May 2001
5 Ibid
6 Brandreth, Gyles, *Philip and Elizabeth: Portrait of a Marriage* (Century, 2004) p363
7 Turner, Graham, *Elizabeth: The Woman and the Queen* (Macmillan, 2002) p5
8 Brandreth, *Philip and Elizabeth* p363
9 Ibid.p362

86. Biblio-Phil

1 Heald, Tim, *The Duke: A Portrait of Prince Philip* (Hodder & Stoughton, 1991) p127
2 Shew, Betty Spencer, *Royal Wedding* (MacDonald & Co., 1947) p22
3 Heald, *The Duke* pp127–8

4 Brandreth, Gyles, *Philip and Elizabeth: Portrait of a Marriage* (Century, 2004) p281

87. North of Watford Gap

1 Yugoslavia, HM Queen Alexandra of, *Prince Philip: A Family Portrait* (Hodder & Stoughton, 1960) p20

88. Prince Philip: The Godfather

1 *Vintage* 19 February 2016
2 metro.co.uk/2019/01/12/prince-charless-godson-gets-engaged-professional-mermaid-8336521/

89. Philip the Good Father

1 Hoey, Brian, *Anne, The Princess Royal* (Grafton, 1989) p78

91. Charity Case

1 Judd, Denis, *Prince Philip: A Biography* (Michael Joseph, 1980) pp142–3
2 Ibid.pp237–8
3 Ibid.p239
4 Boothroyd, Basil, *Prince Philip: An Informal Biography* (McCall, 1971) pp245–6

92. The Death of Diana

1 Smith, Sally Beddell, *Elizabeth the Queen* (Random House, 2012) pp394–406
2 Knatchbull, Timothy, *From a Clear Blue Sky: Surviving the Mountbatten Bomb* (Hutchinson, 2009) p176
3 Smith, *Elizabeth* p296
4 Turner, Graham, *Elizabeth: The Woman and the Queen* (Macmillan, 2002) p158
5 Author interview with the Hon. Mrs Rhodes, September 1997
6 Smith, *Elizabeth* p399
7 Turner, *Elizabeth* p158
8 Ibid.p157
9 Smith, *Elizabeth* p403
10 *An Intimate Portrait of the Queen at 80*, Andrew Marr, BBC, 2006

93. Is There Anyone There? Part 1

1 Dale, John, *The Prince and the Paranormal: The Psychic Bloodline of the Royal Family* (W.H. Allen, 1986)

2 Shawcross, William, *Queen Elizabeth the Queen Mother: The Official Biography* (Macmillan, 2009) p86
3 *Daily Mail* 25 October 2014
4 *Majesty* vol. 13, no. 8, August 1992
94. Is There Anyone There? Part 2
1 Eade, Philip, *Young Prince Philip: His Turbulent Early Life* (Harper Press, 2012) p268
2 *Daily Telegraph* 18 February 2010
3 Ziegler, Philip, *Mountbatten: The Official Biography* (Collins, 1985) p493ff
4 Eade, *Young Prince Philip* p268
5 Ibid.
6 Horsley, Peter, *Sounds from Another Room* (Pen & Sword Books, 1997)
7 Wheen, Francis, *How Mumbo Jumbo Conquered the World,* (Fourth Estate, 2004) p138
95. Cartoon Character
1 Heald, Tim, *The Duke: A Portrait of Prince Philip* (Hodder & Stoughton, 1991) p128
2 *Daily Telegraph* 24 February 2018
97. Fun Phil Facts
1 Hunt, John, *The Ascent of Everest* (Odhams Press, 1954) pp247–8
2 *Daily Telegraph* 22 May 2001
3 Oliver, Charles, *Dinner at Buckingham Palace* (Metro Books, 2003)
4 Richard Stone, email to the author, 13 August 2020
5 Strong, Roy, *The Roy Strong Diaries, 1967–1987* (Weidenfeld & Nicolson, 1997) p247
98. My Husband and I
1 *Daily Telegraph* 21 May 2001
2 *Independent* 13 December 1992
3 Turner, Graham, *Elizabeth: The Woman and the Queen* (Macmillan, 2002) p32

4 Shawcross, William, *Queen Elizabeth the Queen Mother: The Official Biography* (Macmillan, 2009) p631
5 Ibid.p630
6 Brandreth, Gyles, *Philip and Elizabeth: Portrait of a Marriage* (Century, 2004) p209
7 Boothroyd, Basil, *Prince Philip: An Informal Biography* (McCall, 1971) p62
8 Pimlott, Ben, *The Queen* (HarperCollins, 2001) p260
9 Brandreth, *Philip and Elizabeth* p209
10 Lady Pamela Hicks, telephone interview, January 2019
11 *Daily Telegraph* 21 May 2001
12 Pimlott, *The Queen* p270
13 *Independent* 13 December 1992
14 Heald, Tim, *The Duke: A Portrait of Prince Philip* (Hodder & Stoughton, 1991) p231
15 Williams, Charles, *Harold Macmillan* (Weidenfeld & Nicolson, 2009) p359
16 *Independent* 13 December 1992
17 Paxman, Jeremy, *On Royalty* (Penguin, 2007) p291
18 *Daily Mail* 8 March 2016
19 *Daily Telegraph* 21 May 2001
20 Smith, Sally Beddell, *Elizabeth the Queen* (Random House, 2012) ppxvi–xvii
21 *Daily Telegraph* 22 May 2001
22 Brandreth, *Philip and Elizabeth* p283
23 *Daily Telegraph* 21 May 2001
24 Longford, Elizabeth (ed.), *The Oxford Book of Royal Anecdotes* (Oxford University Press, 1990) p510
25 *Sun* 5 October 2019
26 Smith, *Elizabeth* p475
100. I Did It My Way
1 *Daily Telegraph* 22 May 2001
2 *Sunday Telegraph*, 16 May 1999
3 *Ibid.*

BIBLIOGRAPHY

Books

Aston, Sir George, *His Royal Highness the Duke Of Connaught and Strathearn* (George G. Harrap, 1929)

Blair, Tony, *A Journey: My Political Life* (Alfred A. Knopf, 2010)

Boothroyd, Basil, *Prince Philip: An Informal Biography* (McCall, 1971)

Bradford, Sarah, *Diana* (Viking, 2006)

Bradford, Sarah, *Elizabeth* (William Heinemann, 1996)

Bradford, Sarah, *George VI* (Weidenfeld & Nicolson, 1989)

Brandreth, Gyles, *Philip and Elizabeth: Portrait of a Marriage* (Century, 2004)

Carter, Miranda, *Anthony Blunt: His Lives* (Farrar, Strauss & Giroux, 2001)

Catterall, Peter (ed.), *The Macmillan Diaries: The Cabinet Years 1950–1957* (Macmillan, 2003)

Cawthorne, Nigel, *I Know I Am Rude, But It Is Fun* (Gibson Square, 2017)

Crawford, Marion, *The Little Princesses* (Duckworth, 1993)

Curtis, Sarah (ed.), *The Journals of Woodrow Wyatt: Volume Two* (Macmillan, 1999)

Davenport-Hines, Richard, *An English Affair: Sex, Class and Power in the Age of Profumo* (William Collins, 2003)

De Courcy, Anne, *Debs at War: How Wartime Changed Their Lives* (Weidenfeld & Nicolson, 2005)

Dean, John, *HRH Prince Philip, Duke of Edinburgh* (Robert Hale, 1954)

Devonshire, Deborah, *Wait for Me! Memoirs* (Farrar, Straus & Giroux, 2010)

Dimbleby, Jonathan, *The Prince of Wales: A Biography* (Little, Brown and Co., 1994)

Duncan, Andrew, *The Reality of Monarchy* (Heinemann, 1970)

Eade, Philip, *Young Prince Philip: His Turbulent Early Life* (Harper Press, 2012)

Ellis, Jennifer (ed.), *Thatched with Gold: The Memoir of Mabell, Countess of Airlie* (Hutchinson, 1962)

Field, Leslie, *The Queen's Jewels* (Weidenfeld & Nicolson, 1987)

Forster, Margaret, *Daphne du Maurier: The Secret Life of the Renowned Storyteller* (Doubleday, 1993)

George, Don, *Sweet Man: The Real Duke Ellington* (G.P. Putnam's Sons, 1981)

Heald, Tim, *The Duke: A Portrait of Prince Philip* (Hodder & Stoughton, 1991)

Heald, Tim, *Princess Margaret: A Life Unravelled* (Weidenfeld & Nicolson, 2007)

Hibbert, Christopher, *The Court of St James's* (Weidenfeld & Nicolson, 1979)

Higham, Charles and Moseley, Roy, *Princess Merle: The Romantic Life of Merle Oberon* (Coward-McCann, 1983)

Hoey, Brian, *Anne, The Princess Royal* (Grafton, 1989)

Horsley, Peter, *Sounds from Another Room* (Pen & Sword Books, 1997)

Hough, Richard, *Louis and Victoria: The Family History of the Mountbattens*, 2nd edn (Weidenfeld & Nicolson, 1984)

James, Robert Rhodes, *Chips: The Diaries of Sir Henry Channon* (Penguin, 1970)

Jephson, Patrick, *Shadows of a Princess* (HarperCollins, 2000)

Judd, Denis, *Prince Philip: A Biography* (Michael Joseph, 1980)

Keeler, Christine, *Secrets and Lies: The Trials of Christine Keeler* (John Blake, 2014)

Kelly, Kitty, *The Royals* (Warner Books Inc., 1997)

Knatchbull, Timothy, *From a Clear Blue Sky: Surviving the Mountbatten Bomb* (Hutchinson, 2009)

Knightley, Phillip and Kennedy, Caroline, *An Affair of State: The Profumo Case and the Framing of Stephen Ward* (Atheneum, 1987)

Lacey, Robert, *Royal: Her Majesty Queen Elizabeth II* (Little, Brown and Co., 2002)

Lawrence, A.H., *Duke Ellington and his World* (Routledge, 2001)

Lees-Milne, James, *A Mingled Measure, Diaries 1953–1972* (John Murray, 1994)

Leigh, Wendy, *Prince Charming: The John F Kennedy Jr. Story*, rev. edn (Signet, 1999)

Leslie, Ann, *Killing My Own Snakes: A Memoir* (Pan Books, 2009)

Longford, Elizabeth (ed.), *The Oxford Book of Royal Anecdotes* (Oxford University Press, 1990)

Menkes, Suzy, *The Royal Jewels* (Grafton Books, 1985)

Moran, Joe, *On Roads: A Hidden History* (Profile Books, 2010)

Morgan, Janet, *Edwina Mountbatten: A Life of Her Own* (Fontana, 1992)

Oliver, Charles, *Dinner at Buckingham Palace* (Metro Books, 2003)

Parker, Eileen, *Step Aside for Royalty* (Bachman & Turner, 1982)

Parker, John, *Prince Philip: His Secret Life* (St Martin's Press, 1990)

Paxman, Jeremy, *On Royalty* (Penguin, 2007)

Pearson, John, *The Ultimate Family: The Making of the Royal House of Windsor* (Michael Joseph, 1986)

Penrose, Barrie and Freeman, Simon, *Conspiracy of Silence: The Secret Life of Anthony Blunt* (Vintage Books, 1988)

Petropoulos, Jonathan, *Royals and the Reich: The Princes von Hessen in Nazi Germany* (Oxford University Press, 2006)

Pigott, Peter, *Royal Transport: An Inside Look at the History of Royal Travel* (Dundurn, 2005)

Pimlott, Ben, *The Queen* (HarperCollins, 2001)

Radziwill, Lee, *Lee* (Assouline, 2015)

Rhodes, Margaret, *The Final Curtsey* (Umbria Press, 2001)

Sacks, David, *The Alphabet: Unraveling the Mystery of the Alphabet from A to Z* (Arrow Books, 2004)

Shaw, Maud, *White House Nannie: My Years with Caroline and John Kennedy Jr.* (Signet, 1966)

Shawcross, William, *Queen Elizabeth the Queen Mother: The Official Biography* (Macmillan, 2009)

Shew, Betty Spencer, *Royal Wedding* (MacDonald & Co., 1947)

Sinclair, Marianne (ed.), *The Wit and Wisdom of the Royal Family* (Plexus, 1990)

Smith, Charles, *Lord Mountbatten: His Butler's Story* (Stein and Day, 1980)

Smith, Kent, *Duke Ellington* (Melrose Square Publishing, 1992)

Smith, Sally Beddell, *Elizabeth the Queen* (Random House, 2012)

Stourton, James, *Kenneth Clark: Life, Art and Civilisation* (William Collins, 2016)

Strober, Deborah and Gerald, *The Monarchy: An Oral History of Elizabeth II* (Hutchinson, 2002)

Strong, Roy, *The Roy Strong Diaries, 1967–1987* (Weidenfeld & Nicolson, 1997)

Summers, Anthony and Dorril, Stephen, *Honey Trap: The Secret Worlds of Stephen Ward* (Weidenfeld & Nicolson, 1987)

Sutherland, Douglas, *The Great Betrayal: The Definitive Story of Blunt, Philby, Burgess and Maclean* (Times Books, 1980)

Turner, Graham, *Elizabeth: The Woman and the Queen* (Macmillan, 2002)

Vickers, Hugo, *Alice: Princess Andrew of Greece* (Hamish Hamilton, 2000)

Vickers, Hugo, *Cecil Beaton: The Authorized Biography* (Weidenfeld & Nicolson, 1985)

Vidal, Gore, *Palimpsest: A Memoir* (Random House, 1995)

Warwick, Christopher, *Princess Margaret: A Life of Contrasts* (André Deutsch, 2000)

Wharfe, Ken, *Diana: Closely Guarded Secret* (Michael O'Mara, 2002)

Wheeler-Bennett, John W., *George VI: His Life and Reign* (St Martin's Press, 1958)

Wheen, Francis, *How Mumbo Jumbo Conquered the World*, (Fourth Estate, 2004)

Williams, Charles, *Harold Macmillan* (Weidenfeld & Nicolson, 2009)

York, Sarah Duchess of, *My Story* (Simon & Schuster, 1996)

Yugoslavia, HM Queen Alexandra of, *Prince Philip: A Family Portrait* (Hodder & Stoughton, 1960)

Ziegler, Philip, *Mountbatten: The Official Biography* (Collins, 1985)

Ziegler, Philip (ed.), *Personal Diary of Admiral The Lord Louis Mountbatten, 1943–1946* (Collins, 1988)

NEWSPAPERS AND MAGAZINES

Aberdeen Press and Journal
Birmingham Daily Gazette
Daily Herald
Daily Mail
Daily Mirror
Daily Telegraph
Dundee Evening Telegraph
Evening Telegraph and Post (Dundee)
Illustrated London News
Independent
London Gazette
Metro
Sydney Morning Herald,
Tatler
The Times
Washington Post

RADIO AND TV DOCUMENTARIES

An Intimate Portrait of the Queen at 80, Andrew Marr, BBC, 2006

Anne the Princess Royal at 70, ITV, 2020

Confessions of a Prince, BBC World Service, 14 May 2020

Prince Philip: The Plot to Make a King, Channel 4, 2015

The Duke: A Portrait of Prince Philip, ITV, 2008

The Queen's Coronation: Behind Palace Doors, Channel 4, 2008

The Queen's Mother-in-Law, Channel 4, 2012

WEBSITES

www.harpersbazaar.com
www.variety.com

INDEX